Leisure for Leisure

Critical Essays

Edited by
Chris Rojek
Senior Editor in Sociology, Routledge

MACMILLAN
PRESS

First published 1989

Published by
THE MACMILLAN PRESS LTD
Houndmills, Basingstoke, Hampshire RG21 2XS
and London
Companies and representatives
throughout the world

British Library Cataloguing in Publication Data
Leisure for leisure: critical essays.
1. Leisure—Social aspects
I. Rojek, Chris
306'.48   GV181.3
ISBN 0-333-43446-3 (hardcover)
ISBN 0-333-46170-3 (paperback)

Contents

Notes on the Contributors

Jeff Bishop is Lecturer at the School of Advanced Urban Studies, Bristol Unversity.

Fred Coalter is Director. of the Centre for Leisure and Tourism Studies, North London Polytechnic.

Nicholas Dorn is Researcher at the Institute for the Study of Drug Dependence.

Eric Dunning is Senior Lecturer at the Department of Sociology, Leicester University.

Harvie Ferguson is Lecturer at the Department of Sociology, Glasgow University.

David Frisby is Reader in the Department of Sociology, Glasgow University.

Jennifer Hargreaves is Senior Lecturer in Sports Studies, Roehampton Institute, London.

Paul Hoggett is Lecturer at the School of Advanced Urban Studies, Bristol University.

H. F. Moorhouse is Lecturer in the Department of Sociology, Glasgow University.

Chris Rojek is Senior Editor in Sociology at Routledge, London.

Nigel South is Researcher at the Institute for the Study of Drug Dependence.

Introduction
Chris Rojek

I

In societies dominated by instrumental rationality and secularism, where lives are suspended between deadlines and dead-ends, leisure assumes extraordinary ideological significance. Paid employment and family life may be regarded as the main part of 'normal' adult existence. However, leisure, it is said, is the 'necessary' counterpart to work, the 'reward' for effort, the prerequisite for a 'healthy' and 'balanced' lifestyle. It would be absurd to suggest that Western culture presents paid employment and family life as a purgatory of self-denial. On the contrary, it can be said safely that paid employment and family life are widely seen as affirmations of adulthood – that is, people do not think of themselves as real grown-ups until they get a steady job and start a family. However, the pleasures of work and family life, great as they may be, are moderated by the sense of responsibility and self-discipline which both require. In work and family life we may satisfy and surprise ourselves. However, only in leisure are we said to be ourselves.

This is certainly the dominant position in academic sociology. Leisure is consistently associated with positive experience: liberty, fulfilment, choice and growth. For example, Dumazedier, writing in 1967, defined leisure as

> activity – apart from the obligations of work, family and society – to which the individual turns at will for either relaxation, diversion or broadening his knowledge and his spontaneous social participation, the free exercise of his creative capacity.[1]

Kelly's definition, written twenty years later, errs on the side of brevity, but endorses the same view. 'Leisure,' he writes, 'is the *freedom to be*' (emphasis his).[2]

All of the essays in this book take issue with this view. The book is divided into two sections. The first section examines some theoretical perspectives on leisure. The second section is devoted to a

1

consideration of leisure, power and planning. H. F. Moorhouse gets the collection off to a rousing start and also captures the temper of the book. His is indeed a *critical* essay which neatly dissects the pretences of the dominant tradition and the acclamations of the neo-Marxist 'alternative' embodied in the work of Clarke and Critcher. His conclusion raises some pertinent and searching questions about conventional and alternative treatments of the 'work-leisure relation' and the direction of 'leisure studies' as a field of academic enquiry.

In Chapter 2 a specific sociological perspective on leisure and sport is outlined and defended. The perspective is figurational sociology, and counsel for the defence is Eric Dunning. Figurational sociology arouses strong opinions. Some writers argue that it explains everything. Others maintain that it 'explains' nothing and that Elias's 'theory' of the civilising process is merely an empiricist exercise. Eric Dunning begins by considering some of the leading criticisms made of the figurational approach to the study of leisure and sport. Using textual material from Elias's own writings, he disentangles the approach from charges of idealism and evolutionism. Dunning believes passionately in the promise of figurational sociology to produce a genuine, objective understanding of leisure, sport and many aspects of social life besides. In this essay he uses figurational studies of foxhunting and football hooliganism in Britain to illustrate how the approach has been applied.

The work of Sigmund Freud has been neglected in leisure studies. This is careless. The middle-class patients who trooped into his consulting rooms in Vienna revealed psychological burdens which damaged all aspects of their lives, including their 'free' time relations. Moreover, systematic study of the Case Histories alone would yield rich material for considering another neglected question in leisure studies: the question of what constitutes 'deviant' and 'normal' leisure practice. Harvie Ferguson, in his mobile and unconventional essay on Freud, argues that Freud's own leisure habits (orderly/self-improving) must be used as the basis for understanding the relevance of Freud's writings for the study of leisure. Freud lived in a society dominated by the philosophy of possessive individualism – bourgeois society. The market of goods and services found its direct parallel in 'the market of sentiments'. The pursuit of pleasure in bourgeois society, like the pursuit of goods and services, was founded on rational, calculable action. Freud, argues Ferguson, revealed that the bourgeois world of pleasure was based on the systematic repression of 'fun'. The crucial breakthrough here was Freud's 'discovery' of infantile sexuality. In the 'polymorphous perversity' of the infant, Freud discovered 'the primary processes' which precede the orderly, artificial, adult world of bourgeois pleasure. In a subtle and suggestive commentary on the concepts of 'fun', 'pleasure' and 'excitement', Ferguson exposes the unconscious motivations at work in the modern 'leisure industry'. Freud is presented finally as a major, if also reluctant representative of modernist sensibility.

The theme of modernism is continued in the next two essays. Chapter 4 is written by David Frisby and consists of an examination of Simmel and leisure. Georg Simmel's writings are notoriously difficult to categorise. The breadth of his intellectual concerns and his resistance to systematising his thought, contributed to the marginal status meeted out to him as a 'founding father' of sociology. David Frisby has done much to rehabilitate Simmel as a key sociologist of modern times.[3] In this elegant and powerful essay, Frisby explores the place of leisure in Simmel's writings. Simmel's sensitivity to the flow, diversity and interdependency of modern urban-industrial relations would alone guarantee the enduring relevance of his work for the study of leisure. However, added to this is the extraordinary vitality of his substantive works. Simmel's essays on aesthetics, fashion, travel, adventure, the metropolis and exhibitions crackle with unfamiliar ideas and connections regarding leisure practice. Frisby's discussion of Simmel's thought on 'momentary satisfactions' and the individual's quest for 'ever-new stimulations and sensations' is particularly evocative. Simmel died in 1918. Yet here and elsewhere in his writings, he reads like a contemporary observer struggling to explain the friction and restlessness of leisure practice today.

Traditional bourgeois life was founded upon principles of sobriety and delayed gratification. Work was seen as a part of the realm of necessity and was associated, more or less exclusively, with public life. Leisure and family life were seen as parts of the realm of freedom, and were identified with private life. Doubtless the distinctions between necessity and freedom, public and private life, work and leisure, were always challenged. However, in the twentieth century, under the full impact of modernism, they ceased to be tenable. In Chapter 5, Chris Rojek considers the work-leisure relationship in traditional bourgeois society. Using biographical and documentary sources he shows how leisure time and space were regulated. Moreover, he indicates some of the ways in which the traditional bourgeois perspective in leisure practice have been undermined by modernism.

Part II of the book explores substantive issues of power and planning in modern leisure. Chapter 6 focuses on tensions in post-war leisure policy and is written by Fred Coalter. He argues that policy debates and initiatives on leisure have been dominated by two traditions: social democracy and socialism. The conventional assumption in the field is that these two positions are polarised. In this coherent and ironical essay, Coalter questions the validity of this assumption. He works through the main features of each position and concludes that there are major differences regarding the role of the market and consumer sovereignty in leisure activity and provision. Nevertheless, there are also major points of coalescence, notably with respect to the emancipatory potential of the state and the positive role of human agency. Coalter's essay encourages us to critically reassess our orthodox ways of thinking and talking about leisure policy in the post-war period.

We live in patriarchal societies where life chances for women are systematically curtailed and conditions of work and leisure are riddled with disadvantage. In Chapter 7, Jennifer Hargreaves sets out a framework for considering female oppression in leisure and sport. She criticises monolithic models of domination and subordination. Instead, adapting Gramsci's notion of hegemony, she argues that male power in sport and leisure is both constraining *and* enabling. Hargreaves illustrates her argument with detailed examples drawn from women's experience of leisure and sport, and also from the representation of gender images in modern culture. This thorough and principled essay is a valuable and provocative addition to feminist contributions to leisure studies.

In Chapter 8 Jeff Bishop and Paul Hoggett map out the contours of the informal economy; that is, activity outside registered paid employment which is devoted to reducing household expenditure (housework, self-servicing domestic labour), generating additional income or caring for dependants. Like many commentators they recognise the economic significance of activity in the informal economy for the GNP. However, they also maintain that the social aspects of the informal economy are far from negligible and that they have been marginalised in the specialist literature. Voluntary organisations and combinations of unregistered labour operate to reinforce and extend neighbourliness, caring, mutual aid and community action. These 'use' values cannot be quantified accurately. However, there is no doubt that they bulk large in the people's estimates of the real value of everyday life. Bishop and Hoggett apply the concept of the informal economy to undercut conventional ways of treating the work-leisure relationship.

One of the most obvious facts about modern leisure practice is also one of the least commented upon and under-researched in the academic study of leisure. It is, briefly, that many of the regular leisure activities which people engage in are illegal. In Chapter 9 Nicholas Dorn and Nigel South examine the recreational use of drugs. Most studies of drug abuse in the sociology of deviance and youth culture have focused narrowly on the drug-user. Dorn and South, in this important and timely essay, examine responses to the drug-user in the immediate family circle. Aligning themselves with Foucault's work on discourse and power, the authors introduce the concept of the *drugalogue*. They describe this as the pleasure and relief which parents and other members of the family related to the drug-user derive from talking about 'the social problem'. Discussion occurs in the context of both everyday life and anti-drug self-help groups. Dorn and South submit that the drugalogue can become a major influence in the leisure practice of the individual. They show how it can challenge male (father), female (mother) stereotypes in the family. The drugalogue, they conclude, can be seen as part of a deeper shift in modern leisure practice from 'social responsibility' to 'personal discovery'.

The final chapter of the book examines leisure time and leisure space and is written by Chris Rojek. At first sight, questions of time and space might seem abstract and remote from the 'real' world of leisure. Against this, Rojek uses examples of the campaign to prevent Sunday trading and the social reaction to the Stonehenge hippy convoy to illustrate the immediate, concrete and practical issues which occur regularly in delineating and defending leisure time and space. Moreover, he suggests that one of the most intriguing and significant trends in the organisation of modern leisure is the conversion of 'old' work-space into 'new' leisure space.

II

These critical essays are also formative. They point to new directions for discussion and research. Four points must be made. In the first place, leisure relations are regulated by strong notions of social 'health' and 'normality'. These do not determine activity, but they have certainly influenced the ways in which people actually behave in their 'free' time. In the post-war period our understanding of 'normal', 'healthy' and 'responsible' leisure has been challenged by a number of critical social movements, such as the women's movement, the movement for gay rights, the ecology movement and various youth subcultures. We do not know enough about the historical emergence and present-day mediation and development of notions of 'health' and 'normality' in leisure. Structures of class and patriarchy are obviously important. But too often they have been used as metaphors for actual social processes which are certainly more complex and many-sided. Areas ripe for study in this respect include the assumptions and activities of medical theory and practice, the education process in schools , psychoanalysis, social work, the judicial system, alternative medicine and the mass media.

This brings me to my second point. It is fairly well established in the academic study of leisure that leisure practice can pave the way for personal discovery and fulfilment. However, the significance of leisure as a resource for collective consciousness-raising has been under-theorised and under-researched. This is a pity, for palpably leisure is becoming more and more important as a site for collective organisation and action. Reams have been written on the political significance of the new alternative social movements which have emerged in reaction to the established political, military and economic framework of Western capitalism, for example the women's movement, the movement for gay rights, the ecology movement, anti-racist groups, UB40 clubs, welfare rights collectives, and the like. It has been observed that while these groups differ in their immediate political objectives, they share a general dissatisfaction with the bourgeois lifestyle with its emphasis on materialism, conspicuous consumption and privatism. What is noted less frequently is that these movements are pre-eminently *leisure* movements, – that is, that they owe their origins and vitality to meetings, rallies and contacts conducted after work, in the evenings, weekends and holidays.

The third point refers to the question of the state. For much of the post-war period, Western social science has been inflamed by a raging debate on the nature of state power and the role of the state in regulating everyday life. This debate has a chequered history in the study of leisure. The conventional sociology of leisure has ignored it. The radical sociology of leisure has embraced it enthusiastically, but often at the cost of diluting the subtleties of the original sources. In particular, Marxist and neo-Marxist studies must be criticised for identifying the state narrowly with exploitative and repressive functions while neglecting the enabling aspects of state power in leisure practice.[4] Disentangling the real history and operations of state power in the leisure sphere, from the mythical histories and operations attributed to it in the existing literature, is a major task for students of leisure. The state is important because it commands concentrated moral, physical and economic power in society, and claims to use it for the common good as opposed to the advantage of narrow sectional interests. Foucault, and other writers, have recognised that at the heart of state activity is a deep paradox. For, in expanding and guaranteeing the rights of citizens, the state instals new and extended patterns of surveillance and control which necessarily check the freedom of the individual. There are many fronts in modern leisure activity where this paradox can be studied profitably.

I will confine myself here to two examples. The first example relates to the state monopoly over legislation and licensing. This certainly manipulates what the public is entitled to see, hear and experience in leisure time and leisure space. Yet the attempt to improve the moral fibre of the nation through legislation and licensing often has the unintended effect of exacerbating social problems. This was clearly the British experience with regard to drug abuse. The switch to a more draconian policy of sanctions relating to the consumption and controlled use of drugs in the 1960s, acted as the incentive for the growth of an unscrupulous and dangerous black market in the seventies and eighties.

The second example relates to state policy on women and community care. From the earliest days of the welfare state, legislation embodied the explicit assumption that the role of adult women is pre-eminently one of caring and helping in the family. The Beveridge Report (1942) supported this view, while at the same time encouraging the build-up of the official welfare system. As the cost of caring for frail, elderly and severely handicapped individuals has escalated, the state has exercised the option of transferring the burden of care back on to private helpers – daughters, wives, mothers. This has culminated in the present official enthusiasm for ideas of voluntary and community care. Women's leisure, which is already at a premium, is thus eroded still more. Indeed, if one follows the logic of Finch and Groves,[5] argument, the threat to women's leisure posed by the community/ voluntary care bandwagon is potentially devastating. Consider the trends and projections for the size of the elderly populaton alone. In the last twenty-five years the numbers in the 85-or-over group (who make the heaviest demands on services) have increased by 133 per cent. It is estimated that numbers will rise by a further 75 per cent by 2011, bringing the anticipated numbers in this age group to 904 000.[6] Since there is no evidence that the supply of public-sector services will be increased to cater for this rise in demand, it is a fair assumption that married or single women are expected to take up the slack. Thus, state policy which is officially behind the idea of equality for women, works in practice to reinforce inequality, especially in the leisure sphere.

The fourth point refers to the perception and experience of leisure in modern society. Erving Goffman argued, correctly in my opinion, that the most obvious and practical question which people ask themselves in social situations is also the most profound and theoretical question in the study of social life: 'What is it that's going on here?'[7] Goffman's lifelong attempts to answer this question produced some of the most original and stimulating works on the character of immediate and concrete experience in the whole of the social sciences. Yet, in common with much social theory, his preoccupation with issues of social agency takes up so much of the foreground that the dimensions of social structure are reduced to little more than a vague and shadowy backdrop. The same lack of balance is evident in the academic study of leisure. Matters relating to problems of agency, matters concerning the choice, freedom and self-determined goals of the individual, domi- nate the scene. Social structure appears as a transparent, watery presence – obscure in its origins and insubstantial in its effects. This long in my view overlong, spell of domination in the academic study of leisure is now at an end. The proposition that leisure practice is socially constructed is now taken more seriously. Furthermore, there is more openness and interest in examining how processes of social construction occur, for example through studies of structures of class, patriarchy, culture, race, discourse, and so on. These are welcome developments. However, after such a long period of blandness and introspection in leisure studies there is a real danger of over-reaction and overkill. Already studies have appeared which teeter on the brink of structural determinism.[8] It is essential to oppose this tendency before it becomes fashionable. Leisure relations must be studied as relations of power. However, they must also be studied as relations which are both constraining and enabling. The leisure options available to the individual may be heavily conditioned. They are certainly far more heavily conditioned than the conventional sociology of leisure, with its incessant references to 'freedom' and 'self-determination', allows. Yet options do exist. Choice is real. Perhaps the most stimulating and exciting work being done in the study of leisure attempts self- consciously and consistently, to combine agency and structure. It recognises that consciousness of class, gender, culture, etc., changes because the concrete social relationships expressed in these forms change. Action *is* rule-bound; that is, socially constructed. The individual *is* shaped (and also shapes) structures of class, gender, race, culture, discouse and so on. However, actions and rules, individuals and structures do not exist in aspic. They exist in time. The precondition for more realistic views of leisure is to recognise that both our object of study *and* our theories are *social processes*; human relations which are contingent and subject to change. This is the best antidote to the twin blights of essentialism and reification which mar so much work in the field.

III

Leisure is the 'reward' of the many who toil in domestic labour and paid employment for the profit of the few. The pleasure which derives from 'free' time activity is rule-bound and conforms to an historically specific economy of political and cultural regulation. These are two of the basic arguments which run through this book. The title is *Leisure For Leisure: Critical Essays*. An ironical title, for each contributor had to sacrifice a great deal of 'free' time in order to contribute. A doubly ironical title, for in British academic life today, critical and reflective thought on leisure, and much else besides, is not encouraged. Since 1979 the social sciences have been throttled. Government policy has witheld funds for new appointments and research. A net cut in academic staff has been imposed. Since 1981, 10 per cent of academics have left higher education for 'early retirement'. Promotion prospects have been curtailed drastically. Circulation within the system hardly exists. Perhaps most disturbing of all, a whole generation of young social scientists has been lost.

I make these points because they are essential for understanding the tone and content of this book. They form part of the immediate context in which the project was initiated and the contributions prepared and collated. It is a safe bet that the leisure and tourist industry will grow rapidly in the years up to 2000, and will prosper in the next century. Already leisure accounts for between a quarter and a third of all consumer expenditure in Britain. Well over one million people are employed in producing leisure-related goods and services.[9] Moreover, the creation of artificial leisure environments is becoming more and more capital-intensive. For example, as I prepared this introduction, two major schemes of European development were announced. Walt Disney Productions signed a contract to build the

10 *Introduction*

largest leisure park in Europe, 20 miles east of Paris at Marne-la-Vallée. Work on the project will cost £1.25 billion and will provide 20 000 jobs. In London, plans were unveiled to transform Battersea Power Station into a new leisure complex. The scheme is planned to cost £135 million and aims to create 2500 jobs in the first phase, rising up to 4500 jobs when the development is fully operational and complete. In short, we live in times when the leisure industry is one of the main sources of job creation, economic growth and social interest.

Yet the academic study of leisure for recent graduates and postgraduates faces a brick wall. There are disturbing institutional implications in this situation, and they should not be ignored. The lack of job opportunities and circulation within the system has been a lifeline for the old ideas and moulds of thought which have traditionally dominated the academic study of leisure. The leisure establishment is male, white, middle-class and middle-aged.[10] Now, when the ideas of the past are so patently deficient in understanding the conditions of the present, there is the need for critical thought. Leisure is more than freedom, self-determination, life satisfaction and growth. These critical essays explore the world beyond the conventional wisdom.

London   CHRIS ROJEK

Notes

1. J. Dumazedier (1967) *Towards a Society of Leisure*, New York, Free Press, pp. 16–17.
2. J. R. Kelly (1987) *Freedom To Be: A New Sociology of Leisure*, New York, Macmillan, p. 238.
3. See, for example, D. Frisby (1981) *Sociological Impressionism: A Reassessment of Georg Simmel's Social Theory*, London, Heinemann; (1984) *Georg Simmel*, London, Tavistock; (1985) *Fragments of Modernity*, Oxford, Polity Press.
4. See, for example, J. Alt (1976) 'Beyond class: the decline of industrial labour and leisure,' *Telos*, 28: 58–80; Brohm, J. M. (1978) *Sport: A Prison of Measured Time*, London, Interlinks; Rigauer, B. (1981) *Sport and Work*, New York, Columbia University Press.
5. J. Finch and D. Groves (1980) 'Community Care and the Family: a Case for Equal Opportunities?', *Journal of Social Policy*, 9:4, pp. 487–511.
6. Office of Population Censuses and Surveys (1978) *Demographic Review, 1977*, HMSO, London.

7. E. Goffman (1974) *Frame Analysis: An Essay on the Organization of Experience*, Boston, Northeastern University Press, p. 8.

8. From the Marxist and neo-Marxist standpoint see Alt, *op. cit*; Brohm, *op. cit*; Rigauer, *op. cit*. For a rather mechanical view of patriarchy and women's leisure see R. Deem (1986) *All Work and No Play? The Sociology of Women and Leisure*. Milton Keynes, Open University Press.

9. All figures from A. J. Veal (1987) *Leisure and the Future*, London, Allen & Unwin.

10. The situation is, of course, not unique to Britain. International bodies reflect the same bias. For example, see the elected delegates for the 'Executive Board and Board of Directors of the Research Committee on the Sociology of Leisure of the International Sociological Association for the term 1986–90', listed in the International Sociological Association, *Leisure Newsletter*, Vol. XIII, No. 2, Winter 1986 pp. 14–16.

Part I

Theoretical Perspectives on Leisure

1   Models of Work, Models of Leisure

H. F. Moorhouse

The social analysis of 'leisure' is not well developed. In part this reflects the area's marginal status for sociology and Marxism, but this underdevelopment is also due to the failure of those who have been busy in the field to break out. Rather they seem to have been content to clear their own ground and map out the terrain, creating a fraternity of 'leisure studies'.[1] Recently, this contented community has been blasted by loud criticisms.[2] Van Moorst, for example, argues that:

> Theories of leisure have been dogged by three major problems: a series of superficial concepts and spurious distinctions . . . a preoccupation with a desire to *plan* leisure . . . and, thirdly, partly as a result of these an inadequate theoretical base most frequently stemming from a functionalist framework.[3]

These are telling, and valid, criticisms but to them I would add that usually:

1 the so-called 'theories' of leisure are not theories in any scientific sense being untestable as well as untested; they actually occupy the much less lofty analytic heights of 'approaches to', 'typologies of', or 'ways of thinking about' leisure;
2 the self-referring tendency of leisure studies, which Rojek has pointed to,[4] includes an inclination towards an uncritical reporting of other texts so that points at issue between authors remain vague, the basis for beneficial argument obscure;
3 as part of a tendency to privilege evidence derived from survey methodology, the proponents display an ingenious disregard of national differences and cultures, skipping continents with ease, so that 'results' from Australia, Japan, America and the UK are treated as equivalents, as saying something about 'things' called 'work' and 'leisure', with little thought that those might vary

according to certain material histories and specific national value systems;

4 while individual 'states of mind' or 'attributions of meaning' are allocated great prominence in this tradition (often because of the definitional problems authors have riddled themselves into) such texts studiously avoid most of the issues and scholarly discussions concerning the ways meanings are generated, promoted, and sustained in modern society, which is, in part, to say that the avoidance of serious engagement with class relations[5] has been almost as marked in leisure studies as the trivialisation of gender relations which is, I think, now believed to be its Achilles heel.

All in all, the existing leisure studies tradition is an analytical and conceptual morass which can suck in the unwary, and the real problem of the approach is that it now serves as an impediment to the growth and development of the study of both 'leisure' and 'work'. It is a recognition of this inhibiting role that has provoked some of the recent criticisms, but, as I hope to show, some of the critics, by accepting boundaries and issues legitimated in leisure studies, have ultimately failed to pursue their own logic to its ultimate conclusions.

Deem is an interesting recent example. Considering the lives of certain categories of women she realises that there are severe difficulties with the concept 'leisure' itself, and is worried about exactly what it could refer to in the lives of the women. She says:

The definitional problem about leisure cannot be avoided, and indeed there are good reasons not to do so. But, at the same time, it is necessary if one is not to emulate the centipede who started to count his legs but forgot *why* as well as *where* it started, to use the word leisure as though there were a consensus about what it meant, as well as holding open the question of whether existing definitions are the most appropriate in relation to women's lives.[6]

This is rather unsatisfactory and Deem promises to return to 'the insoluble but crucial question of defining leisure'[7] after her substantive chapters, but when she does she actually avoids the issues rather than confronting them, and seeks to hold the concept 'leisure' for reformist political purposes rather than analytical ones.[8] So she ends up in an odd academic position not unlike that of one of the leading lights of leisure studies who can blithely tell readers: 'leisure, itself, defies definition'[9] while writing reams about it.

'LEISURE' AND 'WORK'

A lot of Deem's unease arises from the way leisure studies has tended to define the concept in a reactive or negative way: it is *not* 'work' or 'obligated time' and this 'social space' simply does not seem to exist for a lot of the women Deem studied, though (and another source of her unease) they *did* experience pleasure and enjoyment in their lives.[10] The issue here is much wider than how existing definitions apply to married women.

One of the narrow concerns about 'leisure' which leisure studies has legitimated is its relation to 'work'. Some major theorists of leisure studies disavow the significance of 'work' and argue for the independence of 'leisure'. Yet 'work' remains a vital concept for them as the opposite, the negative, which constitutes what 'leisure' *is*. Roberts defines leisure as 'the relatively freely chosen non-work area of life'[11] and remarks, 'to understand leisure in modern societies it must be seen, in part at least, as the obverse of work'.[12] Kelly argues that 'if something has to be done then it isn't leisure'[13] and that 'leisure is generally understood as chosen activity that is not work'.[14] However, such conceptualisations do lead, as I have noted for Deem, into some difficulties.

Roberts allows that there are activities – 'leisure at work' and 'work in leisure' which seem at odds with his main definitions.[15] Characteristically, he relies on commonsense understandings to solve this flux: most people can easily decide what is 'work' and what is 'leisure'. However, his reliance on popular perceptions and feelings has other consequences for his main definitions, since people can often experience what is objectively necessary or constrained activity as 'leisure'. So, Roberts has to concede, the boundaries of 'work', 'non-work' and 'leisure' are very fluid; 'leisure' can pop up at all time and places, including paid labour, though earlier in his discussion we had been told that employment places and spaces were distinct from those of 'leisure'.[16]

Kelly introduces the rather odd categories of 'interstitial leisure' and coordinated leisure[17] to deal with similar problems but does not really develop these concepts. Indeed, while stressing the independence of 'leisure' and arguing that, to some extent, it is taking over some socially integrative role from 'work', his analysis is in terms of 'disillusionment' and, 'disenchantment' from work, 'mid-career crises' and the like, which seem to assume that work once was, or was promised to be, the most important area of life for most people,[18] which is just the kind of issue which requires discussion.

So even these theorists, who do not pretend to examine 'work', rely on some rather uneasy vision of it and its social role, to highlight their own leisure studies, but Parker, another leading figure in this tradition, has most explicitly tried to relate 'leisure' to 'work'. I want to use aspects of his approach to illustrate crucial deficiencies in the leisure studies tradition and to show how some recent critics actually almost replicate identical inadequacies.

I want to concentrate attention on three, rather crucial, aspects of Parker's texts.[19]

(i) What are his definition and exploration of 'work'?
(ii) What are his definition and exploration of 'leisure'?
(iii) What connections, if any, does he perceive between 'work' and 'leisure'?

Parker has helped constitute the preferred subject of leisure studies as 'the individual', a being oddly shorn of social attachments other than an immediate one of an equally asocial 'family'. The hallmark of his input is a stress on the significance of the individual's 'work' experience for 'leisure' behaviour and attitudes. It has to be said at the outset, though, that this project is fatally flawed by a resolute avoidance of the structures of class and gender relations. There is little, if anything, in Parker's texts of class cultures, occupational ideologies, the social sources of ideologies, various vocabularies of motivation, and so on. Parker attempts to show a connection between 'work' and 'leisure', and simply does not consider whether some third factor or broader structure might encompass both the production of certain kinds of work, attitudes to them *and* certain types of leisure and appropriate attitudes. This myopia is rather touchingly revealed when Parker (and Kelly and Roberts) seek to justify definitions of 'leisure' in part because they accord with 'popular notions' of what 'leisure' is, *as if* such notions were the outcome of untrammelled human existence or individual response to certain inherent needs.[20] The point that the definitions of leisure studies accord with 'the popular mind' because *both* are faithfully vocalising dominant values never seems to occur to its proponents. Rather this alignment is taken as evidence of 'correctness' (which simply does not follow – consider 'race' for example) and so of analytic usefulness.

Parker tries to grasp 'leisure' as it revolves around 'work'. However, even in its programmatic form, and it must be said that, despite what some recent critics seem to believe, very little *evidence* has been provided to substantiate Parker's ideas, let alone appropriate evidence, Parker's attempt is confused and confusing since he operates with at least three definitions of 'work' and two definitions of 'leisure'. The differences between the various conceptualisatons are often left implicit and Parker tends to move, without much worry, between them in his outline of the 'work-leisure' relationship.

The three definitions of 'work' Parker uses are:

(i) work as employment, as paid labour;
(ii) work as any productive, creative activity;
(iii) work as a moral ideal: what men should do to be 'truly human'.

Parker's outline of work–leisure relations turns primarily on the first of these definitions. His contribution to leisure studies would be much more accurately stated as paid labour–leisure relations, but, the cost of adopting this, much more accurate, label would mean losing the moral impetus which lurks in definition (ii) and is exposed in definition (iii). The word 'work' carries a morally-based drive which eases the acceptance of analysis via the taken-for-granted 'rightness' of what is said, rather than by any actual connection forged in logic or by empirical evidence.[21]

On the few occasions Parker does acknowledge that 'work' has the broader meaning of definition (ii)[22] his references are allusions only, and are not tied back into his repeated discussion of work–leisure relations. The problem here is most clearly presented in an additional page in the 1983 revision of his 1971 text when he argues that not all economic activity takes place in the formal economy and that:

> In line with common usage and in order not to be pedantic I have so far used the work 'work' when strictly speaking the reference was to 'employment' or 'the job'.[23]

He says that employment is essentially a social relationship not to be equated with the performance of work, and maintains that when people complain of their employment, they are dissatisfied with the *pay* and *conditions*, not actually 'work', which is, the moral undertones vibrating again, 'the activity . . . upon which all societies depend.'[24] However shallow is this recognition of the problems involved what it certainly does not do is to cause Parker to revise, alter, or even relabel his typology of work–leisure relations. To do so would be both to forfeit that moral charge of the word 'work', *and*, since work occurs at a lot of times and places other than in paid labour, would mean that the actualy dichotomy Parker uses would collapse, so that the walls of the opposition of times and activities could not be maintained.

Generally, Parker utilises definition (i) and the essence of his definition of 'leisure' is that it is not 'work' or is the opposite of 'work'. This is revealed in his 1976 perception of: 'a broad trend in modern society away from work and toward leisure',[25] which becomes in 1983: 'Industrial societies have, at least in some senses, continued to move away from work and – more questionably – towards leisure.'[26] It is also evident in his 1976 definition:

> Leisure is time free from work and other obligations, it also encompasses activities which are characterised by a feeling of comparative freedom.[27]

Trying to hold on to this causes Parker a deal of definitional troubles. These can be seen in his views on domestic labour,[28] his problems with 'the idle rich',[29] or when regarding work done in the home when we are told in places that: 'some part of what would otherwise be spent as leisure time is devoted to DIY work',[30] or 'DIY activities . . . are hardly leisure',[31] and in others that: 'For some people the need for creative expression of workmanship flourishes in leisure, in DIY work, the care of cars or gardens, the inventive puttering of life after work.'[32]

As this might suggest, just as Parker operates with different definitions of what is to be meant by 'work', so he tends to use different definitions of 'leisure'. Mainly he defines it as non-work activity with a perception of freedom, but it is clear here and there that this does not always suit because he is often unwilling to accept the way people choose to spend their time: he does not really approve of consumers, customers or spectators. Here the unresolved issue in his main definition (as it is in Roberts) as to whether people need to make a free choice or merely *feel* they make a 'free choice' becomes too sharp for Parker to sit upon and he abandons his main definition of leisure for higher moral ground. This makes for a host of non-integrated sub-concepts in Parker's accounts such as 'anti-leisure', 'genuine free time', 'true leisure', the essence of leisure, or 'the ideal state of leisure', with which Parker can indicate his disapproval of a lot of the choices real people actually make.[33] Parker's second, rather mystical, view of what 'leisure' is, seems to exclude from the category a lot of what people actually choose to do outside paid labour either because they spectate and are not active or, and quite the reverse because:

many sporting and artistic activities have more in common with
physiologically and mentally demanding work than with the idle and
carefree attitude that is often thought to be the essence of leisure.[34]

Just as Parker cannot keep work out of leisure, so he cannot keep
leisure out of work. He produces a category of 'leisure in work' which
might be thought to take up some of the ways in which paid labour is
actually lived and experienced, but is in fact, rather oddly explained:

> 'Work' and 'leisure in work' may consist of the same activity; the
> difference is that the latter is chosen for its own sake. Thus
> mountaineering is work for the guide but leisure in work for the
> amateur climber. Leisure time and employment time cannot
> overlap, but there is no reason why some of the time that is sold as
> work should not be utilized by the seller . . . for leisure-type
> activities.[35]

Parker does not actually hold to this, as in his musings about people
who are employed doing work they would choose to do even if
financially free, and whether this is 'work' or 'leisure'.[36] Beyond this
however, even for most employees, it is hard to understand why the
flirtations, feuds, jokes, gambling, shopping, and so on that occur all
the time in paid labour are not leisure but only 'leisure-like'. Consider
this outline of a large vehicle manufacturing plant:

> the plant itself is a society in miniature. It provides a variety of
> facilities and activities which are not task based. The consist not only
> of those which formally exist, such as a bar, a canteen, a club,
> snooker tables, but also less formal activities within the place of
> work. We estimate that there are over twenty bookies' runners on
> the shop floor, and there are regular snooker, dominoes, football
> and crib games. From the workers themselves it is possible to buy
> food, cigarettes, fresh fish (at highly competitive prices) meat, shoes
> and clothing, and car spares (including resprays) and to lay bets and
> get your hair cut.[37]

In fact, a lot of the definitional problems arise here because Parker,
and most other students of 'leisure', adopt an extremely unrealistic
view of what paid labour was, and is, like and how it is *actually*
experienced and given meaning. Parker and leisure studies' recent
Marxist critics are keen to hold on to some alienation thesis about most

employment. Parker, eschewing other springs of individual resource, tends to statements like:

> If individuals tend to experience dependence, submission, frustration and short time horizons at work, and if they adapt to these conditions by psychological withdrawal, apathy, and indifference and a decrease in the importance of their worth as human beings, these adaptive activities will become more important in the person's life and they will guide his leisure behaviour outside the workplace.[38]

Well, if they did it might happen (assuming that there are no other sources of meaning and purpose to create identities and meet 'human needs' in society) but there is scarcely a shred of evidence that most worker do feel or adapt in this way.

Another major failing of leisure studies, which could be added to my earlier catalogue, is that it operates with a simplistic and stereotyped view of what most 'work' is like, seeing it as impoverished, routinised, deskilledd, etc., and assumes that direct 'effects' can be read off from this. Debates about such matters raging in industrial sociology simply do not echo in leisure studies, nor do the older, neglected, but very powerful criticisms of any kind of alienation notions which stem from the Affluent Worker study, with its emphasis on *prior* orientations to work, and from the patient observations of Roy, or even Chinoy, at some pains to trace out how paid time, even in the most routinised environments, is given purpose and how meaning comes through the ceremonies and events of shopfloor life or by connection to grander cultural themes.[39] What is a very complicated issue is oversimplified in leisure studies. Certainly the effects of the constant active de-alienation of employment experience and the way that cultural values of various kinds can contextualise and give meaning to employment, find little space in Parker's discussion of 'work' and 'leisure', nor do they in the views of Marxist critics of leisure studies.

Notwithstanding evident difficulties in keeping the two terms discrete, Parker has set out a pattern of 'work–leisure relations'.[40] He distinguishes *an extension relation* where 'leisure' activities are similar in content to 'work' and no sharp distinction is made in what is considered to be 'work' or 'leisure', *an opposition relation* where 'leisure' activities are deliberately unlike 'work', with a sharp distinction drawn, and *a relation of neutrality* where 'leisure' activities generally differ from 'work' but this is not deliberate, and, while a difference between 'spheres' is appreciated, the one is not defined as the absence of the other. Actually, some of this is at odds with Parker's main definition of 'leisure', but rather than resolve such conceptual differences, or provide more reasoning about, or evidence of, the causes of, or the actual existence of, such patterns Parker has chosen to constantly repeat and elaborate this scheme. So, by 1983, both 'work' and 'leisure' have each been broken into three aspects of the possible relation – involvement, activities and attitudes – and each aspect can relate to every other one giving nine possible connections.[41]

However, as Parker dwells on this he is unable or unwilling to suggest some actual causal line or major relation, so we can be told: 'High involvement in work may be positively, negatively or neutrally related to high involvement in leisure',[42] which is another way of saying that there is *no* relation. In his texts Parker provides a plurality of 'levels' and 'aspects' from which it is quite impossible to draw any clear analytical statement. Parker clearly wants to suggest that 'work' causes 'leisure', and he does, occasionally, offer a causal statement, albeit one riddled with moralising. When talking of the neutral pattern, with its detached attitude to work, he says:

> Instead work leaves them comparatively unmarked and free to carry over into leisure the non-involvement and passivity which characterizes their attitude to work. In other words, detachment from any real responsibility for and interest in work leads to detachment from any active and constructive leisure pursuits.[43]

But Parker actually disclaims any causal connection between 'work' and 'leisure', or indeed between various aspects and others.[44] Since, it seems, one occupation can yield all three relations with 'leisure', and all these relations can appear among those involved in one hobby, this is a wise caveat.[45] What Parker claims to have revealed are some associations between 'work' and 'leisure' but even this is not really the case, for the evidence offered is very thin and contradictory, and even if it consisted of the reliable statistical associations Parker claims,[46] correlation is far from causation, and all the academic labour required to turn what is in fact a typology of possibilities into hypotheses capable of being tested in reality remains all to be done. What would be required is the specification of the conditions under which one pattern rather than another could be expected and some argument about probable causes. In fact, as I have tried to suggest before, the stock of causes are most unlikely to be found in immediate 'work' or 'leisure' experiences, and one would need to consider whether broader material and cultural factors might not be producing certain attitudes *both* to work and to leisure. To give a simple example, Parker seems to believe that it is the absorbing 'work' of professionals and managers which produces a spillover into 'leisure', whereas it is part of *learning* to be a 'professional' (and to claim its rewards) to insist that you are absorbed in what you do and have no time free of the demands of your job, and so on.[47]

All in all, it is none too clear what benefit the study of leisure derives from Parker's work. Parker, quite correctly, denies that he is offering a theory, though he does seem to believe that it is a step 'towards a theory'. Others seem to regard Parker's work as one of those (elusive) 'theories of leisure' suggesting that Parker has actually traced some connection between 'work' and 'leisure' whereas, as I have tried to indicate, the two terms of this 'equation' vary, continuously, with a chameleon-like quality in their nature, while no actual connection in fact or theory has been drawn between them. Moreover, there are, via references to other social theory and research, good reasons to believe that the whole project of trying to link 'work' and 'leisure' as discrete and isolated phenomena is misconceived. Even if it were not, then much closer attention would need to be paid to the real rhythms and experience of life on the shop or office floor. Unless leisure studies grasps these matters, and moves away from its own narrowly set range of 'problems' it will deserve to enjoy its marginal status.

THE NEO-MARXIST ALTERNATIVE

And this is a real danger, for, oddly enough, recent Matxist critics of mainsteam leisure studies display similar weaknesses. They have, for example, the same cavalier stance to definitions, claiming both that the sociology of leisure has had an obsession with defining leisure and, in some contradiction, that an arbitrary commonsense concept has been used as an adequate academic concept. These authors abdicate from any attempt at defining their subject. Their work:

> does not attempt to finally lay to rest all those complex definitional questions about what is or is not leisure. We do not believe that these questions can be solved by ever more elaborate analytical juggling.[48]

Instead, they claim this ambiguity is exactly their subject, since it reveals leisure as the site of social conflict:

It is this contradictory and ambiguous status of leisure in British society that interests us. In what follows our task is not to supply a more simple definition of leisure which will remove all those ambiguities, but to understand *how* leisure comes to be the subject of these competing definitions.[49]

This appears to assume that confusions in a concept arise from a social conflict, which is both deterministic and generous, and the authors never really elaborate just why 'leisure' is the kind of concept whose lack of definition should be regarded as a virtue. In practice the authors do use the same commonsense category, with 'leisure' regarded as free time (with or without inverted commas), time left over from 'work', or as non-work, which leads them into some difficulties, as we shall see. The main thrust of Clarke and Critcher's book is along two channels. First, these authors insist that 'work', or employment at least, is *capitalist work*. They are, therefore, even less willing than Parker to allow that paid labour can be, for most, a source of satisfaction, purpose, creativity, qualitative experience, and so on. They are more insistent on voicing the 'radical' stereotype of labour as routinised, degraded, alienated, arduous drudgery and so on:

> The mechanisation, fragmentation and routinisation of work have received extensive analysis from generations of industrial psychologists concerned at the effects of such work experience in creating bored, alienated and dissatisfied workers and their associated problems of low output, poor quality, high absenteeism and high labour turnover . . . Extensive though such efforts have been it seems that they have failed to remove the essential experience as a painful necessity for the majority of workers.[50]

'Leisure', modern 'leisure', is the flip side of this:

> By contrast leisure seems to offer the prospect of being all those things that work is not: the source of satisfactions, gratifications and pleasures. Where work is the realm of dull compulsion, leisure represents freedom, choice and creativity. Where work is that which must be done, leisure is the pursuit of free chosen self interest.[51]

They see life as: 'a daily circuit of misery and pleasure' with 'leisure' as compensation or escape. Capitalist work then is a vital aspect of Clarke and Critcher's account but, as in Parker's work, this crucial experience is not documented but invoked, and the same problem arises for them as for Parker: inside the factory and office, people may be told to accept an alienated role, outside they do not but inject meanings, purpose, pride and prestige into what they have to do.[52] So the many meanings and actual experiences of paid labour are crushed into a stereotype of what it must be like if the theory is to hold. If 'work' is not protrayed accurately and in detail as an experience and *if* it has an intimate connection with 'leisure', then it seems unlikely that the experience of 'leisure' can be protrayed accurately either.

Clarke and Critcher's second stress is to insist that while 'leisure' has been presented (and with a much less certain emphasis accepted) as compensation, in fact the 'self-fulfilment' and 'choice' are illusions. They are limited, controlled, with choice materially and culturally constrained by all manner of social divisions. Clarke and Critcher are quite unwilling to accept the 'happy families' version of 'leisure choice' at the heart of Roberts' account. However, this leads them into two difficulties: firstly, and again like Parker, they do not like some of the choices which the proletariat as consumers make and in which they seem to find 'satisfactions'. So they have to appeal to something 'deeper' than the majority's apparent contentment. Which is to say, in this account, a wide alienation and inhumanity *in* 'leisure' as in 'work' has to be granted by theoretical *fiat*, not by empirical elucidation.[53] Moreover, secondly, there is an unresolved issue here about how the individuals who seem to be the dupes of 'market choice' create cultures, working-class cultures, which roam free and still offer alternatives to what is. In fact it is just this insistence that allows Clarke and Critcher to offer themselves as class-domination theorists, not mass-society ones, whom they deplore as much as Roberts for their supposed unwillingness to spot the signs of struggle and counter-attack all round. But this invocation of resistance in leisure is none too amply documented and while it is comforting to leave the idea that 'the double movement of constraint and creation'[54] somehow leads to a middle path their post-war examples hardly sustain this. They are forced to stress the informal, street, spontaneous elements in leisure as opposed to people's experiences of participation in the commercial mode and so, once again, a book about leisure displays a real lack of detail about what most people actually do or feel in their 'free time'.

Then Clarke and Critcher's outline of capitalism's distinction of employment and leisure into two sets of time, space, and meanings, bumps on to the reef of domestic work in the home, as they recognise;

'The work/leisure categorization is inapplicable to much domestic activity'. It is hard to maintain the segregations, leisure can conceal time spent on domestic labour, it can be both work and satisfying, relaxing and creative. They say:

> it is essential to establish how unsatisfactory the work/leisure dichotomy is when applied to the home and the sexual division of labour and time within it.[55]

This is certainly the issue, though it has a much wider application than domestic labour conceived of as an activity of 'reproduction', but it is rather at odds with much of what the authors have said before which does assume, like Parker, that the crucial, vital, 'work' is employment. Clarke and Critcher scarcely resolve the issue, though in some rather speculative pages about 'play' they do suggest, again at some odds with most of the rest of their text, that:

> The antithesis of work and leisure may, then, be more usefully understood as that of necessary labour and unnecessary play.[56]

The problem with this is that 'unnecessary play' can often involve labour, and, that the contours of what is 'necessary' and 'unnecessary' are hard to perceive and are often, apparently, bound up in the same moment or activity.

DISCUSSION

None of the above would be of much moment were the territory which leisure studies has tried to stake out of no importance, but it is important, in part because more adequate analysis could help shake those preconceptions of a lot of sociology and of most Marxism which help create their inadequacies as general theories. Feminist criticisms have pointed the way here, but in this paper I have focused on a specific, but crucial, joist in the present construction of the analysis of 'leisure' to try to indicate its weaknesses. The real orthodoxy of leisure studies is a conceptual and theoretical confusion coupled with an unwillingness to break out of its own isolation. Rojek has offered four rules of the sociology of leisure[57] but I would put forward two much more specific injunctions for those who really want to grasp the nature of modern life.

First, I think it would be as well to abandon the commonsense categories of 'work' and 'leisure'. Aristotle can hardly be allowed to have had the last word on conceptual development here and those who claim to want to dig beneath the surface of capitalist reality require well-fashioned (as opposed to fashionable) tools so to do. Abandonment of this enticing, but disabling, couplet might provoke a more precise focus on the actual times, and qualities of times, people wish to concentrate on, and would have the bonus of ditching the moral resonances which hang around both terms. This is just what is occurring in other areas of sociology, especially in recent contributions to the study of economic life, where the concept 'work' has come under very close scrutiny.[58] As Pahl puts it in a recent book:

> A problem with many of the scholarly discussions of work, certainly since the time of Adam Smith and Karl Marx, is that too much emphasis has been given to that work narrowly perceived to be connected with a specific conception of production and too little to the other productive work connected with reproduction and consumption.[59]

He conceptualizes the household (that 'family' of leisure studies) as: 'simply units for getting various types of work done', and argues that an insistence on the material and moral significance of one kind of work – employment – is historically inaccurate and contemporarily myopic. Other forms of work which have been both restricted and encouraged by structural and value changes since the war contain, like a lot of waged work, conflicting themes:

> Certainly some self provisioning is a coping response for those with insufficient financial resources to hire labour in the market, but it also provides aesthetic satisfaction, pride in workmanship and a sense of domestic solidarity.[60]

Within a broad duality of production and reproduction Pahl provides a typology of ten types of work, with eleven qualifications or subdivisions. The reproduction aspect itself, a category covering a lot of what other analysts would label 'leisure', contains four kinds of work, with six sub-divisions.

Pahl's study certainly does set out some of the complications of the term 'work' and deals a profound blow to analyses like those of leisure studies and its critics which seek to operate with simple, obvious dualities. However, Pahl's work does contain faults. These turn not on the point, which he acknowledges, that he is considering household not individual strategies (and, despite its stress on the family the actual subject of leisure studies has been the individual) but concern other, deeper, problems about meanings and exactly what the term 'work' is to cover.

Although Pahl begins his study by saying that one of its starting points was people's changing *experience* of 'work' his study is curiously silent about meanings and their sources. The main text presents a rather formal account of 'work' of which the typology just referred to is an example, while a couple of case studies here and there hardly deal with the issue of what messages people are receiving about 'work' and how they interpret them. Pahl falls back on quantitative measurements, not those of quality, to measure significance: 'The assumption must be that, if more time is spent on one activity than another, then that activity ranks as more important or essential'[61] which is a quite unwarranted logical deduction and existentially is obviously untrue. Apart from a few scattered references to advertising and the sales effort Pahl has little to say about how time and activities are given meaning. This is a similar failure to that of the 'leisure studies' approaches and, as I will try to show below, leads Pahl into rather similar definitional problems.

Pahl has little to say about 'leisure'; it is mentioned here and there but is not a vibrant concept in his approach. This then poses the problem which Pahl does well to recognise – in his presentation, is *all* activity 'work'? He takes up the issue by setting out the maximal answer:

> it may be argued, we live in a capitalist social formation, *all* attitudes are concerned with the production and reproduction of that system. According to such an extreme position, productive work is seen as central and all other activities are secondary and subservient to it. Thus, people's leisure free time, or play can be seen as recreating the energy and momentum to return to productive work and somewhat humourlessly re-productive work is seen as serving the function of reproducing the labour power and social relations of the social formation.[62]

Pahl rejects such extreme functionalism (though his use of the production-reproduction couplet does tend to lead to this) and that all human activity is 'work', but it is far from clear just why he does so. A footnote about the above passage notes that 'productive work' is a concept capable of generating immense confusion, as is 'reproduction', and states his position as:

> Some social formations encourage the production of many objects and things which, in turn, implies substantial consumption. Since without this consumption, the raison d'être of production would be condemned, consumption is essential for production and is a necessary form of work in such societies.[63]

This formulation is repeated elsewhere: 'The development of *consumption* as a form of work is, perhaps, the dominant new element that capitalism has imposed on household work strategies'[64] and is one which seems to add to the view that, from his perspective, all activities are work and there would be little space for 'leisure' except as a particular label for forms of work. Pahl's negative answer to the question is to enjoin analysts to look at the social context:

> Specific people in specific circumstances in specific sets of social relations and social relationships can be described precisely in terms of whether they are engaged in work or play. The word work cannot be defined out of context, that, indeed, is the conclusion and answer to the question.[65]

But this is an opaque answer and the only real suggestion Pahl gives to sort out such contexts is the various meanings which people bring to certain tasks, but, as I have said, he provides no systematic account of the production, promotion and acceptance of meanings which (to repeat) is a major failing of leisure studies.

While analyses like Pahl's, which are being developed in other areas of social analysis, will not offer ready-made 'solutions' to the muddle around the 'work–leisure relation', they do indicate the kind of conceptual distinctions required if 'leisure' is to be located and the break that has to be made with the way certain issues have been 'understood' and institutionalised in leisure studies. The separation of time into paid labour, unpaid labour and consumption, and various experiences in these would be a start, but it is a complicated matter, for while it is rarely recognised in leisure studies, the tempo of experience, in any 'category' is not a matter of measuring each mundane moment but of musing on peaks and troughs. So, as well as developing a more precise categorisation of 'life space', analysts also require to grasp exactly what pieces of time and aspects of activities people use to colour in the whole day or life.

This leads to my second injunction, which is that social analysis must start taking a serious interest in fun and pleasure. So far leisure or other studies have provided little sense of what people actually do or feel in pubs, gardens, kitchens, on pitches or package tours. In part, this is a plea about methodology. 'Leisure activities' are social phenomena where ethnography and the detailed study of particular places, enthusiasms and events is both relatively easy *and* highly appropriate, and yet few such studies exist.[66] But such an emphasis would also require a theoretical consideration of exactly how non-work activities are actually organised and informed. Roberts' view: 'the values that stimulate industrialisation tend to devalue spare time, and offer little guidance as to how leisure should be spent'[67] is simply perverse if we cast half an eye at the sales effort of modern capitalism. On the other hand, abstract references to: 'the leisure industries', 'capitalism', 'market provision', 'consumerism', 'hege-mony' and the like merely indicate where detailed analyses might begin and by no means represent analyses in themselves.

One aspect of this would be some further unravelling of the 'work–leisure relation', for ideas about craft, skill and the work ethic, which the practitioners of leisure studies seem to feel once applied to 'work', have been taken up by the commercial and moral entrepeneurs of consumption and applied to the production of pleasure in non-paid activities. People's pleasure in what looks like unpaid and arduous 'work' is a hook which troubles both Deem and Clarke and Critcher, but as there is no intrinsic meaning in any action, scholarship needs to reveal how meanings have been applied, sustained, changed and learned.

I believe there is a route into all this, contained in general social theory via concepts which have been abused or ignored in social analysis. Weber used the concepts of status group and lifestyle to refer to specific patterns of consumption and culturally-based attachments.[68] For Marxism such concepts are simply secondary or inappropriate and while both concepts are sometimes referred to in leisure studies they are used as cavalierly there as they have been in most of sociology.[69] Sobel sums up the use of one of them:

there is almost no agreement either empirically or conceptually as to what constitutes a lifestyle. There is not much explicit disagreement either. Rather, the literature is idiosyncratic . . . Furthermore, virtually no discussions of lifestyle as a phenomenon in its own right are to be found. In short, social scientists use this term to refer to whatever they wish . . . their use is no more informative than the layman's.[70]

The same applies to status and while there is a minor resurgence of interest in the concept recent contributions are trying to claim the concept for the study of employment-based divisions rather than for consumption.[71] A stress on such concepts cracks across a neo-Marxist concern with class relations but, as I have tried to indicate, this involves a preconception and preoccupation about the significance of 'work' in people's lives.

Burns suggested a long time ago that attention to the concepts of status group and lifestyle could be one way to a more academically sophisticated and adequate analysis of relations between employment and non-employment, and the way individuals and groups get tied into projects which order the significance of paid and unpaid time to them.[72] I have tried to argue that the social analysis of 'leisure' is not so far advanced that it can really afford to avoid trying out new analytical pathways and developing routes out of its isolation.

Notes

1. Institutionalised in the Leisure Studies Association (1975), the journal *Leisure Studies*, various series of working papers and books, etc.
2. H. van Moorst (1982) 'Leisure and Social Theory', *Leisure Studies*, 157–69. J. Clarke and C. Critcher (1985) *The Devil Makes Work: Leisure in Capitalist Britain*, London, Macmillan; C. Rojek (1985) *Capitalism and Leisure Theory*, London, Tavistock; R. Deem (1986) *All Work and No Play?*, Milton Keynes, Open University.
3. Van Moorst, op. cit., p. 157.
4. Rojek, op. cit., p. 1.
5. So leisure studies make few if any references to the influential typology of value systems and social sources contained in F. Parkin (1971) *Class Inequality and Political Order*, London, MacGibbon & Kee, even though this was published in the *same sociology series* as S. Parker (1971) *The Future of Work and Leisure*, London, MacGibbon & Kee, a basic text of leisure studies.
6. Deem, op. cit., p. 17.
7. Ibid., p. 19.
8. Ibid., pp. 135–7 and 149.

9. S. Parker (1976) *The Sociology of Leisure*, London, George Allen & Unwin, p. 48–9.
10. Deem, op. cit., pp. 88–9 and 135.
11. K. Roberts (1978) *Contemporary Society and the Growth of Leisure*, London, Longman. p. 3.
12. Ibid., p. 3.
13. J. Kelly (1983) *Leisure Identities and Interactions*, London, George Allen & Unwin, p. 5.
14. Ibid., p. 9.
15. Roberts, op. cit., p. 3.
16. Compare Roberts pp. 3–4 and pp. 6–7.
17. Kelly, op. cit., p. 162 and pp. 9–10.
18. Kelly, op. cit., p. 73–5.
19. S. Parker (1971), S. Parker (1976) and S. Parker (1983) *Leisure and Work*, London, George Allen & Unwin.
20. e.g. Parker (1983) p. 40; Roberts p. 3.
21. The 'work ethic' is one such concept simply accepted, rarely interrogated. It certainly flits in and out of the analyses of leisure studies when something is required to bridge a gap in 'explanation'. See H. F Moorhouse (1987) 'The 'Work' Ethic and 'Leisure' Activity' in P. Joyce (ed.) *The Historical Meanings of Work*, Cambridge, Cambridge University Press.
22. E.g. Parker (1971) p. 19; Parker (1983) pp. 1–2.
23. Parker (1983) p. 32.
24. Parker (1983) pp. 32 and 125.
25. Parker (1976) p. 71.
26. Parker (1983) Preface.
27. Parker (1976) p. 12.
28. E.g.Parker (1983) p. 12, where the lives of housewives are described as 'fuller' than those of other people, which is one way of putting it.
29. Parker (1971) p. 31, where Parker speculates that the 'work' life of the idle rich is even more 'impoverished' than that of prisoners, the unemployed and housewives. This insight is dropped in the 1983 revision.
30. Parker (1976) p. 35.
31. Parker (1971) p. 11 and Parker (1983) p. i.
32. Parker (1971) p. 100 and Parker (1983) p. 87.
33. E.g. Parker (1976) p. 35.
34. Parker (1976) p. 70.
35. Parker (1983) p. 11.
36. Parker's ideal is the 'artist' or 'craftsman' whose activities are both 'work' and 'leisure' as they 'take off' into some 'state of flow'. He writes from the perspective of someone 'lucky enough' to be employed doing what he would choose to do anyway. Which is to say that leisure studies is shot through with the same highly romantic notion of 'the whole man' which has bedevilled analysis in industrial sociology recently.
37. E. Batstone, I. Boraston and S. Frenkel (1977) *Shop Stewards in Action*, Oxford, Basil Blackwell, pp. 127–8.
38. Parker (1976) p. 75, and see e.g. Parker (1983) pp. 31 and 125.

39. J. H. Goldthorpe (1966) 'Attitudes and Behaviour of Car Assembly Workers', *British Journal of Sociology* XVII, pp. 227–44, D. Roy (1959–60) 'Banana Time: Job Satisfaction and Informal Interaction' *Human Organization* XVIII, pp. 158–168, and (1974) 'Sex in the Factory: Informal Heterosexual Relations between Supervisors and Workgroups' in C. Bryant (ed.) *Deviant Behavior*, Chicago, Rand McNally; E. Chinoy (1955) *Automobile Workers and the American Dream*, Boston, Beacon; H. F. Moorhouse (1983) 'American Automobiles and Worker's Dreams', *Sociological Review* XXXI, pp. 403–26.

40. Parker (1971) Chap. 8; Parker (1976) Chap. 5; Parker (1983) pp. 75–80 and Chap. 8.

41. Parker (1883) pp. 75–80. In another differentiation of levels and possible relations Parker gets to 16 'combinations' of the individual and social structure. S. Parker (1981) 'Change, Flexibility, Spontaneity, and Self-Determination in Leisure', *Social Forces* LX, p. 327.

42. Parker (1983) p. 75.

43. Parker (1983) p. 91. In his efforts to show some connection between 'work' and 'leisure' Parker is pushed to some particularly strained 'connections'. The repeated sections on bingo and fishing are good examples. See e.g. Parker (1983) pp. 74 and 84.

44. Parker (1983) pp. 97 and 111.

45. Ibid., p. 93 and 95–6.

46. Ibid., p. 97.

47. There is a whole debate here about the fact that 'skill', 'craft', and 'knowledge' are not 'things' intrinsic in certain tasks or jobs, but are socially constructed labels used in attempts to secure favourable positions in the labour market. C. Cockburn (1983) *Brothers, Male Dominance and Technological Change*, London, Pluto, is a good starting point for the issues here.

48. Clarke and Critcher (1985) p. xiii.

49. Ibid., pp. 11–12.

50. Ibid., p. 2.

51. Ibid., p. 3.

52. K. Kusterer (1978) *Know How On the Job: the Important Working Knowledge of 'Unskilled' Workers*, Boulder, Colorado, Westview, is an excellent and neglected study of this point.

53. The wise words in the Affluent Worker study about appeals to 'alienation' need to be confronted by those who wish to use the concept. J. H. Goldthorpe et al. (1969) *The Affluent Worker in the Class Structure*, Cambridge, Cambridge University Press, pp. 179–87.

54. So this text displays two more general weaknesses of the output of the Centre for Contemporary Cultural Studies. Experience in employment is invoked as vital but is not the subject of detailed study *and* almost any form of deviance is claimed as 'class resistance'. These are necessary qualifications to the adequacy of the Centre's research as it ends to be used in leisure studies as if it were a well-rounded, detailed, empirical set of 'examples' of youth at leisure.

55. Clarke and Critcher (1985) p. 110.

56. Clarke and Critcher (1985) p. 173.

57. Rojek (1985) pp. 180–1.
58. E.g. B. Roberts et al. (eds.) (1985) *New Approaches to Economic Life*, Manchester, Manchester University Press: R. Pahl (1984) *Divisions of Labour*, Oxford, Blackwell.
59. Pahl (1984) p. 19.
60. Ibid., p. 105.
61. Ibid., p. 106.
62. Ibid., pp. 126–8.
63. Ibid., p. 126.
64. Ibid., p. 106.
65. Ibid., p. 128.
66. Consider how little study there is of what professional soccer 'means' to the older, non-hooligan fan, i.e. about 90 per cent of those who watch football.
67. Roberts (1978) p. 90.
68. M. Weber (1948) 'Class, Status and Party' in H. Gerth and C. Wright Mills (eds.) *From Max Weber*, London, Routledge & Kegan Paul, pp. 180–95.
69. Roberts puts some stress on 'lifestyle' as important for the study of leisure, but this tends to be seen as a set of 'tastes' the individual arrives at independently from all the good things on offer. The ideologies and institutions which now promote 'lifestyles', i.e. the power relations of consumer culture, are characteristically downplayed, if not ignored.
70. M. Sobel (1981) *Lifestyle and Social Structure*, New York, Academic Press, p. 2.
71. J. Barbalet (1986) 'The Limitation of Class Theory and the Disappearance of Status', *Sociology* XX, pp. 557–75, and R. Crompton (1987) 'Gender Status and Professionalism', *Sociology* XXI, pp. 413–28.
72. T. Burns (1966) 'The Study of Consumer Behaviour, A Sociological View', *Archives Européennes de Sociologie* VII, pp. 313–29.

2 The Figurational Approach to Leisure and Sport

Eric Dunning

In this essay, I shall illustrate the 'figurational' ('developmental' or 'sociogenetic' and 'psychogenetic') approach to sociology developed by Norbert Elias with special reference to some of the work that Elias and I have done in the field of leisure and sport.[1] As is perhaps well known, this work is mainly concerned with testing and elaborating the theory of civilising processes that Elias began to develop in the 1930s. I shall start by responding to some criticisms of the theory and, after that, I shall present a thumbnail sketch of what the theory actually entails. The theory of the civilising process has been tested in a wide variety of areas. If one limits oneself merely to the field of leisure and sports studies it has been used to examine the quest for excitement in modern leisure relations; the sports of Ancient Greece; the development of rugby football and the growth of formal rules of conduct in activities such as boxing, soccer and cricket.[2] I do not have the space here to go into all of these areas. Therefore I will confine myself to two illustrative case studies: (i) Elias's study of the development of foxhunting;[3] and (ii) the work on football hooliganism that I have been carrying out in collaboration with Patrick Murphy and John Williams.[4]

SOME CRITICISMS OF THE THEORY OF CIVILISING PROCESSES: A CRITICAL RESPONSE

In a recent review of Chris Rojek's *Capitalism and Leisure Theory*, a book in which many aspects of the figurational approach are recommended, Otto Newman refers to 'Elias's notion of the ever-civilising trend of social life'. He continues '. . . in the face of ubiquitous "class warfare, violence on the picket lines, sexual

36

harrassment, genocide, terrorism and abortion" – what of drug abuse,
urban riots, street crime and hooliganism? – even Rojek finds such
generalisations hard to sustain.'[5] Similar criticisms are contained in
recent articles by Jennifer Hargreaves[6] and James Curtis.[7] For
example, Curtis writes:

> As interesting and insightful as Elias' analyses are, his theory has a
> flaw. His assumption of more or less unilinear evolution is very
> questionable. For example, he says that ontogeny repeats
> phylogeny, that societies go through a process of development
> similar to that of humans, from infants (sic) through childhood and
> adulthood. Surely, we must reject this view. One problem is that the
> process of civilization is not as irreversible as biological maturation.[8]

A little later, Curtis continues:

> While reading *The Civilizing Process*, I could not help thinking of all
> the contrary evidence . . . from the past few years: the slaughter of
> Jews in Nazi Germany; the devastation laid on people in Dresden;
> the annihilation provided the people of Hiroshima; the destruction
> of life and property in the bombing of Tokyo; and the massacres at
> Mai Lai and in other places in Vietnam, to name but a very few. How
> do we reconcile these events with the notion that people are moving
> toward a pinnacle in self-restraint of aggression?[9]

Ian Taylor even identifies Elias as an 'evolutionary idealist' and, in an
unsubstantiated attack on the work on football hooliganism that
Patrick Murphy, John Williams and I have been engaged in, writes
dismissively that:

> the project appears to be to find evidence of violent incidents at
> soccer games continuously *throughout* the history of the profession-
> al game and also to locate examples of violence amongst crowds at
> soccer games outside England. One can see why this project is
> helpful to Dunning in his attempt to illustrate the evolutionary and
> idealist social theory of Norbert Elias – but the evidence *is* stretched
> . . . and the theory's stress on an ongoing process of civilization
> *surely* is a very unhelpful framework through which to analyze the
> current condition of working class youth in Britain.[10]

As I shall show later, what we have tried to do in the Leicester project is to trace *variations* in the reported incidence of soccer-spectator misbehaviour over time but Taylor confuses this with a non-developmental notion of an unchanging historical continuity. Moreover, as I also hope to show, *pace* Taylor, Elias's theory provides an *extremely* helpful framework to analyse the current conditions of working-class youth in Britain. However, in order to recognise that, one has to pay attention to what Elias *actually wrote*. Before I provide a thumbnail sketch of one or two key aspects of Elias's sociological work, let me first of all respond briefly to the critical points made by Newman, Hargreaves, Curtis and Taylor.

The first thing to note is that these four authors, but particularly Newman and Curtis with their reference to genocide and so on, fail to take account of the fact that Elias is a German of Jewish descent, that the two volumes of *The Civilizing Process*[11] were written just after he had been forced to flee Nazi Germany, that Elias lost both his parents in the Nazi terror (his mother died in Auschwitz), and that Elias was forced to flee his native Germany and take up residence in England. Either Elias at the time was an individual completely detached from and unaware of what was going on around him, or these scholars have fundamentally misunderstood vital aspects of his theory. As I hope to show, Elias's paradigm has been, from the outset, more reality-orientated than many other approaches at present on offer in sociology. It is, therefore, reasonable to suppose that Newman, Hargreaves, *et al* have either taken Elias's work out of its wider context, or they have simply failed to grasp the range, complexity and subtlety of his theory. Let me push this point a little further.

The common strand in these attacks is the identification of Elias's theory of civilising processes as a theory of 'unilinear evolution'. Beyond that, the critiques of Taylor and Curtis, the most elaborate of the four, are different. Taylor attacks the theory as 'idealist', whilst Curtis attacks it for allegedly asserting that 'ontogeny repeats phylogeny'. Taylor is evidently so attached to the idea of Marxist materialism as the *only* form of radical commitment that he is unable to appreciate a theory which strives to transcend the crude dichotomy between 'the material' and 'the ideal'.[12] For his part, Curtis is evidently so attached to the idea that *any* developmental theory must *necessarily* take the form of an eighteenth- and nineteenth-century theory of 'unilinear progress' that he equates Elias with Auguste Comte. A modification of aspects of Comte's theory is certainly *one* of the bases from which Elias's emergent synthesis has been built.[13] However, whilst it may be correct to criticise Comte for mistakenly believing that the 'law of the three stages' as a social process replicates the stages through which the thinking of an individual human being passes, it is difficult to see how such a 'flaw' can be attributed to Elias. Again and again, he takes pains to stress not only the evolutionary connections between, but also the relative autonomy of, structures at the physical, biological and social levels. One of Elias's clearest statements on the relative autonomy of the social came when he wrote:

in sociology distinct and specific forms of integration and disintegration, patterns of order and disorder, and types of structure and function are encountered which differ from those on all previous levels of integration and cannot be reduced to them, even though the forms found on all levels constitute ontogenetically a single, if subdivided, developmental continuum.[14]

One implication of this is that, while the sequence of biological stages through which an individual human being or any other organism passes on its way from birth to death is necessary and irreversible, the compulsions involved in a process of social development do not have the same character of inevitability and irreversibility. That is in large part because the processes at work in a human society depend on learning. They may, for example, lead it to become more differentiated and integrated at a higher level, less differentiated and integrated at a lower level, or to remain for a greater or lesser time fixed at a given level of differentiation and integration. But these are relatively autonomous *social* processes and they have to be understood as such. The point, of course, is that, although it is a developmental theory and although Elias focuses primarily on Western European developments, his theory of civilising processes is a twentieth-century synthesis which seeks to avoid eighteenth- and nineteenth-century mistakes. It is, therefore, fully attuned to the occurrence of shorter and longer term 'regressions', 'counter civilizing-developments' or 'de-civilizing spurts'. For example, Elias writes:

this movement of society and civilization certainly does not follow a straight line. Within the overall movement there are repeatedly greater or lesser counter-movements in which the contrasts in society and the fluctuations in the behaviour of individuals, their affective outbreaks, increase again.[15]

there is no 'zero-point' of civilisation, no 'absolutely uncivilized' human society or group, either today or in the past.[16] Moreover, societies or groups which are more 'advanced' in this regard are not 'civilized' absolutely. As Elias puts it:

> We cannot expect of people who live in the midst of (present) tensions, who are thus driven guiltlessly to incur guilt upon guilt against each other, that they should behave to each other in a manner representing – as seems so often to be believed today – an ultimate pinnacle of 'civilised' conduct. The continuous intertwining of human activities again and again acts as a lever which over the centuries produces changes in human conduct in the direction of our standard. The same pressures quite clearly operate in our society towards changes transcending present standards of conduct and sentiment in the same direction – although, today as in the past, these trends can go at any time into reverse gear. No more than our kind of social structure is our kind of conduct, our level of constraints, prohibitions and anxieties something definitive, still less a pinnacle.[17]

Elias's critics appear to ignore one of the basic principles of the figurational approach: the principle that, like all other aspects of known reality, human figurations are *inherently processual*. Life itself is a process and the living human beings who form figurations are not only interdependent with each other but have to act and interact – both with each other and with 'extra-human nature' – in order to produce and reproduce their lives. Over time, the interweaving of their actions unintentionally produces changes and, since the dawn of time, the rate of change has been tending more or less constantly to increase. However, the concept of change is too general to capture adequately the complexity of such processes. As a minimum, concepts are needed, firstly to convey the fact that social processes can involve changes in different directions, for example, towards higher or lower levels of differentiation and integration, or towards higher or lower levels of 'civilization'; and secondly, in order to capture the connections between stages in such processes. The concept of 'development' refers, in a minimum sense, to a change towards higher levels of differentiation and integration; the concept of 'regression' refers to a change in the opposite direction; and the adjective, 'developmental', refers to a study that is concerned to trace such changes over time and to explain the connections between prior and subsequent stages. But there is no commitment in the 'Eliasian paradigm' to the idea that such processes 'necessarily' involve changes in a single direction.

As Zygmunt Bauman recognises, Elias has sought to develop an 'explanatory device better geared to the needs of sociology than naturalistic causal explanations.'[18] That is, Elias rejects the common *analytical* approach in which societies are broken down into sets of 'factors', 'variables' or 'spheres' (such as 'the political factor', 'the education variable' or 'the economic sphere'), and in which the attempt is made to assess the relative 'causal weights' of these 'factors', 'variables' or 'spheres' in the social process or some aspect of it. He is concerned, rather, to discover 'the immanent dynamics of figurations'. What is meant by 'immanent dynamics' is that the dynamics of a social figuration are inherent in its structure and in the 'make-up' and motivations of the people who comprise it. 'Structure' and 'process', however, are different sides of the same coin, not separate 'things' that affect each other. Nor are figurations separate and apart from the people who comprise them. Struggles between individuals and among groups – for control of the economy or the state, for material goods and services, for income and wealth, for access to occupations and occupational advancement, for control over the production and dissemination of knowledge, for prestige, for love and erotic gratification, for excitement, and so on – are crucial in this connection. Such struggles are chiefly influenced and channelled by: (i) a society's size; (ii) the length and structure of the interdependency chains within it and between it and other societies; (iii) the balance within it between 'centripetal' and 'centrifugal' pressures; that is, the degree of effectiveness with which stable centralisation has been secured; (iv) the form taken by the state (whether, for example, it is a private or public monopoly, oligarchic or democratic, capitalist or socialist); (v) whether the society has a 'natural' (that it, a subsistence or barter) economy or a money economy, an agricultural economy or an industrial one, and, whatever its form, whether and how far it is integrated into an inter-societal framework; and (vi) the structurally-determined balance between its constituent groups. This latter balance is fundamentally affected by the degree to which a society's interdependency chains facilitate 'functional democratisation', namely the exercise of reciprocal controls within and between groups. It is also affected by the degree to which the position of groups within the overall system of interdependencies facilitates communication, organisation and 'solidarity' among their members and gives them access to key institutions and their resources, including access to strategically significant knowledge.

In the long-term, the immanent dynamics of figurations tend to have a 'blind' or 'unplanned' character largely because they are the unintended outcome of the interweaving of the actions of innumerable interdependent groups and individuals. However, though unplanned, they have a determinable structure and direction. That is because the structure of a figuration at any given stage forms a necessary – though not a sufficient – condition for the formation of its structure at a later stage. The developmental focus of figurational sociology is concerned with tracing such connections between stages in the longer-term 'figurational flow'. It is *not*, as I said earlier, committed to the view that this 'flow' has necessarily to change in a given direction. In the societies of Western Europe between the Middle Ages and the early twentieth century, however, the structure and direction of the longer-term figurational flow took, on balance, the form of a 'civilising' process'. Since the theory of civilising processes is the cornerstone of figurational sociology – Elias himself refers to it as 'a central theory' – it is to that issue that I now wish to turn.

THE THEORY OF CIVILISING PROCESSES

The theory of the civilising processes is based on the observation that, in Western Europe societies since the Middle Ages, a more or less continuous elaboration and refinement of manners and social standards can be shown to have taken place. Over the same time there has been an increase in the social pressure on people to exercise greater self-control over their emotions and in more and more fields of social relations. Correlatively, there has occurred at the level of personality an increase in the importance of conscience ('super-ego') as a regulator of behaviour. That is to say, social standards and taboos have come to be more deeply internalised. No value-judgement, no statement of 'better' or 'worse', is intended by this diagnosis. It is simply an attempt to express a process which can be demonstrably said to have occurred.

A crucial aspect of this process, and one that is central to the figurational study of leisure and sport, has consisted of a long-term decline in people's propensity for obtaining pleasure from directly engaging in and witnessing violent acts. Elias speaks of 'a dampening of *Angriffslust*', literally a decline in the lust for attacking, in people's desire and capacity for obtaining pleasure from doing violence to others. This has entailed, firstly, an advance in the 'threshold of repugnance' (*Peinlichkeitsschwelle*) regarding bloodshed and other direct manifestations of physical violence; and secondly, the internalisation of a stricter taboo on violence as part of the 'super-ego'. A consequence of this is that guilt-feelings are liable to be aroused whenever this taboo is violated. At the same time, there has occurred a tendency to push violence increasingly behind the scenes and, as part of it, to describe people who openly derive pleasure from violence in terms of the language of psychopathology, punishing them by means of stigmatization, hospitalisation or imprisonment.

Powerful elites standing at the nodal points of complex networks of interdependence, such as royal courts and large trading and manufacturing establishments, have, so far, been the principal standard-setting groups in this long-term civilising process from whom standards have subsequently diffused. Their social situation has entailed increasing pressure to exercise self-control and foresight. That is, basically because of the centrality of their role in the interdependency networks in which they occupy a dominant position and because they have found themselves more and more trapped in an unintended 'pincer movement' involving, on the one hand, the growing power of the state and, on the other, the growing power of lower social strata, they have been constrained generally to exercise greater self-restraint over their behaviour and their feelings. Of central importance here has been the following complex of long-term developments: economic growth; the lengthening of interdependency chains (in more conventional sociological language, the growth of the 'division of labour') and the increasing 'monetisation' of social relationships; state formation, especially the formation of stable monopolies of force and taxation, a process that has involved, as one of its central 'moments' the decreasing privatisation of these monopolies and their subjection to increasing public control; and 'functional democratisation'; that is, growing pressure on higher strata 'from below' as increasing interdependence leads to a growth in the power-chances of lower social strata. Conflict and violence have, throughout, been central to the unfolding of these processes. For example, 'elimination struggles' between contenders for the 'royal position' were crucial for the formation of the earliest tax and force monopolies, and functional democratisation, to the extent that it has been resisted by dominant groups, has regularly led, at least in the short term, to increasing conflict and violence. Moreover, as is characteristic of social processes generally because of the part played in them by learning, none of these crucial developments, to the extent that they are replicated elsewhere, should be mechanically read as always and everywhere likely to produce identical results. One can speak of probabilities in that connection, but not of law-like certainties. One can also add that the theory logically implies a theory of 'de-civilisation'. That is, it leads one, *ceteris paribus*, to anticipate that 'counter-civilising' developments will occur in a society that experiences economic decline, a shortening of interdependency chains, diminishing state monopolies over force and taxation, and growing inequality in the balance of power between classes and other groups. Again, of course, since all social processes depend upon learning, any such 'regression', however great its duration and extent, is unlikely to replicate in reverse the details and phasing of its progressive counterpart.

I shall return to the theory of the civilising process when I come to discuss football hooliganism. For the moment, this brief and necessarily rather abstract summary must suffice. I now want to illustrate how the theory has been applied in the field of studies into sport and leisure relations. My first example refers to Elias' work on the development of fox hunting in England.

THE DEVELOPMENT OF FOXHUNTING

Foxhunting is widely considered to be a marginal form of leisure. It is widely regarded as 'uncivilised' and a campaign exists to ban it. However, in the eighteenth century, it was one of the first activities to which the term 'sport', became attached and, as Elias has shown, it emerged as an early form of sport in conjunction with a civilising spurt. In earlier forms of hunting, the excitement of the hunt itself had formed 'a kind of forepleasure experienced in anticipation of the real pleasures, the pleasures of killing and eating'.[19] The pleasure of killing animals, that is to say, was enhanced by its utility and these forms of hunting imposed on their followers few restraints. They were directly in at the kill, killed with whatever weapons they could and, and even though they may have set out with a particular quarry in mind, were liable to kill whatever edible prey they came across. Foxhunting as it was developed by the English aristocracy and gentry in the eighteenth century, however, was very different in all of these respects. Foxes were killed 'for sport' and not for any utilitarian reason such as for food or the protection of poultry. Moreover, they were killed 'by proxy', that is, by the hounds and not by the hunting 'gentlemen' themselves. The hounds were trained specifically to follow the scent of the fox.

Other animals were not hunted. How can one explain a development of this type?

According to Elias the changes in the manner of hunting can only be adequately explained in terms of the framework of civilizing processes. In the seventeenth century, Elias observes, England experienced a cycle of violence as evidence, *inter alia*, in the Civil War, the regicide and the 'Glorious Revolution'. At the heart of this were the struggles between Protestants and Catholics, between the monarchy and sections of the landed upper classes as the former tried to impose absolutist rule and the latter strove to resist it, and between members of the landed upper classes and rising bourgeois groups. In the eighteenth century, however, the cycle of violence gradually calmed down and political conflicts came to be conducted more in terms of a set of non-violent rules and rituals, the rules and rituals of Parliament. According to Elias, the 'parliamentarisation' of political conflict went hand in hand with the 'sportisation' of pastimes. The self-same ruling groups who devised means for conducting political struggles non-violently, devised means for reducing the violence of their pastimes. In both of these regards, their conscience underwent a civilising change. That, in a nutshell, is why the more civilised and restrained English foxhunting ritual (and with it the earliest forms of cricket and more civilised forms of boxing) developed. However, parliamentarisation did not 'cause' sportisation. Both were aspects of the same overall transformation in social and personality structures.

That this initial process of sportisation should have taken place in England rather than, for example, France, was connected with the fact that in England, as opposed to France, Parliament and the relatively autonomous 'countryhouse network' of the landed aristocracy and gentry were of greater importance than the court as civilising agencies. That, in turn, reflected the fact that English monarchs failed in their efforts to introduce absolutist rule, hence enabling free associations of 'gentlemen', that is members of the landed upper classes, to pursue, codify and civilise their pastimes relatively independently of autocratic interference.

Let me now turn to the issue of football hooliganism. On the face of it, that might seem to be an even less auspicious subject than foxhunting for the theory of civilising processes. Indeed, as I stated earlier, Ian Taylor has voiced such a sentiment explicitly. Let me now try to show how, *pace* Taylor, the theory of civilising processes represents a very useful framework to analyse football hooliganism.

THE SOCIOGENESIS OF FOOTBALL HOOLIGANISM IN BRITAIN

It is commonly believed that football hooliganism first became a 'social problem' in Britain in the 1960s. However, research shows that no decade in the history of the professional game – professional clubs began to emerge in the late 1870s and the Football League was formed in 1888 – has gone by without the occurrence of disorderliness on a substantial scale.[20] In fact, its incidence has tended to follow a U-shaped curve. It was relatively high before the First World War, fell between the wars and remained relatively low until the mid-1950s. Then, in the 1960s, it increased, escalating fairly rapidly from the mid-1960s onwards, coming to form an almost 'normal' accompaniment of the professional game.

Despite such variations in its incidence over time, a recurrent feature of football hooliganism is physical violence. This can take the form of assaults on players and referees, or of clashes between rival fans. Before the Second World War, assaults on match officials tended to predominate, but it is clashes between rival fan groups, often with the police involved, that are the dominant form of football hooligan violence in its present phase. In fact, a significant proportion of the fans who attract the 'football hooligan' label appear to be as, or more, interested in fighting as they are in watching football. For them, the match is principally about expressing their *machismo*, either factually by inflicting defeat on the rival fans and making them run away, or symbolically via the medium of aggressive and demasculinising songs and chants. How is one to explain that?

The available evidence suggests that the majority of hard-core football hooligans came from the socio-economically worst-off sections of the working class (see Table 2.1).

What is it about the membership of the lowest levels of the working class that leads to the recurrent generation of an intense *macho* form of masculine identity, what one might call a 'violent' or 'aggressive masculine style', a form of masculine identity that is in large part determined by willingness and ability to fight and in terms of which physical confrontations form a central source of pleasure and meaning in life? How is one to explain the persistence of this form of masculinity in the face of the civilising pressures which, Elias has hypothesised, have been built into the process of state formation in Britain and the lengthening of interdependency chains and consequent functional democratisation that have been attendant on industrialisation and urbanisation?

Table 2.1 Social class membership of football hooligans (Registrar-General's
Classification)

	Numbers	%
1 Professionals, etc.	2	0.38
2 Intermediate	13	2.50
3 Skilled non-manual	29	5.58
4 Skilled manual	98	18.88
4 Partly unskilled	132	25.43
5 Unskilled	245	47.2
Total	519	

Source: Dunning, Murphy, Williams, *The Social Roots of Football
Hooliganism*, Routledge & Kegan Paul (1988).

The first thing to note is the fact that, according to Elias, powerful
elites standing at the hub of complex interdependency networks have,
so far, been the main 'model-makers' in the European civilising
process. By contrast, members of the lower working class, to the
extent that they are able to find employment, do not work in
occupations which demand for their performance to anything like the
same extent a permanent effort of foresight and a steady control of
conduct.[21] They live in a world of 'dense and extensive bonds of
interdependence'[22] but, in that context, they have fewer power
resources than other groups. Far more than groups higher up the social
scale, they are relatively 'passive objects of these interdependencies',
being affected by distant events without being easily able to influence
or even perceive them.[23] They are not, in short, subjected to anything
like the same extent as groups higher in the social hierarchy to civilising
pressures. Added to this, their life-circumstances keep the overwhelming majority of them trapped in relative poverty and they are more
subject than other groups to the regular experience of violence in
various forms. Let me elaborate on this by returning to Elias's own
exposition.

According to Elias, in a society with a relatively stable monopoly of
physical force people generally, not just the members of elites, are
largely protected from sudden attack, from the irruption of physical
violence into their lives. At the same time, they are forced to suppress
their own impulses to attack others physically. Increasingly, parents
demand this suppression of aggression in their children from an early
age. As a result, fear, both of one's own aggressiveness and of a
punitive response to it from powerful others, becomes internalised, a
deep-rooted feature of the personality:

In such a society physical violence is confined to barracks; and from this store-house it breaks out only in extreme cases, in times of war or social upheaval, into individual life. As a monopoly of certain specialist groups it is normally excluded from the life of others; and these specialists, the whole monopoly organizaton of force, now stand guard only in the margin of social life as a control on individual conduct.[24]

Under such conditions, social life becomes more secure, more regular and more calculable. People learn from an early age to exercise greater rationality and foresight in steering their conduct through the complex networks of interdependency in which they find themselves enmeshed. Fear of social degradation, expressed through feelings of embarrassment and shame, comes increasingly to the fore in place of the fear of physical attack or of a sudden reversal of fortunes that is more common in a society without a stable monopoly of force. In a more civilised society, people become more sensitive, among other things, towards committing and, at a later stage, even towards witnessing violent acts. At the same time, official and many other forms of violence are pushed increasingly behind the scenes, and violent acts lead to the arousal of the anxieties and guilt-feelings which are typically instilled in people in societies of this sort.

In a synthesising statement, Elias outlines a fundamental precondition for the occurrence of a civilising process. It is, he suggests:

a rise in the standard of living and security, or, in other words, increased protection from physical attack or destruction and thus from the uncontrollable fears which erupt far more powerfully and frequently in societies with less stable monopolies of force and a lower division of functions. At present we are so accustomed to the existence of these more stable monopolies of force and the greater predictability of violence resulting from them, that we scarcely see their importance for the structure of our conduct and our personality. We scarcely realize how quickly what we call 'reason', this relatively farsighted and differentiated steering of our conduct, with its high degree of affect-control, would crumble or collapse if the anxiety-inducing tensions in and around us changed, if the fears affecting our lives suddenly became much stronger.[25]

Over the past hundred years, a dominant tendency in British society has been the growing affluence and increasing 'incorporation' into dominant values of more and more sections of the working class. The diminishing numbers[26] who have remained relatively unincorporated, however, have had to contend with the regular irruption of specific forms of physical violence into their lives. Their economic circumst-ances, too, have been generally insecure. Growing affluence and increasing incorporation may have had civilising effects on the majority of working-class men and women but what is today the relatively unincorporated and relatively impoverished 'rougher' working-class minority, the social segment from which the football hooligans are principally recruited, is faced, from early in life, not only with economic insecurity but also with the regular irruption of violence from a variety of sources: when they are children, from their parents; as they grow up, from their peers in the street and at school; as adolescents, from gangs within their own and from neighbouring communities; as young adults, from prowling gangs on their nights 'down town'; and on Saturdays, from invading 'fighting crews' who support a visiting football team. And, of course, in all these settings, because they tend to deviate in public from dominant social standards, they are liable to experience violence at the hands of the police. That is to say, for them, the civil branch of society's 'monopoly of force' is not normally 'confined to barracks' to anything like the extent that is usually the case for members of the higher, more 'respectable' social strata. On the contrary, it is a regular and, as far as its specific manifestations are concerned, in many ways unpredictable feature of their lives.

The fact that members of the 'rougher' sections of the working class grew up in a situation of severely limited power chances (I am using the term in its widest sense to include the 'economic' aspects of power), live with a level of violence in excess of that which is usually experienced by groups higher up the social scale and that many of them experience rough treatment at the hands of the police, has manifold consequences for their personality, their social standards and the structure of the communities that they form.[27] In the circumstances in which they live, a highly developed sensitivity towards the committing and witnessing of violent acts, a strict and prohibiting 'conscience' or 'super-ego' in that regard, would be liable in many contexts to be a disadvantage. They have tended to respond to attack with counter-attack. That is, they are constrained to adjust to the fact that the public expression of violence is a regular feature of their lives. This is reflected in their personalities. Moreover, their standards and values accord prestige to males who display loyalty and bravery in physical confrontations, and their involvement in and enjoyment of fighting are reinforced by the poverty of opportunities available to them in other spheres.

That, in a nutshell, is why football hooligans fight. They develop relatively aggressive personalities, firstly because their involvement in the complex interdependency networks of modern society does not lead to pressure to exercise foresight and restraint to the same extent as other groups, and secondly because their communities receive less protection from the monopoly of violence than other groups. Indeed, because of their structurally-generated deviance from dominant social standards, they regularly experience violence at the hands of the state. Moreover, for lower-working-class males, fighting provides one of the few opportunities for obtaining status, meaning and pleasurable excitement. They have chosen football as one of the arenas for acting out their masculinity rituals because it, too, is an arena in which working-class masculine identities are at stake. Football also provides a context where there is relative immunity from arrest and where an 'enemy' is regularly provided, the fans of the opposing team.

Thus, even though it has not been possible for me to give a complete account here, I think I have said enough to show that, far from constituting a refutation of the theory of civilising processes or being a form of behaviour that cannot be fruitfully explored from such a standpoint, a complete understanding of football hooliganism is only possible in its terms. Football hooliganism is indicative of the structurally-generated unevenness with which the British civilising process has taken and is taking place. The public reaction to football hooligan violence is understandable as the reaction of the dominant, 'respectable' majority to the behaviour of people whose standards deviate for structurally identifiable reasons from their own. They experience it as repugnant because it is indicative of the fact that the people who engage in it are, in Elias's technical sense, less civilised than they. However, the frequency with which such more civilised people demand draconian punishments in order to combat football hooliganism shows clearly the insecure foundations on which their civilised behaviour is based and how far they have to go before they can claim to have reached a 'pinnacle' in this regard.

Notes

1. For statements of the figurational approach see, above all, Norbert Elias, *What is Sociology?* (1978) London, Hutchinson; *The Civilizing Process* (1978) Oxford, BLackwell; and *State Formation and Civilization* (1982) Oxford, Blackwell. Detailed examples of the application of the figurational approach in leisure and sport can be found in Norbert Elias and Eric Dunning, *Quest for Excitement: Sport and Leisure in the Civilizing Process* (1986) Oxford, Blackwell.
2. See Elias and Dunning, ibid.
3. Norbert Elias (1986) 'An Essay on Sport and Violence', in Elias and Dunning, pp. 150–74.
4. See Eric Dunning, Patrick Murphy and John Williams, *The Roots of Football Hooliganism: an Historical and Sociological Study*, London, Routledge & Kegan Paul (1988).
5. Chris Rojek (1985) *Capitalism and Leisure Theory* Tavistock, London, reviewed by Otto Newman in *Sociology*, Vol. 20, No. 2, p. 322. The quotation is from page 172 of Rojek's book.
6. Jennifer Hargreaves (1986) 'Where's the Virtue? Where's the Grace? A Discussion of the Social Production of Gender Relations in and through Sport', *Theory, Culture and Society*, Vol. 3, No. 1, pp. 109–21.
7. James Curtis (1986) 'Isn't it Difficult to Support some Notions of "The Civilizing Process"? A Response to Dunning', in C. Roger Rees and Andrew W. Miracle (eds), *Sport and Social Theory*, Champaign, Illinois, Human Kinetics Publishers, pp. 57–66.
8. Ibid. p. 59.
9. Ibid. pp. 59–60.
10. Ian Taylor (1987) 'Putting the Boot into a Working Class: British Soccer After Bradford and Brussels, *Sociology of Sport Journal*, Vol. 4, pp. 171–91.
11. Although translated into English as *The Civilising Process: the History of Manners* and *State Formation and Civilization*, the German title of Elias' two-volume work is *Uber den Prozess der Zivilization: Soziogenetische und Psychogenetische Untersuchungen*. Vol. 1 is subtitled, *Wandlungen des Verhaltens in den Weltlichen Oberschichten des Abendlandes*, and Vol. 2, *Wandlungen der Gesellschaft: Entwurf zu einer Theorie der Zivilization*. Literally translated, the overall title is: 'On the Civilizing Process: Sociogenetic and Psychogenetic Explorations'. Literal translations of the subtitles are: 'Changes in the Behaviour of the Secular Upper Classes of the West', and 'Changes in Society: Attempt at a Theory of Civilisation'.
12. See Elias, *State Formation and Civilization*, pp. 282ff. for an instance of the way in which he strives to transcend this crude dichotomy.
13. For example, Chapter 1 of *What is Sociology?* is entitled: 'Sociology: the Questions Asked by Comte'.
14. Elias, *What is Sociology?* p. 107. Elias also explicitly attacks the notion in a footnote on pp. xiii and xiv of *The Civilizing Process*.
15. Elias, *State Formation and Civilization* p. 253.
16. Newborn babies are, of course, uncivilised and, as a result, a problem for

52   *The Figurational Approach to Leisure and Sport*

the civilising process is posed by each new generation. This is only a different way of pointing to the centrality of learning in such processes and of reinforcing the fact that they cannot be conceived of as necessary and law-like in character.

17. Elias, op. cit. p. 331.
18. Zygmunt Bauman (1979) 'The Phenomenon of Norbert Elias', *Sociology*, Vol. 13, No. 1, pp. 117–25.
19. Norbert Elias (1986) 'An Essay on Sport and Violence' in Elias and Dunning op. cit. 150–74. See also Elias's introduction to this volume, pp. 19–62.
20. See Eric Dunning, Patrick Murphy and John Wlliams, op. cit.
21. As one can see from Table 1, the majority of the football hooligans on whom we have data are employed. Although there are complex linkages between football hooliganism and unemployment, one cannot say that the latter 'causes' the former. Its causal role is more indirect, operating principally by means of the way in which unemployment is one factor in the perpetuation of a 'rough' subculture.
22. Elias, *State Formation and Civilization*, p. 248.
23. Ibid pp. 248–9.
24. Ibid p. 238.
25. Ibid p. 326.
26. Current trends, especially the continuing high rates of unemployment and the increase of relative poverty may be contributing to an increase in the size of the 'unincorporated' working class.
27. There is insufficient space here to go into all the details but, in *The Roots of Football Hooliganism*, we also use Suttles' concept of 'ordered segmentation' in order to explain the sociogenesis of gangs and, correlatively, of aggressive masculinity.

3 Sigmund Freud and the Pursuit of Pleasure

Harvie Ferguson

The term 'leisure' does not appear in the General Subject Index of Volume XXIV, *Indexes and Bibliographies*, of *The Standard Edition of the Complete Psychological Works of Sigmund Freud* (Freud, 1974; see the Bibliography which follows the Notes to this chapter). It is all the more tempting, then, to claim for the idea of leisure a central role in the interpretation of the Freudian *oeuvre*, and correspondingly, to look to his writings for a key to the understanding of leisure in its specifically modern forms. To suggest, in fact, that he deserves a pre-eminent position among the notably small number of writers to have seriously proposed a leisure theory.

The absence of any explicit reference to the concept in Freud's own work is, of course, only a minor obstacle to such a claim. The term 'class', similarly, is missing from the index to the Penguin Edition of Volume I of *Capital* (Marx, 1976), and no one supposes the concept plays no part in his critique of political economy. An irresistible verbal transition, besides, of the sort familiar to us from the analyses of jokes, parapraxes, hysterical symptoms and dreams, effortlessly replaces the missing term 'leisure' with a substitute, 'pleasure', bringing with it the entire edifice of the remaining twenty-three volumes.

Such a procedure, however, reaches its conclusion too swiftly. It is just such displacements, so much a feature of everyday thinking, that rouse accusations of incoherence and arbitrariness. There is something to be said, in addition, for keeping Freud's texts at a manageable distance for a little longer. The theoretical 'emptiness' of leisure is not necessarily an inferior starting-point to the overwhelming but disordered richness of pleasure.

The two, clearly, are related without being synonymous. Sociologists have investigated numerous aspects of leisure, elaborating divergent theoretical 'positions', without reference to any subjective dispositions whatever (Rojek, 1985, 85–139); and the experience of pleasure, obviously, is not restricted to leisure relations. It is the purpose of what follows to define more precisely the nature of this affinity.

FREUD AND LEISURE

It may be helpful to approach the matter biographically and contextually, that is to say in a leisurely fashion. We can begin obliquely with Freud's own leisure activities, with his own pleasures; and first of all with his own dislikes.

Surprisingly Sigmund Freud hated Vienna; or claimed at least that he did so. For example, in letters to his friend Wilhelm Fliess, the Berlin rhinologist who played such an important but obscure part during the 1890s in encouraging Freud's analytic work, he declared that Vienna disgusted him. He found the city 'physically repulsive' and often blamed his periodic bouts of despondency on the necessity of having to make a living there. 'It is misery to live here', he wrote, 'this is no atmosphere in which one can maintain the hope of achieving anything difficult.' A judgment he repeated much later in life, 'I have lived here for fifty years', he maintained, 'and have never come across a new idea here' (Jones, 1953, I, 323).[1]

Freud occasionally gave the impression that his unease in and with Vienna was a consequence of the anti-semitism which effectively blocked his university career there. Ellenberger, however, has convincingly demonstrated that he must have known his modest academic success could not be blamed on prejudice (Ellenberger, 1971, 454).

Superficially he preferred Berlin, and especially Paris, which he visited for several months in 1885 to study under Charcot.[2] To his future sister-in-law Minna Bernays he wrote of being 'under the full impact of Paris'. He was astonished as any other visitor by 'the brilliant exterior, the swarming crowds, the infinite variety of attractively displayed goods, the streets stretching for miles, the flood of light in the evening.' The splendid facade, however, was peopled by, 'a different species to ourselves'. Modern urbanities whom 'I don't think know the meaning of shame or fear.' And later in the same letter he confesses that 'my heart is German provincial and it hasn't accompanied me here' (*Letters*, Ed. Ernst Freud, 199). His fascination with any city was shortlived and gave way to expressions of longing for the tranquil simplicity of his childhood home in Freiberg.[3]

Yet it was just this urbanity of manners, chaotic emotions and hectic, fragmented experience which, transcribed into the idiom of personal reminiscence, surfaced, like repressed wishes in the practice of psychoanalysis. The cultural world of the Ringstrasse, the crucible of modernism, was its specific milieu (Schorske, 1980, Ch. II).

When occasions arose when he might have moved permanently to Paris, or Berlin, or London, he found, not surprisingly, that he was unable to make the effort.

A sense of loss, combined with a feeling of strangeness and unfamiliarity in the city, prompted a continual longing to be on the move. Freud took, he wrote to Martha, 'a childish delight in being somewhere else' (Jones, 1953, I, 198). A fascination with ephemeral and evanescent sensations which was, in fact, quite typical of Viennese culture (Johnstone, 1972, 172) and the general disposition which underlay his dislike of the city.

Travel, consequently, became Freud's major leisure interest, and an activity he pursued with great determination. Following his first visit to England, at the age of nineteen, a year rarely went by without some more or less extended holiday, academic excursion or sightseeing trip. After his marriage in 1886, Martha and the children spent two months of each summer away from Vienna. Freud visited at weekends, if they were relatively near by, and made more ambitious excursions in the company of his brother Alexander, or, unencumbered by young children, his sister-in-law, Minna. In 1896, for example, at a time when Freud felt his money worries to be far from over, he visited Fliess in Dresden for a three-day 'congress' in April, spent a month with the family at Aussee in Styria, afterwards joining Alexander for a tour of Northern Italy which included Bologna and Venice, followed by a week in Florence where they stayed in the upper storey of the Galileo museum, and met Fliess again in Salzburg at the end of August (Jones, 1953, I, 323). He travelled even more extensively in 1897.

At other times, when fully occupied with his work in the city, he satisfied his wish to contact with foreign cultures by indulging a passion for collecting antiques. His 'fondness for the prehistoric', he accounted his one extravagance and 'a source of extraordinary refreshment' (Jones, 1953, I, 315).

In a recent, highly detailed, reconstruction of Freud's self-analysis, the French analyst Anzieu remarks that, 'Holidays were a time when he could rest, be on the move, and think, all at the same time: he cathected them as a period when he could be free, i.e. fulfil his wishes in life and in his dreams more freely, and also as a time when he expected to come up with some new discovery (Anzieu, 1986, 337).

His insight into a method for interpreting dreams, for example, took place at Bellevue, on the outskirts of Vienna, immediately upon his arrival there for the family holiday in the summer of 1895. Freud wrote at once to Fliess with a preliminary description and analysis of the famous 'Dream of Irma's Injection', which was to serve as the initial specimen for his dreambook. He later wondered, only half-jokingly we suspect, if a plaque commemorating the discovery might one day be erected on the spot (Freud, 1954, 322). The Oedipus complex, similarly, fell to the 1897 holiday season.

It was not simply that being somewhere else, perusing ancient relics, provided the spiritual recreation essential to creative effort; holidays and antiquities, Freud's leisure, entered formally and substantially into psychoanalysis.

The psychoanalytic hour became the recreative break in an otherwise routine day. Freud acted as a kind of psychic travel agent; extending, in the withdrawn security of his consulting room, the opportunities for relaxation and cultivation which he had discovered on holiday. Bergasse 19 became a place to which one journeyed, physically and symbolically, with the anticipation more usually reserved for the boarding of a train destined for some previously unvisited country.

The holiday is among the most ideal of modern leisure forms. A period set apart, and preferably physically distant, from the rest of life. It should be devoted to nothing in particular; a playful interlude to be enjoyed from moment to moment without the necessity of an edifying purpose. On his own holidays Freud was incredibly active – no one could keep up the pace he set in sightseeing and hillwalking; but he allowed each day to set its own limits, to reveal each new wonder in turn, as if unanticipated.

The psychoanalyst aims to recreate the interior condition of the holiday. The 'golden rule' of analysis, frequently enunciated by Freud, was that the patient should speak without constraint, follow no preconceived path and remain unconcerned by apparent incoherence or lack of connectedness in their recollections. Nothing must be deemed too trivial, remote or disgusting to be mentioned. The analyst, resisting all temptation to lead, must remain silent and listen to follow the complicated and unpredictable route towards self-revelation.[4]

Freud developed his analytic technique only gradually over a period of about ten years. He had begun in the early 1890s, under the influence of Joseph Breuer,[5] treating patients with nervous diseases by the less leisurely method of hypnosis. After Breuer's pioneering case of 'Anna O', retrospectively claimed by Freud to have been the first patient of psychoanalysis, Freud adopted the 'cathartic' technique; discovering under hypnosis the traumatic root of each sympton and 'abreacting' it through direct suggestion. The method, however, quickly proved laborious and unreliable; the patient frequently developing a bewildering array of new symptons that, parodying the original condition, threatened to outrun the physician's therapeutic stamina (Breuer and Freud, 1895, Standard Edition, II).

The more active the analyst, the more complicated the case became. The practice of a mutually relaxed consciousness was the best guarantee of success. The doctor, Freud urged, 'should simply listen and not bother about whether he is keeping anything in mind.' The leisurely approach (justifying our own discretion), was the only sure method. If strictly followed the 'golden rule' would continue to throw up fresh material for analysis, prolonging the encounter to the extent required for its clarification. It was a method which existed to repeat, 'simply in not directing one's attention to anything in particular and in maintaining the same evenly-suspended attention' (Freud, 1974, XII, 112).

And what should we discover on such psychic holidays but relics? Personal remains; the unmistakeable archaeological evidence of a forgotten, antique existence which in being brought back to life, piece by piece, fits the patient once again for the chaos of everyday life.

The holiday image might be extended somewhat to give us direct access, at last, to the main body of Freud's theoretical work. On holiday we are temporarily relieved of the burden of making a living. We need not work and, hence, the rational and necessary lose their dominion over us. The psychoanalytic hour, through its analagous freedom, provided Freud with the trivial fragments of experience more usually ignored in scheming acts of consciousness. It was in leisure, then, that Freud sought the nature, first of the psychoneuroses, and subsequently of the field of mental functioning as a whole.

It would not be unreasonable to view psychoanalysis as the theory of the leisure class. As a theory of human nature it is rooted in the practice of leisure, and as a medical technique it is leisurely to the point of negligence. Freud at the outset claimed for psychoanalysis the modest therapeutic aim of 'transforming neurotic misery into common unhappiness' – an ambition which towards the end of his life, thoroughly imbued with the 'therapeutic nihilism' (Johnstone, 1972, 223) characteristic not simply of Viennese academic medicine, but of

Viennese culture as a whole, he seemed to regard as recklessly optimistic.[6] The psychoanalytic hour became a habit, less strenuous and theatrical than the daily appearance in café or drawing room (Johnstone, 1972: 115). For Freud's clientele, the majority of whom, having no need to work, had become trapped in a perpetual holiday, psychoanalysis, recapturing the innocence of leisure, must have been a salve rather than a cure.

Freud's psychological writings, following his own 'golden rule', insisted upon the significance of trivia. The dream, the slip of the tongue or the joke; these were the privileged debris of consciousness from which he sought to recover an underlying psychic reality. Any such fragment, indeed, could provide a beginning because each carried, inscribed upon it, the key to its own decipherment. In the place of a systematic causal theory of consciousness there emerged an incomplete series of technqiues and methods; a kind of do-it-yourself psychology kit, as allusive, disjointed and modern as a contemporary townscape. The facts of consciousness were a facade which, in the holiday atmosphere of the consulting room, could be stripped away. Each spontaneously recollected, but inconspicuous fragment, expanding magically before the astonished onlookers, assumed the dignity of a primordial, and unsuspected, reality.

Leisure, even for the leisure class, is but a fragment of life; and Freud's theory remained unashamedly a theory of the fragment. His writing therefore, departed radically from the scientific tradition within which he had been superbly trained. His case studies, for example, had recourse to all the formal trickery of the contemporary novel. Steven Marcus, noticing the similarity, describes the author of the 'Fragment of an Analysis of a Case of Hysteria', as, 'like some familiar "unreliable narrator" in modernist fiction' (Marcus, 1984, 55.)[7] And his most complete work, an interpretation of his own dreams, remained, in spite of continuous additions over the years, essentially incomplete as a self-portrait.

The method of the fragment, however, did not aim, in the shadow of Rousseau, to reconstitute the concrete uniqueness of the individual. Each isolated recollection is traced, instead, to a common store of forgotten experience, to a universal prehistory. The 'Dream of Irma's Injection' was made the emblem common to all minds bent upon genuine self-knowledge. The rational psychologist, misled by the organised structure of consciousness, and the stable relations upon which it was based, failed to penetrate to the levels revealed by a more superficial approach.

But what, we are entitled to ask, was the result of such an interpretive endeavour? Could a leisure theory uncover anything new? Are evanescent recollections not properly neglected alongside the fullness of reasoned memory? Our contemporary vocabulary of corroded and facile subjectivity hardly does justice to Freud's insistence upon the point. Terms such as pleasure, enjoyment, gratification retain for us neither a precise scientific meaning nor a usefully differentiated range of associations. It is worth recalling that Freud in addition to exploiting the corpus of medical theory, drew extensively on the literary tradition. His psychology stems from the work of Shakespeare and Goethe (whose characters figured in his dreams) as well as those of Darwin, Haeckel and Brücke. The tendency of much contemporary writing on Freud has been to domesticate his subversive method and reformulate his interpretive revelations as causal hypotheses.[8] To grasp anew Freud's original insight we must first recover, in its historical context, the bourgeois notion of pleasure.

PLEASURE AND THE BOURGEOIS EGO

The notion of pleasure has, more than any other of the bourgeoisie's linguistic totems (capital, work, rationality), proved resistant to self-criticism. This has not halted history in its tracks; it has meant simply that, much of the time, we misuse words. By making of pleasure an undisclosed inner state we have removed it from the glare of public discussion; like the choice of a holiday destination it has been treated as a purely private matter. What Freud has shown us, if we are interested enough to look, is that our vocabulary is already anachronistic.

The idea of pleasure within the bourgeois world is erected upon the firm foundation of classical political economy, and the scientific worldview of which it formed a part.

Society, upon such a view, can be likened to a mechanical contrivance constructed unwittingly by the interaction of individuals intent upon their own activities.[9] Each individual should be considered, ideally at least (that is to say for 'theoretical purposes'), as an isolated 'atom' within the social cosmos; a free and separate agent. Such elementary particles are moved by the rational pursuit of their own private interest to interact. And private interests can be defined only in relation to the pleasure which is posited as its *telos*. Pleasure is the aim and motive of all action, and is attained by the satisfaction of 'wants'. To want is to simultaneously lack and long for something beyond our immediate grasp, and within the utilitarian tradition the relationship between these terms was reduced to a form of mechanical necessity.

The category of 'want' is admitted to be peculiarly human. 'Man's original wants', notes Adam Ferguson, 'are more numerous and his supply more scanty, than those of any other animal' (Ferguson, 1792, I, 242). Pleasure, therefore, as the satisfaction of such wants, is the spur to human action. The pursuit of pleasure is, in essence, a humanising endeavour.

Success in the pursuit of pleasure, however, depends upon the use of the uniquely human attribute of reason. 'To have an object or purpose, and to employ means for the attainment of it, is the distinctive condition of mind or Intelligence' (Ferguson, 1792, I, 2).

Reason and pleasure belong together as the distinguishing features of human action. In a famous discussion Parsons (1937) has argued that such a tradition, defining rationality exclusively in terms of the relationship between means and ends, excluded any systematic consideration of ends themselves (i.e. of pleasure). All action terminating in irrational inwardness could be analysed with respect only to its 'objectivity' as a means.

Convincing as Parsons's analysis remains it reveals contradictions within utilitarian thought which remained latent during the formation of classical bourgeois culture. The Scottish Moralists, for example, had little doubt that the satisfaction of wants depended (apart from the subjective stimulus) upon characteristics intrinsic to the objects of desire. 'We are pleased,' Ferguson puts it directly, 'with beauty and excellence.' And while cultivation of the senses is a prerequisite for the recognition of beauty and excellence, those values are presumed to reside in the nature of objects themselves. Pleasure then becomes the possession of valued objects; of goods, that is to say, which, by virtue of their own properties, have the capacity, in satisfying our wants, to bestow pleasure.

Within the world of potentially pleasing objects none is more highly valued than another person. A person's capacity to bestow pleasure far exceeds that of any other object. In seeking pleasure through a relationship with another person we do not seek to possess the entire person, but rather, their 'approbation'.[10] Adam Smith (1759, 56) thus remarks that 'the chief part of human happiness arises from the consciousness of being beloved.' It is 'sympathy', the ability imaginatively to put ourselves in the place of another, that is the root of our sociability and makes the feelings of others part of the calculation of our own pleasure.

A market in sentiments, that is to say, as well as in physical goods has been established. And like any other market it is the foundation for rational, calculable action. It both requires and establishes 'stable' personal relationships and leads to the moderation of our demands by civilised manners as a method of maximising our chances of coming to possess that most valued of goods, another's affection.

The rational instrumentality of the market and the interior pursuit of pleasure only appear much later to represent separate orders of reality. Adam Smith and his contemporaries had no difficulty in visualising their common root and uniform logic in possessive individualism, the core of bourgeois culture.

Rational psychology, and here Parsons is quite correct, was unstable. It required no profound historical convulsion to procure, as its mirror image, a 'passionate' individualism which developed as part of a bourgeois protest against capitalism.[11]

Confronted by the chaos of potentially pleasing objects, the infinite variety of possible actions, the rationality of the market-place breaks down. The secret of individual action is to be sought instead in acts of a non-rational will. All actions, however, are not in consequence to be viewed as arbitrary. Every action expresses an underlying selfhood which emerges through repeated and unconscious movements of the will. All choices can be seen, therefore, as choices of and for the self. Between subject and object a self-expanding, circular relationship is set up. Each individual, that is to say, remains sovereign with respect to his own 'object-choice'.[12]

But if the subject must himself define the objects whose possession will bestow pleasure, is this pleasure not, properly speaking, part of the subject in the first place? The original act of discrimination, identifying the prized object, must be a process of projecting into something beyond the individual, an element of his own subjectivity. The object is sought because it has become desired, and is desired because it contains part of ourselves. We always posses, in other words, a little in advance of ourselves, the things for which we most long. We come to attach ourselves to objects by an obscure inner movement, an interior gesture over which we have little control but which remains, for all that, the means by which we most completely express our uniqueness.

Our pursuit of pleasure is really a pursuit of ourselves. Kierkegaard, in particular, had revealed, prior to Freud, the self-reference in all forms of experience. And throughout the nineteenth century a number of such writings recur, each rediscovering in isolation from the others the peculiar spiritual pain of inwardness. A disconnected tradition that ended in the solipsistic heroes of Dostoevsky's 'polyphonic novels' and the radical nihilism of Nietzsche's philosophy.[13]

For the bourgeois ego pleasure was a form of possession. It was the emptiness opened up between subject and object (or subject and subject, or subject and itself), that was felt as passion. The greater this distance the more intense the longing required to sustain the relationship and the greater the subsequent pleasure experienced in closing it. Taken to its logical and irrational extreme the object of desire might be removed to an inconceivable remoteness; to infinity. The most passionate of writers, thus, is Kierkegaard; recklessly flinging himself at God, in pursuit of 'the single one' he had, never sensing its presence within him, allowed to escape. Passionate individualism, becoming romantically entangled with the void, celebrated nothingness.[14]

FREUD AND PLEASURE

It would be altogether too simple to argue that Freud, intellectually trained within the scientific tradition of utilitarian psychology, on the one hand, and attuned to the insights of passionate individualism through his literary sensitivity (and through living in its decadent momument, Vienna), on the other, was able to effect a synthesis of their divergent ideas of pleasure.

Freud, certainly, was brought up in the most advanced of scientific cultures, and the first fifteen years of his professional life were spent in anatomical and histological research. During the 1890s, however, and in particular with the abandonment of the 'Project for a Scientific Psychology', written for Fliess in the autumn of 1895 (Freud, 1954) he gradually but relentlessly broadened the scope of his enquiries and methods to accommodate his humanistic interests. This 'development' has given rise (rather as it has in the case of Marx) to a debate between proponents of the 'young' versus champions of the 'mature', Freud. Sulloway, for example, in a revealingly subtitled book, *Freud, Biologist of the Mind*, argues that, while rejecting a materialist-reductionist psychology, he never abandoned the programme of evolutionary biology. 'Seen in its proper historical perspective', he claims, 'Freud's theory of mind is the embodiment of a scientific age imbued with the rising tide of Darwinism' (Sulloway, 1980, 497). Ricoeur, with an equally symptomatic subtitle to his *Freud and Philosophy: An Essay in Interpretation*, offers, alternatively, a view of Freud engaged upon 'a reinterpretation of all psychical productions pertaining to culture'; an endeavour which promises the hope of a 'unification of human discourse' (Ricoeur, 1970, 177), and a vision of psychoanalysis as a means 'to set free the interplay of references between signs.'

We cannot readily identify in these divergent exegetical tendencies, however, any chronological shift in the balance of Freud's *psychology*. The problem is more acute than that. In the same text, however fragmented, both the scientific and the literary, the utilitarian and the passionate, appear together, resisting union. *The Interpretation of Dreams*, takes up, along with the task of uncovering hidden meanings, the 'economic problem' of the psychical apparatus. In its celebrated seventh chapter the defunct 'Project', shorn of its physiological impedimenta, was given a new lease of life. The conception of a 'psychical apparatus', an essential theoretical fiction sustaining the market image of the psyche, subsequently made its sometimes rather awkward appearance in Freud's interpretive, systematic and expository works.[15] And in the 'Papers on Metapsychology' where we might expect a fresh and undivided reality to emerge, Freud insists upon a carefully controlled use of three different modes of analysis, the dynamic, the structural and the economic (Breuer and Freud, Standard Edition, 1985, XIV).

In proposing a 'leisure' theory (i.e. in being a modern writer), Freud sensed the self-destructive character of any systematically unified theory of human subjectivity. At one with modernity in science and in literature he applied, instead, separate and incompatible perspectives to the same problem; relativising and partial abstractions which exposed in succession radically heterogeneous aspects of reality. The utilitarian and the passionate forms of bourgeois egoism exist side by side in his work. Freud's psychology, however, equally resists the easy reduction to simple formulas such as 'pleasure principle' versus 'reality principle'. Breaking free of both forms of individualism he describes pleasure in new ways.

Emerging from *The Interpretation of Dreams*, *Three Essays on Sexuality* and *Jokes and Their Relation to the Unconscious*, is a view of pleasure as fun.

This refers first of all to a universal and original source of gratification in the organism's enjoyment of its own life process. Prior to any other form of enjoyment there is a primordial indwelling delight in our own physical processes. This is an immediate sensuality unrestrained by moral preconception or calculative endeavour. The 'polymorph perversity' of the infant, suddenly obvious to everyone after Freud had drawn attention to it, attested to an uninhibited and playful world of experience. A constitution, 'containing the germs of all the perversions, will only be demonstrable in *children*', Freud wrote in 1905 (Standard Edition, VII, 172). He developed his ideas on the nature and significance of fun, what he termed 'the primary process' through direct observation of children, analytic reconstructions of early experience, and by way of general theoretical considerations. In the form of 'primary narcissism' it posed the first and most serious question of psychological 'development'.[16] If our existence begins as fun, how can we be persuaded to give it up in favour of the anxious uncertainties of mere pleasure? The myth of Oedipus provided a clue to an initial solution of the problem. Consequent upon an original act of cruelty inflicted upon us by adults unwilling to maintain the context of our infantile paradise, we are forced beyond ourselves towards a genuine 'object-choice'.

The world of fun is repressed. A process of progressive inhibition organises absolute somatic liberty into a clearly bifurcated world of object and subject. The world of objects, Freud insists, is created psychologically from the energised totality which is at first confined within the body. Reality is created and sustained for us, in other words, through our being forced to alienate from ourselves a portion of an originally undivided world of fun.

Between the world of fun and that of individuated objects we exist for a time in narcissistic twilight. But in recognising ourselves as enclosures we simultaneously posit the existence of an 'outside world' and draw a distinctive immanent with the subsequent 'development' of an individuated ego.[17]

In his initial formulations (still influenced by the language of the 'Project') Freud borrowed Fechner's 'Constancy Principle' and applied it to the nascent psychical apparatus. In the primary process stimulation was internal to the system, but the apparatus, guided by a blind attachment to its own gratification, sought to rid itself of excess 'excitation' through 'conversion' into motor activity. Freud's use of this principle is easily misunderstood. He is not supposing that the primordial world of fun is regulated by a 'natural' reserve of any kind; that there is, so to speak, a limit to how much enjoyment we can tolerate. He is simply trying to express, in terms of scientific physiology, the underlying principle of play; a tendency to mobility, to undirected and spontaneous physical activity without purpose or intention in the outside world. The 'Constancy Principle', in fact, is the reason for the exuberance of childhood; its direct and open physicality.[18]

There is in a broader sense no limit to the quantity, just as there is no restraint upon the form, in which fun may indulge us. Freud's characterisation of such a world of primitive experience has been elaborated with a novel historical dimension by Bakhtin in his pioneering book on Rabelais (Bakhtin, 1965). It might be read, indeed, as a 'Fourth Essay' on Sexuality. His depiction of the medieval carnival amounts to a rediscovery, in the form of a collective ritual, of the primary process. The carnival proclaims, if not with its rudimentary innocence, then still with some of its original vigour, perversity and excess, the original distribution of bodily gratification.

Such a world must be forgotten. It cannot even be permitted to linger in degraded and incomplete forms. The world of objects does not simply deny the plenitude of fun, it undermines its possibility. Fun is all or nothing. The incipient rationality of the object world is intolerant of any competitor and, once repressed, its absolute inner freedom can be recalled only briefly in moments of unaccountable ecstasy.

The ego, its sketchy existence grudgingly wrenched from the greater liberty of the playworld is not formed, in Freud's view (though he has been frequently credited with such a view), through the repression of pleasure, but rather, by the inhibition of fun. The distinction is important. In fun there is no logic, no contradiction and no restraint imposed by an unyielding exterior reality. And assuredly there is not, either, any pleasure. Freud as clearly as the greatest of his nineteenth-century predecessors, Søren Kierkegaard, saw the pursuit of pleasure as the means to the emergence of the self. The ego is the agency of pleasure, and in the hermetic sensorium of the primary process there is no ego.[19] The means to experience pleasure must await, through the dissolution of the primary process, the simultaneous creation of both the ego and its objects. The inhibition of fun is the origin of the ego, the beginning, rather than the end, of the pursuit of pleasure, and the source of innumerable maladies.

Much of Freud's most important theoretical writing was guided by a simple question; where does pleasure come from?[20] What is its source? For the most part our everyday pleasures appear to have unproblematic origins. The satisfaction of various appetites, however cultivated, is experienced as pleasurable. And our desire for goods and affection beyond the limits of 'natural' wants could be accounted for, within the framework of bourgeois egoism, in terms of a possessive and passionate 'inflation' of individualism. In trying to trace pleasure to its source, however, Freud was forced to abandon bourgeois psychology. Underlying all pleasure, as its psychic precondition, was fun. The immediacy of the primary process was lost, but, mediated through the differentiations of everyday counsciousness, its primordial reality persists in our every action.

It was, so to speak, on the other side of the ego, however, that Freud came upon the specifically modern deviation of pleasure. For convenience it might be termed excitement.

Excitement is characteristically unanticipated, momentary and arbitrary in nature. It is evidently hoped for in the urgent quest for new impressions; and though it is 'set off' by such novelties as train journeys, exhibitions, department stores, sporting events, its specific exhilaration belongs to none of these. We can plan the pleasures of a holiday or other diversion, but we must simply remain 'on the look-out' for excitement. As such it is, in the modern period, the transformation of the subject most ardently awaited; a temporary relief from boredom (rather than work). It satisfies a quite general, childish wish (and what wish is not childish?) to be 'somewhere else'.

Excitement is the unexpected fulfilment of a wish, often an unsuspected wish. And as all wishes radiate from the primary process, wishing, in an adult, is essentially nostalgic; each specific wish is just a means of expressing the general wish to experience once again the limitless possibilities of fun. In it the 'self' is both lost and found; dissolved into nothing and reconstituted from its foundation. Whatever its specific mechanism the 'exciting' is a brief reminiscence of the abandoned world of fun, recollecting through a complex web of associations our common 'prehistoric' era.

The dreamwork, the jokework, the subversive parapraxes are all techniques of eluding our 'self-composure'. They form, through a series of links too complex to be consciously controlled, a relationship with our forgotten past and its forbidden gratifications. As the unconscious recollection of fun, however, excitement deserves to be treated as a form of gratification *sui generis*. It is not in itself fun, it is not even like fun; excitement exists as a relation of signification in which we gain a momentary relief from ourselves. There is in excitement, therefore, none of the sense of achievement which accompanies our pleasures, nor the easy taken-for-grantedness with which we once enjoyed fun. Its characteristic bewilderment, even though we are continually receptive to its incidental catalysts, always takes us a little by surprise.

The dream or the joke is not readily understood. It does not 'appeal' to consciousness. It is a code, and that in the everyday sense of a concealed message rather than the modern linguists' usage as a 'structure'.[21] The origin of excitement must remain hidden from us; its very nature is concealment.

It is the nature of excitement, it might be noted, which is the reason for Freud's often regretted 'unscientific' method of analysis. As the original source of gratification becomes distant the chain of trivial signifiers we form to reach it, dissolving our ego in its inner complexity, becomes incoherent and logically perverse. Effective associations cannot be predicted in advance but only, and with considerable difficulty, unravelled in retrospect.

In fun and excitement there is none of that inner tension we know as desire. There is no absence into which or across which the ego longs to expand.

In fun there is, literally, nothing beyond immediacy; the world in its entirety is directly sensed. Children, for a time, being absorbed in play, succeed in its precarious symbolic extension. Play, effortless, arbitrary and inconsequential, expresses the mobility of insincere wishes. It is the least constrained of activities and, as nothing resists its inner movement, it is not passionate.

With excitement, again, there is no space between subject and object. The world, indeed is filled with objects other than ourselves but they are not, as they are for the ego, a means to pleasure. Transformed into a personal hieroglyph they form, rather, the leisurely route back to our origins. From its arbitrary terminus in the present the world grows dense with recollections, making accessible (provided we 'give way' to it) an image of the primary process.[22] The 'object', that is to say, is not an object at all but a subject, the subject anterior to the ego; the universal subject.

The neurotic ego, we might say, overly reluctant to admit to anything before itself, clings tenaciously to its object world and halts regressive associations by forming them into symptoms. Freud at first held that 'Hysterics suffer mainly from reminiscences' (Bruer and Freud, 1895, 7), but the trauma to which symptoms appeared traceable gave way, in more relaxed analysis, to the fantasies which preceded it. They suffered, that is to say, from incomplete reminiscences.

At the core of Freud's psychology, then, is the wish rather than desire; fun rather than pleasure. The divergent views of Freud, exemplified by the work of Sulloway and Ricoeur, do not represent a shift in his writing from a 'young/scientific' to a 'mature/literary' mode of thought; nor a movement from a 'possessive' to a 'passionate' view of pleasure; it is a consequence, rather, of his attempt to describe two qualitatively different, but biographically linked, forms of gratification. Fun, a somatic totality, he most frequently described in medico-scientific language; and excitement, its fragmented recapitulation, to which he alluded with a novelist's technique.

Freud's patients suffered from disturbances in the mechanisms of wish-fulfilment (repression, disguise, displacement), rather than from deranged passions. The nature of man is to wish, and only when we have been forced to abandon the wish can we learn to desire. Now, dissatisfied in the pursuit of pleasure, we would like to wish again. But we cannot. We must console ourselves, instead, with fun's vicarious existence in the excitement of spontaneous and uncontrolled recollections; or become ill.

The wish, passive, patient and melancholic, then inexplicably effervescent is typically, though not uniquely, Viennese. Excitement has become the sole diversion for the 'man without qualities'.

If late capitalism has degenerated into a passionless, introverted affair, why should it persist? To return to the simplistic economic question; what is the gain in abandoning the pursuit of pleasure for the chance of excitement?

To pose such a question, however, is still to accept the validity of the bourgeois ego. The pursuit of pleasure is an aspect of that egoism and occurs only when people are convinced there is something 'real' (i.e. transcendental and imaginary) about each unique personality. They must believe in the possibility of 'realising' their 'true nature'; that they might really become Kierkegaard's 'single one' or Stirner's dechristianised but equally religious 'absolute ego'. The secularisation required for the operation of social life elsewhere, however, cannot be conveniently halted at the metaphysical enclosure which is the human body. And though the concept of 'pleasure' as a 'qualification of inwardness' for a long time almost succeeded in effecting such a philosophic sleight of hand, Freud's work itself, in its slow, spasmodic, assimilation, helped to dissolve the boundary. There has been, in other words, little alternative but to accept modernity's welcoming embrace and fall in with the practice of leisure.

THE END OF PLEASURE?

It is no doubt premature to announce the death of bourgeois egoism and the forms of subjectivity it supports. Marx's perceptive comment on the 'categories of bourgeois economics', that 'They are forms of thought which are socially valid, and therefore objective' (Marx, 1976, 169) could to a large extent still be applied to bourgeois psychology as a whole. The 'categories of bourgeois psychology' are not in any simple sense mistaken. Defended as orthodoxy they describe a particular reality.

Marx, of course, was at pains to expose the peculiar inversion at the root of such a reality. Commodities, being produced purely in respect of their use-value, entered the world as alien objects, their presence oppressive to those who had laboured to produce them. The commodity, which is nothing but the embodiment of 'definite social relations between men', comes to, 'assume, for them, the fantastic form of a relation between things' (Marx, 1976, 165). The producer, consequently, became lost in the world of alienated labour.

It is just this 'objectivity' which justified the utilitarian tradition in psychology, and, viewing the individual as a consumer rather than a producer, regarded pleasure as the consequence of possessing valued objects; commodities that had been released into the realm of infinite circulation.

Passionate individualism, also, regards pleasure as a form of possession; self-possession. The 'real' object underlying the pursuit of pleasure is the 'self', whose fictive presence colours the object-choice with its own desirability. Self and other, master and slave, consciousness and self-consciousness, depend upon a mute third party to complete their dialectical circuits. This deeper form of individualism is the perfection of the bourgeois ego. Private, narcissistic and subjective it can be tolerated, even applauded within a capitalist order left undisturbed by the retreat from public, collective life.

Fun and its recollection in excitement appear evanescent by comparison. The pursuit of pleasure still dominates our conscious effort. Their significance, however, is no less real for being concealed.

Fun is devoted to perpetual consumption, but its physical forms, being parts of the body or their 'anaclitic' extension as toys, do not require to be 'possessed'.[23] In being used they are never 'used up', and as receptacles of wishes they are infinitely plastic. And though such immediacy is quickly abolished, modern leisure relations attempt to reinstate a certain element of playfulness into the rational world of commodities. An unease with utilitarian psychology, and even more a recognition of the limitations upon consumption which it represented (desire is serious, possession invokes moral constraint, the longed-for object must be 'worthwhile') has prompted a leisurely and superficial image of consumption.

Consumption has become exciting. The new shops, large department stores, were among the first things to attract Freud's attention on his 1885 visit to Paris. Their displays, as remote from the process of manufacture as dreams from their hidden wishes, held out a new image of sensuous liberty. It recalls the world of pure and continuous consumption. Possession, of course, remains its prerequisite (capitalism is not about to dissolve), but necessity is held in abeyance. A new realm of wish fulfilment, as inexhaustible as its fecund prototype, approaches ever closer to an illusion of reality.

Douglas and Isherwood (1980, 59) in asking the pertinent anthropological question, 'Why do we want goods?' propose that, 'Instead of supposing that goods are primarily needed for subsistence plus competitive display, let us assume that they are needed for making visible the categories of culture.' The culture of classical capitalism was intent upon possession, but that of modernity seeks excitement. Commodities need no longer be collected as marks of personal distinction. Rather than 'realising' ourselves through ownership we can 'lose' ourselves in the excitement of consumption.[24]

Modern consumer toys, like all playthings, are essentially indistinguishable from one another. The ideal commodity has become standardised, easily packaged and infinitely reproducible. A hi-tech box that (again like a toy) in being consumed is not 'used up'. It is watched, listened to, admired. It sets up entire industries to furnish it with the images which it circulates.

This only appears to be irrational. The comparative longevity of modern goods is overwhelmed by the wish for continual newness. Our attachment to commodities, partaking of a diffuse eroticism, has the advantage of any wish in being intense but insincere. The 'leisurework' succeeds in displacing, condensing and distorting our endlessly renewable wishes, attaching them first to one image, then to another, making us, like children, excited only by the latest and most up-to-date 'model'.

Classical capitalism succeeded, by the alienation of labour, in making of the commodity an object of desire; its monopolistic successor seeks, through the alienation of leisure, to rediscover in its object-world the innocence of neglected wishes.

Notes

1. Ernest Jones in writing Freud's official biography had access to many unpublished letters and papers, including the Fliess correspondence. It was to Fliess that Freud sent his first attempt at a synthesis of psychological theory, 'Project for a Scientific Psychology', in the autumn of 1895. It was subsequently published (Freud, 1954) together with a selection of the letters, and made its appearance in the *Standard Edition* (Vol. I, 1966) For discussions of the significance of the Fliess relationship, see Ernst Kris (1954) 'Introduction' to Freud, *Origins*; the editor's comments in the *Standard Edition*; Sulloway (1980); Anzieu (1986). A complete edition of Freud's letters to Fliess has recently appeared, Masson (1986).
2. For a full account see Jones Vol. I (1953); Ellenberger (1971).
3. Anzieu (1986, Ch 1), in particular, stresses the ineradicable impact of the physical and domestic circumstances of Freud's early years.
4. The most important of Freud's writings on analytic technique are contained in Vol. XII of the *Standard Edition*. The quotations cited are from 'Recommendations to Physicians Practising Psycho-Analysis' (1912). Ch. XXVIII 'Analytic Therapy' of the *Introductory Lectures on Psycho-Analysis* (1917) *Standard Edition* XVI, and 'Analysis Terminable and Interminable' (1937), *Standard Edition XXIII*, are also significant.
5. A scholarly reassessment of Breuer's part in the origins of psychoanalysis is offered in Sulloway (1980).
6. 'It almost looks as if analysis were the third of those "impossible" professions in which one can be sure beforehand of achieving unsatisfying results. The other two, which have been known much longer, are education and government'. 'Analysis Terminable and Interminable' (1937) *Standard Edition* XXIII, 248.
7. Marcus, interestingly, likens his technique to Nabokov's. It is worth remembering that the other leading psychologists of modernity were novelists, Dostoevsky and Proust.
8. See, for example, Kline (1981).
9. For insightful discussions see, in addition to Parsons (1937), Macpherson (1962) and particularly Unger (1975).
10. Lovejoy (1961), Chs IV and V, offers an interesting analysis of 'Approbativeness' in seventeenth- and eighteenth-century writers.
11. What is here called 'passionate individualism' refers particularly to the work of Søren Kierkegaard, see his *Either/Or, Repetition*, and *Training in Christianity*. A good introduction has been provided by Malantschuk (1971) and, from a more sociological viewpoint Löwith (1964). Carroll's (1974) neglect of Kierkegaard in his *Break-Out from the Crystal Palace* seriously weakens his attempt to define a nineteenth-century *tradition* of 'anarcho-psychological' writing.
12. See, for example, Kierkegaard (1971, originally 1843), 'Equilibrium Between the Aesthetical and the Ethical in the Composition of Personality'.
13. On Dostoevsky see particularly Bakhtin (1973, 1929) Ch 1 and 2 and

Mochulsky (1967) Freud was interested enough in Dostoevsky as a psychologist to devote an essay to him, 'Dostoevsky and Parricide', *Standard Edition XXI*.

Freud claimed never to have read Nietzsche, 'with the deliberate object of not being hampered in working out the impressions received in psycho-analysis by any sort of anticipatory ideas.' *On the History of the Psycho-Analytic Movement* (1914), *Standard Edition*, XIV, 15–16.

14. Camus (1951) *The Rebel* remains the indispensible guide.
15. See, e.g. *Jokes and Their Relation to the Unconscious* (1905) *Standard Edition* VIII, Ch. IV.

    'Formulation on the 'Two Principles of Mental Functioning' (1911) *Standard Edition* XII.

    'Psycho-Analytic Notes on an Autobiographical Account of a Case of Paranoia' (1911), The Schreber case. *Standard Edition* XII, 59–82.
16. See *The Interpretation of Dreams* (1900 *Standard Edition* IV, 261–63.
17. Melanie Klein (1980) has enormously enriched the psychoanalytic literature on the early body image.
18. For a fuller discussion of the formal characteristics of play see Ferguson (1983), Part II.
19. Commentators such as Brown (1959) and Rieff (1960) who see in Freud's stress on 'internal conflict' a form of philosophical dualism miss, it seems to me, the centrality of the 'primary process' in the construction of Freud's psychology.
20. It is the explicitness of this question in *Jokes and their Relation to the Unconscious*, which makes it, though one of Freud's least-read books, one of the most valuable. See in this connection, exceptionally, Spector (1972).
21. A 'hardening' of the meaning which epitomises Lacan's 'structuralist' reading of Freud. See especially Lacan (1977), Chs 3 and 9.
22. The density of *signs* filling the associative field between the subject and himself can be contrasted to the *hierarchy* of *symbols* through which the medieval penitent strove for *happiness*. The practice of humility was a slow ascent towards God, in whom a final abandonment of the ego became possible. See, for an overview of monastic psychology, Leclerq (1979).
23. A helpful discussion can be found in Winnicott (1971).
24. We have reached, apparently, and by a somewhat different route, Marcuse's concept of 'repressive desublimation', Marcuse (1964), 58. Insisting, however, upon the distinction between pleasure/desire, on the one hand, and fun/excitement/the wish, on the other, makes it difficult to claim that my argument is corroborative.

References

Anzieu, Didier (1986) *Freud's Self-Analysis*, London, The Hogarth Press and the Institute of Psycho-Analysis.

Bakhtin, M. (1929, 1973) *Problems of Dostoevsky's Poetics*, London, Ardis. (1965) *Rabelais and His World*, tr. H. Iswolsky, MIT Press.

Breuer, J. and Freud, S. (1895, 1974) *Studies on Hysteria, Standard Edition* Vol II. See Freud (1974) below.
Brown, Norman O. (1959) *Life Against Death*, London, Routledge and Kegan Paul.
Camus, Albert (1962, 1951) *The Rebel*, Harmondsworth, Penguin.
Carroll, J. (1974) *Break-Out from the Crystal Palace*, London, Routledge & Kegan Paul.
Douglas, M. and Baron Isherwood (1980) *The World of Goods*, London, Harmonsworth, Penguin.
Ellenberger, H. (1971) *The Discovery of the Unconscious*, London, Allen Lane, The Penguin Press.
Ferguson, Adam (1792, 1976) *Principles of Social and Political Science*, Edinburgh.
Ferguson, Harvie (1983) *Essays in Experimental Psychology*, London, Macmillan.
Freud, S. (1954) *The Origins of Psycho-Analysis* (eds. Marie Bonaparte, Anna Freud, Ernst Kris), London, Imago.
(1960) *Letters of Sigmund Freud, 1873–1939*, (ed. Ernst Freud), London, The Hogarth Press.
(1974) *The Standard Edition of the Complete Psychological Works of Sigmund Freud*, 25 vols, London, The Hogarth Press and the Institute of Psycho-Analysis.
(1985) *The Complete Letters of Sigmund Freud to Wilhelm Fliess* (tr. and ed. J. M. Masson), London/Harvard, Harvard University Press.
Johnstone, W. (1972) *The Austrian Mind: An Intellectual and Social History*, London, University of California Press.
Jones, E. (1953–55) *The Life and Work of Sigmund Freud* London, The Hogarth Press and the Institute of Psycho-Analysis.
Kierkgaard, S. (1843, 1959) *Either/Or*, Princeton, Princeton University Press.
(1844, 1964) *Repetition: An Essay on Experimental Psychology*, New York, Harper.
(1850, 1967) *Training in Christianity*, Princeton, Princeton University Press.
Klein, M.(1980) *The Psycho-Analysis of Children*, London, The Hogarth Press and The Institute of Psycho-Analysis.
Kline, P. (1981) *Fact and Fantasy in Freudian Theory*, London, Methuen.
Lacan, J. (1977) *Écrits: A Selection*, London, Tavistock.
Leclerq, J. (1979) *The Love of Learning and the Desire for God*, Fordham University Press.
Lovejoy, A. O. (1961) *Reflections on Human Nature*, Baltimore, The Johns Hopkins Press.
Löwith, K. (1964) *From Hegel to Nietzsche: The Revolution in Nineteenth Century Thought*, London, Constable.
Macpherson, C. B. (1962) *The Political Theory of Possessive Individualism* Oxford, Oxford University Press.
Malantschuk, G. (1971) *Kierkegaard's Thought*, Princeton, Princeton University Press.
Marcus, S. (1984) *Freud and the Culture of Psychoanalysis*, Boston, Allen and Unwin.

74   *Sigmund Freud and the Pursuit of Pleasure*

Marcuse, H. (1964) *One Dimensional Man*, London, Routledge & Kegan
Paul.
(1972) *Eros and Civilisation*, London, Abacus.
Marx, K. (1976) *Capital Volume One*, Harmondsworth, Penguin.
Mochulsky, K. (1967) *Dostoevsky: His Life and Work*, Princeton, Princeton
University Press.
Nietzsche, F. (1969) *On the Genealogy of Morals*, New York, Vintage Books.
Parsons, T. (1937) *The Structure of Social Action*, New York, The Free Press.
Ricoeur, P. (1970) *Freud and Philosophy: An Essay on Interpretation*, New
Haven, Yale University Press.
Rieff, P. (1960) *Freud: The Mind of the Moralist*, London, Methuen.
Rojek, C. (1985) *Capitalism and Leisure Theory*, London, Tavistock.
Schorske, C. (1980) *Fin-de-Siècle Vienna: Politics and Culture* London,
Weidenfeld & Nicolson.
Smith, Adam (1759, 1973) *Theory of Moral Sentiments*, Edinburgh.
Spector, J. (1972) *The Aesthetics of Freud: A Study in Psychoanalysis and Art*,
London, Allen Lane, The Penguin Press.
Sulloway, F. (1980) *Freud, Biologist of the Mind*, London, Fontana.
Unger, R. (1975) *Knowledge and Politics*, New York, The Free Press.
Winnicott, D. W. (1971) *Playing and Reality*, London, Tavistock.

4 Simmel and Leisure
David Frisby

> The mere possibility of happiness, even if its realisation is sparse and fragmentary in actual life, englobes our existence in light.
>
> Georg Simmel, *Schopenhauer and Nietzsche*

> Just as it has been said that the history of women has the peculiar characteristic that it is not the history of women but of men, so one can say that, viewed more closely, the history of recreations, of play, of enjoyments is the history of work and of the serious side of life.
>
> Georg Simmel, 'Infélices possidentes'

I

It should not be surprising that Georg Simmel (1858–1918), one of the first sociological analysts of modernity and metropolitan experience, should also have concerned himself in direct and roundabout ways with the problem of modern leisure. This is not least because his social theory, grounded in the study of forms of social interaction or sociation, enabled him to view society as the totality of social interactions, as a complex web of interrelationships and social interactions, within which one could legitimately focus on any interaction, however fleeting and insignificant, and both arrive at its connection with any other interaction as well as view it as the locus of the meaning of the totality of interactions.[1] Simmel's aesthetic sensitivity to the tempo, rhythm and symmetry of social interactions, so distinctive a feature of much of his sociological writings – especially after his seminal article on 'Sociological Aesthetics' (1896)[2] – suggests the influence of an aesthetic distance which he himself practised. Was it perhaps part of the psychological defence mechanisms with which he argued metropolitan dwellers should go armed in order to withstand the tumultuous shocks of endlessly new impressions and encounters in big-city life? Certainly leisure is often seen as an escape, a distancing, either physical, social, mental or aesthetic, from the demands of external life, or as Simmel would have it, from the growing objective culture. But Simmel was a sufficiently astute social theorist to recognise that this did not mean that leisure was therefore to be located solely in what he termed subjective culture, that realm wherein genuine individuality might still be created in a context of growing materialism and individualism. The organisation of leisure, however individual its form, was also permeated by the objective, material culture, by the social. Indeed, as we shall see, one of the most universal forms of leisure – sociability itself and conversation – was viewed by Simmel not merely as 'the play form of society' but also as a pure form of what he understood to be society.

Indeed, as with many of the themes of Simmel's reflections, it is impossible to view them as detached from his own activities and experiences. From what we know of Simmel's life, his own leisure activities at first sight reflect those of certain strata of Berlin bourgeois intelligentsia at the turn of the century. In Berlin itself, Simmel valued the institutional arrangements for sociability that were soon to become anachronistic: the intellectual salons. But even here one should be careful to distinguish 'the intersecting of social circles'. When Simmel himself had become established as a leading intellectual figure after the turn of the century then the 'salons' conducted in his own home might contain figures from a variety of spheres: philosophers, poets, artists and so on.[3] At the Simmel family's weekly 'jours', Simmel's favourite students might be in attendance, so that they took on the atmosphere of a 'Privatisimum'.[4] But earlier in his career, in the early 1890s, Simmel probably also attended the so-called 'Red Salon' of Leo Arons – an active socialist academic dismissed from Berlin University who was also the inventor of the neon lamp (whose shrill light was to illuminate the showplaces of modernity a few decades later) – where he would have come into contact with Mehring, Kautsky and other more dangerous figures.[5] Much later in his life, Simmel's own thirst for sociability was reflected in arrangements to meet and converse with friends even for an hour at railway stations and elsewhere, even in the darkened days of the First World War.

The latter suggests that Simmel was prepared to travel to meet his friends. Certainly Simmel and his wife Gertrud would visit the Webers in Heidelberg and mix with their social and intellectual circle. But even when he was academically established, Simmel did not always attend academic congresses. Perhaps his appearance to give the opening address to the first meeting of the German Sociological Association in

Frankfurt in 1910 on 'The Sociology of Sociability' was an exception.[6] Maybe that fusion of leisure and work, signalled even in its title, was too uncomfortable to be often repeated. More typical of Simmel's activities was his summer travel, for instance, to work on his writing at one of his uncle's residences on the Reichenau on Lake Constance. In keeping with his strong aesthetic interests, Simmel visited art exhibitions (the subject of one of his essays that is examined below) and trade exhibitions (another theme examined below) in Berlin. In 1902, Simmel travelled to the Rodin exhibition in Prague, in 1905 to Paris to visit Rodin himself. His vignettes of the Alps, Rome, Florence and Venice indicate the activities of an extensive railway traveller, accompanied sometimes by his family or by his students such as Ernst Bloch (to Florence) or Margaretta Susman. Occasionally, these visits prompted another of Simmel's leisure activities: the writing of poems, aphorisms and snapshots which usually appeared in the leading German *Jugendstil* journal, *Jugend*, and included one of his longest poems 'Autumn on the Rhine' (1897).[7]

But however compelling Simmel's aesthetic interests may have been – he was also a collector of Japanese vases at the turn of the century – and however widely he travelled to attractive rural or urban settings, his interests remained those of a cosmopolitan urban intellectual. Unlike Tönnies, for instance, who hated cities and above all Berlin, Simmel was completely at home in his native city. Even a bizzare attack on his life in 1886 in the streets of Berlin whilst collecting the rent on one of his uncle's properties did not deter him from making that city his life's focus.[8] When he was finally appointed to a chair of philosophy at Strasbourg University in 1914, he very soon felt the loss of the metropolitan context for his work. And that metropolitan context was for Simmel a crucial source of the modern search for new leisure forms, of the thirst for ever-new excitements.

II

The social space of the metropolis might well constitute a starting-point for an examination of Simmel's treatment of leisure. It is both the source of the metropolitan personality type and the focal point of the money economy and the modern division of labour in production and consumption. For Simmel, the metropolis is the showplace of modernity, extending its effects – like the money economy itself which also symbolises the complex networks of interaction in the spheres of circulation and exchange – far into the hinterland. Indeed, the metropolis and the mature money economy together constitute a central constellation within which we can understand Simmel's reflections upon leisure.

The metropolis is 'the genuine showplace of this culture' of objectified material entities, of objective culture which Simmel saw as having advanced so rapidly in the later decades of the nineteenth century. Yet this complex network and labyrinth of social interactions witin the ever-changing, disintegrating and reconstituting social space of the metropolis, facilitating as it does an increase in 'the material enjoyment of life', also requires the creation of new responses by human beings to the complexities of functional differentiation, to 'the most advanced economic division of labour', to the levelling effect of the money economy which 'dominates the metropolis' and, above all, to 'the tumult of the metropolis', to 'the jostling crowdedness', to 'the motley disorder of metropolitan communcation'.

As 'seats of the most developed economic division of labour', in which 'city life has transformed the struggle with nature for livelihood into a struggle with other human beings for gain, which is here not granted by nature but by human beings',[9] metropolitan centres are also sites of production as well as of consumption, circulation and exchange. Elsewhere, in a manner sometimes reminiscent of the early Marx, Simmel argues that modern production is not the site of creativity, of individuality, of pleasure. Indeed, the personality of the individual worker 'often even becomes stunted' through its frag- mented specialisation. The separation of the worker from the means of production and from work activity itself 'as purely objective and autonomous', indicates that 'labour now shares the same character, mode of valuation and fate with all other commodities'.[10] Since Simmel was more interested in the circulation, exchange and consumption dimensions, it is legitimate to inquire whether the sphere of consumption was any more satisfying.

The sphere of consumption and the circulation of individuals as customers or as commodities is also concentrated in the metropolis. The sphere of non-work, ostensibly that of leisure, can also be filled out by consumption and by circulation in search of what is new. Where a 'mass' of consumers has been created, commodities can be sold for their price rather than their quality. Simmel sees this as the attraction of 'the "fifty cents bazaar"', as part of the cycle of 'the production of cheap trash', and in turn 'a broadening of consumption [which] corresponds to the specialisation of production'.[11]

The other dimension of mass consumption to which Simmel indirectly draws attention is the creation of customers' needs, since

the seller must always seek to call forth new and differentiated needs of the lured customer. In order to find a source of income which is not yet exhausted, and to find a function which cannot readily be displaced, it is necessary to specialise in one's services. This process promotes differentiation, refinement and the enrichment of the public's needs.[12]

It is a process which does not necessarily enrich the individual. At first sight it seems as if, in the metropolis 'life is made infinitely easy for the personality in that stimulations, interests, *fillings in of time and consciousness [Ausfüllungen von Zeit und Bewusstsein]* are offered to it from all sides. They carry the person, *as if in a stream*, and one needs hardly to swim for oneself'.[13] Yet such passivity on the part of the individual consumer signalises 'the atrophy of individual culture through the hypertrophy of objective culture'.

What does this signify? Simmel indicates a whole range of areas of economic and social life in which subjectivity is threatened: *production* is not the sphere of 'the harmonious growth of the self'; the 'subjective aura of the *product* also disappears' in mass production; in *exchange* relations, 'subjectivity is destroyed and transposed into cool reserve and anonymous objectivity'; in the sphere of *consumption*, 'by their independent, impersonal mobility, objects complete the final stage of their separation from people. The slot machine is the ultimate example of the mechanical character of the modern economy'; as part of 'the objectivity of the *life-style*' of the modern metropolis, 'the externalities of life . . . confront us as autonomous objects' and the objectification process 'invades even the more intimate aspects of our daily life'.[14] This objectified, reified world presents itself to us 'at an ever increasing distance'.

Not surprisingly, the impact of this reified world of the metropolis and the money economy upon individuals is all the greater because human subjects are themselves compelled to respond to their 'particularly abstract existence' only by attempting to distance themselves from it. Above all, they must respond to the shock of 'the rapid and unbroken change in external and internal stimuli' that is experienced 'with every crossing of the street, with the speed and diversity of economic, professional and social life', as 'the rapid crowding of changing images, the sharp discontinuity in the grasp of a single glance, and the unexpectedness of onrushing impressions'.[15] This accounts, Simmel argues, for the 'increase in nervous life', the neurasthenia of modern human beings, including its pathological forms of agoraphobia and hyperaesthesia, and the 'psychological distance' created by the intellect as a defence mechanism for the emotions against the endless shock experience of urban existence. Similarly, the heightening of intellectual defence mechanisms is matched by an acceleration and heightening of emotional responses that remain unsatisfied by the 'stimulations, interests, fillings-in of time and consciousness' that are offered. The permanent 'feeling of tension, expectation and unreleased intense desires', the 'secret restlessness' results in our endless neurotic search for

> momentary satisfaction in ever-new stimulations, sensations and external activities . . . we become entangled in the instability and helplessness that manifests itself as the tumult of the metropolis, as the mania for travelling, as the wild pursuit of competition and as the typical modern disloyalty with regard to taste, style, opinions and personal relationships.[16]

By implication, then 'the inner barrier . . . between people . . . that is indispensable for the modern form of life', 'the mutual reserve and indifference', 'the specifically metropolitan excesses of aloofness, caprice and fastidiousness' are ultimately ineffective against the experience of modernity as the discontinuity and disintegration of the modes of experiencing time, space and causality (including the teleology of means and ends). Alienated forms of existence become the objective forms within which we exist.

The most typical form of existence, 'unreservedly associated with the metropolis' and the mature money economy dominated by commodity circulation and exchange, is that which is dominated by the blasé attitude resulting from 'the rapidly changing and closely compressed contrasting stimulations of the nerves' and culminating in 'an incapacity to react to new sensations with the appropriate energy'. Where individuals themselves circulate as commodities and where all values have been reduced to exchange values, the blasé individual 'experiences all things as being of an equally dull and grey hue, as not worth getting excited about'.[17] This does not remove the thirst for more amusement and excitement since it has not been satisfied. Hence, 'the craving today for excitement, for extreme impressions, for the greatest speed in its change . . . for "stimulation" as such in impressions, relationships and information – without thinking it important for us to find out why these stimulate us'.[18]

It is against this background that we can now examine those 'fillings-in of time and consciousness' that ostensibly lie outside the sphere of work and constitute 'leisure'. Where the stimulations and distractions of leisure are directly located in the sphere of the consumption of commodities – and Simmel already posited the extension of commodification to the personal sphere, to the sale of 'experiences' as commodities – it is difficult to see how they can rise beyond this sphere and contribute to the realisation of the elusive creative subjectivity and individuality which Simmel sought. And, as we shall see, even when the stimulations and distractions of leisure seemed to be distanced from this sphere, it was not always the case that they were truly satisfying as far as the promulgation of subjective culture was concerned.

Since Simmel produced no elaborate treatise on leisure, what is offered in the first case is a series of vignettes illustrating the phenomenal life of the commodity in the consumption sphere: the pursuit of fashion (the commodity's new face), places of entertainment or enjoyment [*Vergnügungstätten*] and prostitution, the exhibition of aesthetic and commercial commodities (art exhibitions and trade exhibitions). As instances of those forms of leisure activity which are apparently distanced from the commodity sphere Simmel offers us sociability and the adventure.

III

The 'immense abundance . . . of machines, products and supra-individual organisations of contemporary culture' offers us 'endless habits, endless distractions and endless superficial needs'.[19] Individuals, however, wish to assert their individuality and differentiation, to set themselves apart from the mass whilst at the same time adhering to the style of life of their social group. Simmel sees this tension between differentiation and imitation in the pursuit of fashion and style. The 'individualistic fragmentation' typical of modernity requires its counterpart in the homogeneity of fashions and styles. But one feature of adherence to fashions in contemporary society as an instance of the filling-in of time and consciousness is the increasing rapidity of the 'turnover-time' of fashions themselves, a reflection of 'the specific "impatient" tempo of modern life', of the breaking-up of the rhythm of life into ever-shorter fragments:

> The fact that fashion takes on an unprecedented upper hand in contemporary culture – breaking into hitherto untouched areas, becoming more obsessive in existing ones, i.e. incessantly increasing the speed of changes in fashion – is merely the coalescing of a contemporary psychological trait. Our internal rhythm requires increasingly shorter pauses in the change of impressions; or, expressed differently, the accent of attraction is transferred to an increasing extent from its substantive centre to its starting and finishing points.[20]

Fashion is then an instance of the transitory pursuit which 'gives us such a strong sense of presentness' but its reflection of 'the fleeting and changeable elements of life'. Its dedicated followers are those individuals 'who are inwardly lacking in independence and needing support', who use fashion as a means of expressing their absent individuality and content. And although 'each individual fashion to a certain extent emerges as if it wishes to live for eternity', its 'illusory nature' manifests itself in the rapidity with which each fashion disappears. Yet the 'seed of death' that is contained in fashion's moment of appearance is not some autonomous, organic process but rather arises out of the process of the production and circulation of commodities, in which 'articles are produced for the express purpose of being fashionable. At certain intervals of time, a new fashion is required *a priori* and now there exist creators and industries which exclusively carry out this task'.[21]

New fashions for old distractions and stimulations constitute an essential part of leisure-time consumption. In 1893 (under the pseudonym of Paul Liesegang), Simmel published a short essay entitled 'Infélices possidentes!' (Unhappy Dwellers)[22] which reflects upon Berlin 'places of entertainment' [*Vergnügungstätten*], devoted to 'the titillation of the senses and intoxication of the nerves'. The entertainment which they provide must stimulate the nerves: 'it requires glamour for the eyes, in which the establishments breathlessly excel in providing, while the bourgeois sits by and waits, with the ease of the spectator at the gladiators' match or of the owner of a harem, to see which of his slaves to pleasure amuses him the most and, at the same time, makes him the most comfortable'. Such entertainment as is offered requires both 'the removal of any deeper content' and that everything remain on the surface of superficiality. This amusement or play is the obverse of the 'dreadful, shocking, tragic' nature of modern life. If modern human beings are pushed to and fro 'between the passion to gain everything and the fear of losing everything' in 'the feverish pursuit of daily labours', then 'what does the evening look like?'

What inner forces still remain after the day has used up what was available in activity, tension and concentration? . . . Because every day life has completely exhausted the individual's energy, only that may be offered to him or her as relaxation which lays claim to absolutely no energy for its assimilation; the nerves, exhausted by the bustle and anxiety of the day, no longer react any more to stimulations, except to those which are, as it were, directly physiological, to which the organism itself still responds if all its sensitivities have been blunted: the attractions of light and of colourful glamour, light music, finally and above all the excitement of sexual feelings.[23]

In this context, then, the history of forms of leisure is the history of labour and the serious things in life. The exhaustion of our mental and physical energies in work lead us to require only one thing of our leisure: 'we must be made comfortable'; 'we only wish to be amused'. This Simmel sees as 'the complete poverty of the nature of our entertainment'. We must relax, enjoy our leisure, 'according to the principle of energy-saving'.

This ban upon seriousness in the leisure sphere can also have a political motivation. Simmel reports in the same year of the restriction on staging Gerhardt Hauptmann's *Weaver*, initially forbidden to the public and shown only to a restricted audience. In contrast, the police

allow the Berlin Residenztheatre year after year to present the basest French burlesques which, by the titillation of sexual feelings and the emphatic concentration of all life – interests upon these particular pleasures, may exercise their educational effect upon our people; in the Panoptikum a series of waxworks of bloody deeds is offered to the public under the title 'For those with strong nerves!'[24]

In contrast, a play such as Hauptmann's, challenging the illusions of the day, is not viewed as part of the 'aesthetic education' of the people. This hypocrisy is highlighted in Simmel's early treatment of prostitution (1892). The moral indignation of 'good society' at the widespread prostitution in the late nineteenth century is expressed, Simmel argues, as if it were not the result of social and economic conditions that are the consequences of that same good society's own interests. It also of course treats 'elegant and impoverished prostitution' in a different manner and hides its negative response to the latter in mystifying forms of description:

> There exists no more false expression than when one terms this impoverished creature 'joy girl' [*Freudenmädchen*] and hence believes that she lives out enjoyment; perhaps the joy of others, but certainly not that of her own. Or does one believe that it is a pleasure to wander the streets evening after evening, regardless of whether it is hot, raining or cold in order to serve as the spoils of some particular man, perhaps a repulsive one, to serve as an ejaculation mechanism?[25]

Leisure for some is labour for others. Like Simmel's other discussion of leisure, he also highlights prostitution's connection with the money economy. For this 'completely fleeting inconsequential relationship' between prostitute and client, 'only money . . . is the appropriate equivalent to the fleetingly intensified and just as fleetingly extinguished sexual appetite that is served by prostitution'.[26]

If prostitution serves as Simmel's crucial instance of the commodification of human values, then perhaps the exhibition of material commodities indicates a social location for leisure that is equally exemplary. The display of the phantasmagoria of commodities had become increasingly popular ever since the first World Exhibition of 1851 in London. The marvel of the serialised display of 'dead' commodities to which the visitor was to passively respond merely by observation did, of course, hide a further intention beyond this mesmerised response, namely to be brought back to life again through their purchase.

Such exhibitions were therefore also trade exhibitions and Simmel himself responded to 'The Berlin Trade Exhibition' (1896)[27], which many saw as signifying Berlin's elevation to a world metropolis. The effect of the concentration of a world of commodities in a confined space is similar to that of the effect of the tumult of the metropolis. The visitor 'will be overpowered and feel disorientated by the mass effect of what is offered here', whilst the wealth and colourfulness of the impressions is itself 'appropriate to over-excited and exhausted nerves' need for stimulation'. The overall effect is that of entering a dream-world since 'the close proximity within which the most heterogeneous industrial products are confined produces a paralysis in the capacity for perception, *a true hypnosis*'. In addition, 'in its fragmentation of weak impressions, there remains in the memory the notion that *one should amuse oneself here*'. This impression is accentuated by the arrangement of the exhibition into smaller galleries with entrance fees, so that the excitement and anticipation is constantly renewed and the amusement effect is both heightened and toned down.

Such exhibitions were housed in newer architectural forms which, in keeping with the fleeting life of the commodity, also reflected this transitoriness. Indeed, 'the conscious negation of the monumental style' was complemented by giving the building structures 'the character of a creation for transitoriness'. The layout of such exhibitions enhanced their 'aesthetic productivity' through 'the increase in what one might term the shop-window quality of things that is evoked by exhibitions . . . one must attempt to excite the interest of the buyer by means of the external attraction of the object, even indeed by means of the form of its arrangement'.

At the end of the previous decade, Simmel had reflected upon an earlier leisure activity which was achieving greater popularity and which possessed many common features to the world exhibitions, namely visits to art exhibitions. In 'On Art Exhibitions' (1890),[28] Simmel views the art exhibition as a symbolic microcosm of 'the colourfulness of metropolitan life on the street and in the salon' which brings together for the viewer, in a series of small spaces and 'in the same concentration, the whole wealth of feelings that art as a whole can awaken in him'. However, this very wealth of impressions and images induces two modern responses to this concentrated diversity: 'the blasé attitude and superficiality'. The 'overburdening' of impressions and the 'fleeting character of art exibitions' that resides in 'the immediately consecutive viewing of that which is contradictory' produces only a superficial overview of the whole. In place of recognition of the individuality of works of art there emerges 'more and more the influence of the mass'. In short, the display of works of art does not escape the developing features of modern metropolitan existence. In this respect, the structure and organisation of art exhibitions fails to realise what for Simmel is one of the crucial features of the work of art: 'art brings us closer to reality; it places us in a more immediate relationship to its distinctive and innermost meanings . . . In addition, however, all art brings about a distancing from the immediacy of things; it allows the concreteness of stimuli to recede and stretches a veil between us and them just like the fine bluish haze that envelops distant mountains.'[29]

And yet we cannot escape to 'distant mountains' either in order to recover our genuine individuality. Although the flight from the present can take a spatial as well as a temporal form – which Simmel examines in 'The Adventure' – a return to nature as a crucial dimension of leisure activity is also deeply compromised. In 'Alpine Journeys' (1895),[30] – discarding his interest in yodeling from over a decade earlier[31] – Simmel examines the consequences of opening up areas of landscape for leisure by the extension of railways 'to goals which were otherwise only accessible to solitary wandering'. The Swiss Alps were undergoing changes that had earlier taken place in the Black Forest: the extension of tourism to previously inaccessible places and, within tourist resorts, the further extension of railways and other forms of communication up the mountains themselves. This particular form of the process of the domination of nature creates a new environment, a new nature for the tourist: 'In more than a merely external analogy to our economic development, one could term it the large-scale enterprise of the enjoyment of nature'. The romantic solitary communion with nature (which was also a social construct) is now replaced by that of a 'colourless mass' experiencing a 'standard enjoyment' of nature. This 'socialising large-scale enterprise, compared with the individual enterprise of alpinism', does open up nature to many more people. But, 'the power of capitalism also extends over concepts', such as that of the creative formation [*Bildung*] of individuals which was associated with the image of communion with nature. Instead of an effect upon the total personality – physical, intellectual and moral – Simmel detects its fragmentation into differentiated elements associated with 'subjective–egoistic enjoyment'. The latter replaces any formative and moral value of our relationship to nature and is to be found in alpine sports and the ideology of the alpine clubs which assume that overcoming dangerous physical difficulties is morally meritorious. The egoistic risk to one's life, the gamble with the forces of nature does bring excitement, but an excitement that is intimately associated with the modern drive towards greater stimulations.

IV

Are there any forms of leisure activity which escape the reduction to forms of empty filling-in of time and consciousness? Aside, perhaps from total idleness, which Simmel satirises in his 'Metaphysics of Laziness' (1900)[32] as the total saving of energy, there are two, almost ideal-typical instances of leisure activity which are removed from the contents of everyday existence: sociability and the adventure.

At first sight, sociability seems to be the mere filling-in of time. Yet as 'the play form' of society it has a much greater significance. It is 'the pure form, the free-playing interacting interdependence of individuals' that is 'freed of substance' and 'spared the frictional relations of real life; but out of its formal relations to real life, sociability . . . takes on a symbolically playing fullness of life . . . it alone presents the pure, abstract play of form'.[33] The activity of sociability, then, 'plays at the forms of society', a 'social game' with whose help 'people actually "play" society'. This is only possible because sociability possesses 'no ulterior end, no content, and no result outside itself, it is oriented completely around personalities', but without any excessive emphasis upon individuality and egoism which would destroy sociability as a form. Sociability, then, is 'a pure interaction', 'an ideal sociological world, for in it . . . the pleasure of the individual is always contingent on the joy of others' and each participant '"acts" as though all were equal'.

The social game of sociability is found in various forms. At a universal level, it is to be found 'in that most extensive instrument of all human common life, *conversation*', in which 'talking is an end in itself', indeed 'a legitimate end in itself'. In interaction between the sexes, too, 'eroticism has elaborated a form of play: *coquetry*, which finds in sociability its highest, most playful, and yet its widest realisation'. Just as 'sociability plays at the forms of society, so coquetry plays out the forms of eroticism'. But where the play forms of sociability become too rigid, as in over-elaborated forms of *etiquette*, they become a caricature of themselves and sociability dissolves.

If sociability as the play form of society is, in principle, a universal form, especially as conversation, in everyday existence, then Simmel's typification of the experience of the adventure[34] is of that form of experience which is dissociated from everyday existence. Indeed, 'the most general form of adventure is its dropping-out of the continuity of life', 'the exclave of the life-context, that which has been torn away [*das Abgerissene*]', 'something alien, untouchable, out of the ordinary', 'an island in life which determines its beginning and end according to its own formative powers'.

In the adventure, we experience the synthesis of activity and passivity, 'we forcibly pull the world into ourselves'. Simmel contrasts this experience with work which

> has an organic relation to the world. In a conscious fashion, it develops the world's forces and materials toward their culmination in the human purpose, whereas in adventure we have a non-organic relation to the world. Adventure has the gesture of the conqueror, the quick seizure of opportunity, regardless of whether the portion we carve out is harmonious or disharmonious with us, with the world, or with the relation between us and the world. On the other hand, however, in the adventure we abandon ourselves to the world with fewer defenses and reserves than in any other relation.[35]

Like sociability, the adventure is 'a *form of experiencing*. The *content* of the experience does not make the adventure'. It is a 'closed entity' which is momentarily detached from the reified everyday existence. The adventurer gives himself or herself to the moment, to 'a fragmentary incident'. Hence the time-consciousness within which the adventure is lived out is that of

> unconditional presentness, the quickening of the process of life to a point that possesses neither past nor future and therefore contains life within itself with an intensity that, compared with the content of what has gone before, is often relatively indifferent.[36]

When the adventure is recalled in our memory it takes on 'the nuance of dreaming'; the character of 'a remembrance which is connected with fewer strands than other experiences to the unified and continuous process of life . . . The more "adventurous" an adventure is . . . the more "dream like" it will be for our memory'.[37] The more the adventure accords with its concept, the more it comes to stand 'over and above life'. Insofar as this is the case, it has an affinity with the work of art:

> Precisely because the work of art and the adventure stand juxtaposed to life . . . the one and the other are analogous to the totality of life itself, as it is presented in the brief outline and the condensation of the dream experience. Thereby, *the adventurer is also the most powerful example of the unhistorical person, of the contemporary essence. On the one hand, he is determined by no past . . . on the other, the future does not exist for him.*[38]

The ambiguity of the adventure is present here in its encapsulation of the experience of modernity as immediate presentness and in its promise of an external presentness. Somewhat cryptically, Simmel wishes to see it as 'admixed with all practical human existence' whilst at the same time recognising that 'so much of life is hostile to adventure'.

V

Were Simmel able to look forward to the images of sociability and the adventure that are so central to the marketing strategies of the leisure and tourist industries today, he would have difficulty in not recognising that their ideologically permeated forms have also been incorporated into the world of the commodity.[39] Indeed, had he been reflecting upon sociability and the adventure a decade earlier (both essays were written in 1910), his presentation might well have been closer to those which we outlined earlier. At all events, Simmel's earlier reflections on leisure, on 'the fillings-in of time and consciousness', would find accord with more recent judgements that 'the social spaces of distraction and display become as vital to urban culture as the spaces of working and living'.[40]

Notes

1. On Simmel's methodology see D. Frisby (1084) *Georg Simmel*, Chichester/London/New York/, Ellis Horwood/ Tavistock/Methuen, Ch. 3.
2. G. Simmel (1968), 'Sociological Aesthetics', in K. P. Etzkorn (ed.) *Georg Simmel, The Conflict in Modern Culture and Other Essays*, New York, Teachers College Press, pp. 68–80.
3. See D. Frisby, op. cit., Ch. 2. See also D. Frisby (1981) *Sociological Impressionism*, London, Heinemann.
4. Ibid.
5. This corresponds to the period when Simmel was publishing in such socialist journals as *Die neue Zeit*.
6. See G. Simmel (1971), 'Sociability' in G. Simmel, *On Individuality and Social Forms*, Chicago/London, University of Chicago. Press, 1971, pp. 127–40.
7. G. Simmel (1897) 'Herbst am Rhein', *Jugend*, No. 4, p. 54.

8. K. C. Köhnke (1983), 'Murderous Attack upon Georg Simmel', *European Journal of Sociology*, 24, 2, p. 349.
9. K. H. Wolff (ed.) (1964) *The Sociology of Georg Simmel*, 2nd ed., New York/London, Free Press, p. 420. Translation amended.
10. G. Simmel (1978) *The Philosophy of Money*, London/Henley/Boston, Routledge & Kegan Paul, p. 456. On Simmel's theory of modernity as a whole see D. Frisby (1986) *Fragments of Modernity*, Oxford, Polity, Ch. 2.
11. Ibid. pp. 393–4 and 455.
12. K. H. Wolff (ed.), op. cit., p. 420.
13. Ibid., p. 422. Translation amended and my emphasis.
14. G. Simmel, *The Philosophy of Money*, op. cit., pp. 459–61.
15. K. H. Wolff (ed.), op. cit., p. 410. Translation amended.
16. G. Simmel, *The Philosophy of Money*, op. cit., p. 484.
17. Ibid., p. 256.
18. Ibid., p. 257.
19. Ibid., p. 483.
20. G. Simmel (1923), 'Die Mode' in *Philosophische Kultur*, 3rd ed., Potsdam: Kiepenheuer, p. 42.
21. Ibid., p. 36
22. P. Liesegang (1893), 'Infélices Possidentes!', *Die Zukunft*, 3, pp. 82–4.
23. Ibid., p. 83.
24. G. Simmel (1892–3), 'Gehardt Hauptmanns "Weber"', *Sozialpolitisches Centralblatt*, 2, pp. 283–4.
25. G. Simmel (1985), 'Einiges über die Prostitution in Gegenwart und Zukunft', in G. Simmel, *Schriften zur Philosophie und Soziologie der Geschlechter* (Frankfurt: Suhrkamp, p. 60.
26. G. Simmel, *The Philosophy of Money*, op. cit., p. 376.
27. G. Simmel (1896) 'Berliner Gewerbe-Ausstellung', *Die Zeit*, 8, 25 July 1896.
28. G. Simmel (1890), 'Ueber Kunstausstellungen', *Unsere Zeit*, 26, pp. 474–80.
29. G. Simmel, *The Philosophy of Money*, op. cit., p. 473.
30. G. Simmel (1895), 'Alpenreisen', *Die Zeit*, 7, 13 July 1895.
31. See 'Questionnaire on Yodeling by George Simmel' in K. P. Etzkorn (ed.), *George Simmel, The Conflict in Modern Culture and Other Essays*, op. cit., pp. 134–6. The original was published in 1879.
32. G. Simmel (1900), 'Metaphysik der Faulheit', *Jugend*, 20, pp. 337–9.
33. G. Simmel, 'Sociability' loc. cit., p. 129.
34. G. Simmell, 'The Adventure', in K. H. Wolff (ed.) (1965) *Essays on Sociology, Philosophy and Aesthetics by Georg Simmel et al.*, 2nd ed., New York, Harper & Row, pp. 243–58.
35. Ibid., p. 248. In this context, the significance of railway journeys should be emphasised. See W. Schivelbusch (1986) *The Railway Journey*, Leamington Spa/Hamburg/New York, Berg.
36. Ibid., p. 254. Translation amended.
37. Ibid., p. 244.
38. Ibid., p. 245. Translation amended.

39. See D. MacCannell (1976), *The Tourist: A New Theory of the Leisure Class*, New York, Schocken Books.
40. D. Harvey (1986), *Consciousness and the Urban Experience*, Oxford; Blackwell, p. 256.

5 Leisure and 'The Ruins of the Bourgeois World'
Chris Rojek

Fate as doom is a familiar and notorious motif in Marxist accounts of bourgeois society. Without doubt the canonical text is *The Communist Manifesto* with its mordant observations on bourgeois 'progress', and its bitter prophecy. 'What the bourgeoisie produces, above all,' wrote Marx and Engels,[1] 'is its own gravediggers. Its fall and the victory of the proletariat are equally inevitable.'

1848: the year of spectres and the consolidation of bourgeois rule. Only three years later, in 1851, the Great International Exhibition opened in Hyde Park. It was housed in the Crystal Palace, a massive structure of glass and iron. This building, which was dismantled and reassembled again in an enlarged version on Sydenham Hill in 1854, became one of the towering images of modernity. It was a worldwide landmark, attracting tourists from every country who sought progress and a glimpse of their own future. Moreover, this extraordinary edifice was quite as captivating for the working class. Ordinary people flocked to it and it can be rightly claimed as one of the first clear examples of popular capitalism. Berman captures something of the popular enthusiasm:

> Long after the Great International Exhibition was over, the masses embraced it as a site for family outings, for children's play, for romantic encounters and assignations. Far from milling around quietly and being reduced to silence, they seem to have found all their energies aroused and engaged; no building in modern times, up to that point seems to have had the Crystal Palace's capacity to excite people.[2]

Excitement in the audacity and realisation of what was, essentially a bourgeois dream, was not confined to the visitors who peered at the glass panes of the Crystal Palace. Benjamin writes of Paris as the first city of modernity.[3] And, indeed, scarcely ten years after 1848 when bourgeois rule appeared to be tottering on the brink, the bourgeoisie began to remake Paris in its own image. Baron Haussmann, under a mandate from Napoleon III, embarked on his scheme to rebuild Paris. Large boulevards cut a swathe through the narrow streets of the medieval city. Old irregular buildings were replaced with new, regular apartments of six, seven and eight stories high. Mobility and leisure space in the city was deliberately transformed.

If Paris was the first city of modernity, it was also the first modern city in which the bourgeoisie had systematically designed public space as a full-scale arena for state surveillance and control. Haussmann had praised the long straight boulevards for opening up mobility and 'breathing space' for the populace. However, they were also built with numerous oblique intersections to facilitate covert troop movement. The boulevards were like bowling alleys down which troops could race and knock down rioters and troublemakers as if they were skittles.

Haussmann's Paris and the Crystal Palace are metaphors of modernity. The bourgeois financiers, designers and contractors who combined to build them, built them to last forever as pinnacles of high tech. In the event, both suffered the modern fate of being surpassed within one generation. It will be said against this that Paris remains a city of daring design with a notable *avant garde* in the arts, fashion and humanities. After all, Foucault, Barthes, Derrida and Lacan were the quintessential Paris intellectuals of the last decade and their ideas are talked about all over the world. There is truth in this objection. However, the 'progressiveness' of Paris is no longer palpable. Its 'revolutionary' exuberance has dwindled into a delightful, but nonetheless whimsical, elegance. As a chronically 'modern' place it has been replaced, first, and briefly, by Berlin, and later by New York. The fate of the Crystal Palace was more severe. No sooner had the structure been reassembled on Sydenham Hill as the world's most modern building, than other buildings, in other countries, began to cast their shadows over it. The Eiffel Tower was built in 1889. The invention of the electric lift (by von Siemens in 1880) made the construction of tall office buildings possible. In 1888–9 a height of 349 feet was reached by the Pulitzer Building in New York. It was rapidly succeeded by taller high-rises. The designs of Louis Sullivan and Frank Lloyd Wright transformed the skyline of American cities. In the process our consciousness of modernity was itself transformed. The teeming skyscrapers of New York and Chicago became the fabled archetype of the 'modern' city. As for the modernity of the Crystal Palace, it was conclusively eclipsed. In 1936 the building was destroyed by a fire. It was not rebuilt.

MODERNITY, THE BOURGEOISIE AND LEISURE

The attitude that the existing achievements of modern design constitute a limit which must be surpassed finds its direct parallel in work relations. The desire to secure market advantage requires the continual search for cost-cutting instruments of production. New technologies and new systems of work sweep over the workforce in a succession of waves. The social consequences are enormous and far-reaching. Marx wrote of the industrial worker as a casualty of the new innovations. Certainly, if one examines the principles of F. W. Taylor's famous system of 'scientific management' the worker is presented as little more than a wealth-creating machine. His work-tasks are defined by management, his skills are mechanical and repetitive, and his energies are controlled by a comprehensive bonus and incentive system.[4]

An extensive literature has grown up around the theme that modern work relations are dehumanising and maiming.[5] This is a central preoccupation in the discussion of modern life. However, to emphasise only the negative side of modernity is to minimise the aching ambiguity of the concept. In trying to pinpoint modernity, Simmel wrote of 'the *dynamic* vital character of the modern life-feeling and the fact that it is manifested to us as a form of vital *movement*, consumed in a continuous flux in spite of all persistence and faithfulness, and adhering to a rhythm that is always new'[6] [emphasis his]. These words are certainly very evocative. The lure of ever-changing leisure-related commodities, the constant search for new excitment, fun or mere distraction, are prominent and familiar features of modern leisure experience.

Traditionally, the study of leisure has been dominated by an interest in problems of agency. The choices and actions of actors have been centre-stage. Where questions of social structure have come in, they have been alluded to in general and vague terms. For example, leisure is said to occur in the context of 'industrial society' or 'class society'. Yet no attempt to specify what industrial society or class society means is made. This tradition is now being challenged vigorously. A number of critical studies have been published which argue that the structural characteristics of the society in which leisure practice occurs are vital for understanding what people actually do in their leisure.[7] Here I will make the first instalment in a planned series of publications which will argue that modernity is the essential context for approaching and understanding leisure.

However, before coming to the matter of modernity, something needs to be said about the idea of 'the bourgeois world of leisure'. For it is certainly.the case that a crucial argument in the Marxist and neo-Marxist tradition in leisure studies is that modern leisure is dominated by the bourgeois class. This is evident, it is said, in the bourgeois ownership and control of the means of production, the state apparatus and the media. Leisure relations, it is said, are structured to fragment working-class consciousness, disperse excess energies and paralyse meaningful opposition to bourgeois rule. 'Leisure activities', writes Brohm 'in fact constitute the best way of dulling and intellectually neutralizing the masses.'[8] Brohm maintains that leisure relations give the illusion of personal freedom and self-determination. However, in reality, they function to make the working class (i.e. the real creators of wealth) into a disorganised mass of docile and atomised bodies. The broad brushstrokes of the argument are evident in other Marxist and neo-Marxist contributions to leisure studies and I have commented upon them elsewhere.[9] What I want to concentrate upon at this stage in my discussion is the concept of the bourgeois world of leisure. For while it is often argued that bourgeois class domination is a palpable fact in modern leisure relations, the content of this bourgeois world of leisure is somewhat ignored.

Actually, Marx gave a very clear, albeit rather schematic statement on the bourgeois attitude to leisure. For the bourgeois, Marx writes,

pleasure is only a side issue – recreation – something subordinate to production; at the same time it is a *calculated* and, therefore, itself an *economical* pleasure. For he debits it to his capital's expense account, and what is squandered on his pleasure must therefore amount to no more than will be replaced with profit through the reproduction of capital. Pleasure is therefore subsumed under capital, and the pleasure-taking individual under the capital-accumulating individual.[10]

This passage identifies the basic feature of the bourgeois attitude to leisure, i.e. leisure is said to be distinct from the 'serious' side of life (capital-accumulating employment) and rendered subordinate to it. However, it is quite wrong to deduce from this that leisure has no place in the bourgeois scheme of existence. The great testaments and essays of self-consciousness of the bourgeois class in the late eighteenth and early nineteenth century reserve a valued place for leisure and relaxation. It is generally acknowledged that one of the most powerful representatives of the bourgeois worldview was Benjamin Franklin (1706–90). Franklin had definite views on the place of leisure in a healthy life and he wrote about them in his *Autobiography*.[11] In that work he describes his 'Project of Moral Improvement'. This is based on thirteen Virtues which, Franklin maintains, are indispensable for the cultivation of a socially useful and personally rewarding life. The Virtues are, *Temperance, Silence, Order, Regulation, Frugality, Industry, Sincerity, Justice, Moderation, Cleanliness, Tranquility, Chastity* and *Humility*. Franklin described these as the self-evident facts of common sense. However, in retrospect they read like the basic features of rising bourgeois class-consciousness. At any rate, there is the clear assumption in Franklin's writings that lives which are not spent in obedience to the thirteen Virtues are aimless and degenerate. For each Virtue, Franklin devised some precepts which were intended to act as practical aids in the day-to-day management of life. For example, under *Order* he wrote 'Let all your Things have their Place. Let each Part of your Business have its Time.' He continued under *Industry*, 'Lose no Time. Be always employ'd in something useful. Cut off all unnecessary Actions.' Franklin meant his 'Project' to be taken seriously. His *Autobiography* includes a *Scheme of Employment* which assigns fixed times for work, eating and recreation. The *Scheme* is reproduced in Figure 5.1.

There is consoling evidence to show that Franklin deviated from the stringency of this self-appointed code in his private life.[12] However, his writings, notably *Advice to a Young Merchant* and *Necessary Hints to Those that would be Rich*, were widely circulated and influenced the attitudes of many rising businessmen and industrialists.[13] Weber certainly recognised Franklin as a leading exponent of bourgeois values. In his study *The Protestant Ethic and the Spirit of Capitalism*[14] he pays particular attention to Franklin's famous remark in the *Advice to a Young Merchant*:

> Remember that *time* is money. He that can earn ten shillings a day by his labour, and goes abroad, or sits idle, one half of that day, though he spends but sixpence during his diversion or idleness, ought not to reckon *that* the only expense; he has really spent, or rather thrown away, five shillings besides [emphasis his].[15]

Time is money: the sentiment is fundamental in classic bourgeois attitudes to work and leisure. Indeed, during the late eighteenth century and all through the nineteenth century, a steady flow of

Figure 5.1   The scheme of employment

	a.m.	
The Morning	5	Rise, wash and address *Powerful Goodness*;
Question, What		Contrive Day's Business and take
Good Shall I Do	6	the resolution of the Day;
This Day?		prosecute the present Study;
	7	and breakfast?
	8	
	9	
		Work
	10	
	11	
	12	Read or overlook my
		Accounts and dine.
	p.m.	
	1	
	2	
	3	
		Work
	4	
	5	
	6	
		Put Things in their Places,
	7	Supper, Music or Diversion
		or Conversation.
	8	
		Examination of the Day
	9	
The Evening	10	
Question, What		
Good have I	11	
done today?	12	
	1	Sleep
	2	
	3	
	4	

Source: Benjamin Franklin (1896) *The Autobiography and Others Writings*, p. 97.

Essays, Enquiries, Testaments and *Guides* offering practical advice on the subject ebbed into the public domain. Of these, perhaps the most influential was Samuel Smiles' famous book of 'common sense', *Self Help* (1859). The book is laced with advice on the responsible and healthy use of time, including leisure time. 'An economical use of time', declares Smiles, 'is the true mode of securing leisure.'[16] Elsewhere, he refers to the dangers inherent in the overdevelopment of the faculties for pleasure, recreation and amusement. He writes:

> Amusement in moderation is wholesome, and to be commended; but amusement in excess vitiates the whole nature, and is a thing to be carefully guarded against. The maxim is often quoted 'All work and no play makes Jack a dull boy'; but all play and no work makes him something greatly worse.[17]

The principles of self-improvement that Smiles advocated were not confined to any age group. Yet the potential fruits were richest for the young. The Victorians were troubled by the working-class 'loafers' and 'wild boys' who hung around street corners. Smiles recognised the 'danger' and argued that it found its counterpart in the lassitude of young men from privileged homes. He writes:

> We find among students a tendency towards discontent, unhappiness, inaction and reverie – displaying itself in contempt for real life and disgust at the beaten tracks of men. . . . Dr Channing noted the same growth in America, which led him to make the remark that 'too many young men grow in the school of despair.' The only remedy for this green-sickness in youth is physical exercise – action, work and bodily occupation.[18]

The belief that a natural balance exists between work and leisure is the cornerstone of the bourgeois view. Both Franklin and Smiles refer to it, and it is the counterpart of the bourgeois belief that the natural condition of society is order. However, the bourgeois view of leisure should not be seen as a mere exercise in self-discipline which is restricted to the propertied class and their families. On the contrary, the rational recreation movements which began to emerge in the closing decades of the nineteenth century sought to instill the bourgeois attitude to leisure in the hearts, minds and bodies of the young. The main target group in this respect was working-class male youth, and the key institutional mechanism of training was the youth brigade. The Church Lads' Brigade was form in a Fulham Parish Church in 1891; the Jewish Lads' Bridgade followed it in 1895. These were followed by the Church Boys' Brigade in Bermondsey in 1896, and the Boys' Life Brigade in Nottingham in 1899. However, the organisational model for all these units was certainly the Boys' Brigade which was founded by William Smith in Glasgow in 1883. The aim of the Boys' Brigade was to channel youthful energies in the 'right' direction. Instead of being allowed to run wild, boys were to be trained in the habits of Reverence, Discipline, Self-Respect, Civic Duty and all 'that tends towards a true Christian manliness'. Smith desired to create, and the phrase is his, 'the working boy'. The mechanisms of character-formation were standardised and overtly militaristic. The boys were taught 'elementary drill, physical exercises, obedience to the word of command, punctuality and cleanliness.'[19] Organised games and the Boys' Brigade uniform were used to generate *esprit de corps*. Figure 5.2 shows a typical Boy's Brigade camp timetable. The parallel with Franklins' Scheme and its close attention to time and balanced activity is inescapable.

It would be possible to continue with additional examples. However, perhaps enough has been said to indicate the validity of Marx's characterisation of bourgeois leisure as sober, economical and calculating. For Franklin, Smiles and writers like them, the unrestrained pleasure-seeker is an object of contempt. People who devote themselves to seeking fun and excitement are seen as irresponsible and dangerous characters. Lives of leisure are associated with inauthenticity, disorder and immorality.

Such sentiments continue to be influential. Although the bourgeoisie often refers to the leisure society as a desirable goal, its attainment is privately viewed with deep ambivalence. The bourgeois feels bruising discomfort at the prospect of a society in which the majority do not work in paid employment. For where there is no paid employment, there is no means of consumption and hence no personal stake in the preservation of society. Yet the new technologies of capitalism are now so successful that up to one-sixth of the working population in the advanced economies is surplus to requirement. One solution, much canvassed, is to create a state credit fund which would supply the workless with an income to lead meaningful lives of leisure in consumer society.[20] However, this solution is passionately resisted by many sections of the propertied class, who maintain that the provision of a state credit fund would be a massive general disincentive to work in paid employment and therefore create a generation of loafers and scroungers. There is nothing new in this argument. If we scratch it deep enough we find the prosaic bourgeois belief that a natural balance exists between work and leisure and, moreover, that its disturbance is a menace to society.

Figure 5.2   Timetable of events at Boys' Brigade Camp

6	Reveille
7	Bathing Parade (Boats) and
8	Service of biscuits
	First Bathing Bugle
9.15	Breakfast
9.45	Morning Prayers
10.45	Dress Bugle
11.00	Inspection of Camp and Full Dress Parade
p.m.	
1.15	First Dinner Bugle
1.30	Dinner
5.45	First Tea Bugle
6.00	Tea
7.00	Fishing Parade (Boats)
9.30	Evening Prayers
9.45	Tattoo
10.00	Lights Out

Source: D. McFarlan (1982) *First For Boys: The Story of the Boys' Brigade 1883–1983*, Collins, Glasgow.

BOURGEOIS CLASS UNITY

Discussions of the bourgeois influence on leisure relations have a marked tendency to support some version of the dominant ideology thesis. This thesis, in brief, contends that the ideas of the bourgeois class are the ruling ideas in society. Implicitly, and sometimes in quite explicit ways, subordinate classes are obliged to comply with bourgeois domination. Such thought is evident in many Marxist and neo-Marxist contributions to leisure studies. Springhall's study of the rational recreation movement in Britain can serve as an example.[21] Commenting on bourgeois involvement in working-class youth-training and character-formation movements, he writes, 'the patronizing rejection of urban working-class culture and values suggests that the middle-class benefactors or activists involved in youth movements set out to mould the leisure of the "unenlightened" young into the more amenable and familiar shape of their own "superior" way of life.'[22] The dominant ideology thesis, and the assumptions which underpin it, have come under increasing fire in recent years.[23] For example, it has been pointed out that the thesis produces a one-sided picture of class relations in which the bourgeois class is presented as the active oppressor and the working class is presented as the passive victim of oppression. Moreover, it has been argued that the dominant ideology thesis wrongly assumes that dominant ideologies are clear, coherent and effective. Against this, it is maintained that close historical scrutiny shows the ideological structure to be far more complex and ambivalent.[24]

With regard to the moral regulation of social life in general, and the shaping of leisure relations in particular, the dominant ideology thesis is extremely problematic. Within the propertied class, divisions have always existed between 'educated' and 'uneducated' opinion, 'wet' and 'dry' attitudes. Smiles certainly recognised them. In the 1886 Preface to his book he grumbled at those sections of 'respectable' opinion that had attacked his philosophy as 'a eulogy of selfishness'. It is undoubtedly true that some of the most powerful critics of bourgeois attitudes in the Victorian period were themselves bourgeois. One thinks, for example, of John Ruskin, William Morris, Robert Owen and, of course, Marx and Engels.

Certainly, if one considers conditions in the present day, the dominant ideology thesis becomes transcendent in its implausibility. Bourdieu, in his outstanding study of taste, distinguishes between the 'new bourgeoisie' and the 'old bourgeoisie'.[25] The new bourgeoisie, argues Bourdieu, tends to be employed in knowledge-based industries. They are more likely to be graduates and to have reached positions of authority at an early age. They are less wedded to notions of 'respectable society' and 'sober conduct' than the old bourgeoisie. Indeed, their lifestyle is often very critical of old bourgeois attitudes and values. As Bourdieu puts it:

the new bourgeoisie denounce the 'up-tight' 'stuffed shirt' rigour of the old bourgeoisie and preach 'relaxation' and a 'laid back' life-style, the old bourgeoisie condemns the 'sloppy' life-style of the new bourgeoisie and calls for more restraint in language and morals.[26]

Bourdieu suggests that leisure is an important transmission belt for registering distinctions in lifestyle. The leisure of the new bourgeoisie is more expressive, outward-looking and frivolous than is the case with the old bourgeoisie. Typical forms include alternative comedy, critical cinema, protest music, fringe theatre, third-world travel, the recreational use of soft drugs, consciousness-raising groups, and so on. The new bourgeoisie is far more likely to seek personal satisfaction in leisure and non-work relationships. Paid employment is more likely to be treated as a means to finance leisure and private interests rather than an end itself.

It would be absurd to claim that bourgeois class attitudes do not exist or that the bourgeois class is incapable of collective action. In the field of leisure there is no doubt that both the old and the new bourgeoisie have been prominent campaigners, e.g. in the movement to extend access to the countryside, to conserve the national heritage, to liberalise the laws on Sunday trading, etc. However, these campaigns can hardly be said to exhibit an urgent, distinctive class character. Rather, they are quite palpably fragmentary, particularisitic movements which employ cross-cultural and inter-class alliances to pursue their ends. They are not examples of solo-class agitation. However, it is also true, and very important to state, that they occur in the context of a general historical struggle for social justice and the recognition of human rights, notably the right to engage in pleasurable activity. As Habermas shows in his study of the emergence of 'the public sphere' in society, the antecedents of this struggle have a marked class character.[27]

THE BOURGEOIS PHILOSOPHY OF PLEASURE

Bourgeois political economy never generated a theory of leisure. However, in its obsessive concern with moral principles and ethical behaviour it dealt regularly with questions of pleasure and happiness which are central to leisure. For example, Bentham's philosophy of utilitarianism had an enormous influence on bourgeois thought.

Bentham argued that man is driven by a desire to gain pleasure and avoid pain. This desire, continued Bentham, is common to all human actions. It is therefore an appropriate basis to compare the worth of actions. In fact, ·Bentham maintained, it is possible to judge every human action as either praiseworthy or reprehensible according to the degree to which it either increased or decreased the sum of human happiness. The task of philosophy was simply to devise a clear set of rules that would enable anyone to decide infallibly the worth of every action.

Utilitarianism was indeed the quintessential bourgeois philosophy. For it sought to produce an orderly account of an orderly world which was said to be regulated by timeless, universal laws. Moreover, in attempting to produce a definitive science of pleasure it endorsed the proposition that human emotion can be quantified and compared in terms of a common denominator (pleasure). Thus, emotions are reduced to a mere exchange value.

The regular and serious objection to this whole approach is that the value of pleasure is multi-dimensional. Since it means different things to different people it cannot serve as the basis for a uniform scale of comparison. For example, listening to music is a pleasurably activity. But the pleasure which an opera-lover derives fom opera is quite different from the pleasure that a fan of heavy metal music gets from listening to heavy metal. One person's pleasure may even be another person's pain. The fact of multi-dimensionality is generally held to falsify the claim of utilitarianism to serve as a practical philosophy of moral value in human affairs. Utilitarianism is rejected as a reductive, essentialist philosophy which falsely treats individuals as abstract and basically uniform actors in the juridical system.

By the end of the nineteenth century the vision of the orderly, law-bound and secure world which bourgeois philosophy endorsed ceased to be tenable. 'Balzac', observed Benjamin in his study of Baudelaire and modernity, 'was the first to speak of the ruins of the bourgeoisie.'[28] This is a colourful phrase which is evocative of an important development, but which requires clarification and qualification. For example, to speak of the ruins of the bourgeois world is very different from maintaining that all forms of social life are in ruins. On the contrary, one of the most palpable facts of modern society is the tenacious routine of everyday life. Work and leisure relations change, but they do so within massive, established configurations of repetitive social and economic practice. Moreover, the proposition that the bourgeois world is in ruins does not necessarily mean that the bourgeois class has disappeared. There have been drastic changes in bourgeois class-formation, and I have alluded to them in this chapter. Nevertheless, from time to time, elements of the bourgeoisie still takes steps to 'clean up' society by waging campaigns against perceived slackness, disorder and immorality. The courts, the police, the church and moralistic pressure groups like the National Viewers' and Listeners' Association keep a watch on society and regularly move to stamp out behaviour which is judged to be 'grossly offensive'. The bourgeoisie still has its sabres and it continues to rattle them against the 'permissive' society.

If so much can be said to remain it may seem inconsistent to conclude that the bourgeois world has collapsed and that the old bourgeois categories of order and stability are no longer tenable with regard to leisure. What then is the basis for this conclusion?

CONCLUSION: MODERNISM AND LEISURE

I have argued that in classic bourgeois society work and leisure are polarised. Work is seen as the serious side of life, the realm of necessity. For all practical purposes work is treated as synonymous with paid employment. In contrast, leisure is regarded as voluntaristic activity, a realm of freedom which is devoted to mental and physical relaxation, refreshment and self-improvement. It is the 'reward', the 'exchange', for the necessary exertions incurred in leading a productive and worthwhile life.

To a large degree the bourgeoisie were themselves responsible for undermining all of this. In pushing back existing standards, in making private life a market resource, and in challenging the validity of all limits, the bourgeoisie created a world without limit. Through literature, painting and music, and with more sobriety but no less self-consciousness in disciplines like sociology, philosophy and psychoanalysis, the perception arose that the world is socially constructed and subject to constant movement. If classic bourgeois thought emphasised order and security, the new perspective fastened upon change and conflict.

Modernism is the name usually given to this new development. Modernism is a multi-faceted phenomenon. However, at its heart is a critical and sometimes wholly pessimistic view of objectivity and authority. Knowledge, it is said, cannot be divorced from the social interests that give it expression and credence. The human being makes sense of the world through language and communication. Under modernism, language and communication is 'read' as a sign system composed of meanings which are always ambiguous and subject to change.[29] Thus, meaning is said to be non-meaning. The real becomes unreal. Classic bourgeois thought believed in definite representation, fixed meaning and universal laws of cause and effect. Modernism turned this world upside down. These are abstract matters and I am well aware that many readers will criticise them for being remote from the 'real world of leisure. I therefore propose to draw on an example from Lowe's[30] work on the history of bourgeois perception to illustrate the modernist influence in contemporary leisure practice. The example will be used as an entrée to a wider discussion of the modernist destruction of the classic bourgeois perspective on leisure.

Lowe argues that in classic bourgeois society the main characteristic of perception was linearity. Events were said to be chained together by universal laws of cause and effect. Furthermore, each event was regarded to be unique, irreversible and stacked in the cumulative order of temporality. According to Lowe, the rise of the electronic media in communications and as a leisure resource has changed all of this. For example, television regularly uses close-up, fade, playback, flashback, freeze-frame, cueing and a variety of other editing techniques, to produce a planned effect in the viewer. Moreover, television does not rely exclusively on a unilinear cumulative storyline to hold our interest. Drama, documentary, sport, comedy and even the news, can engage us fully by inverting the sequence in which things actually happen or playing back a single event, such as the scoring of a goal in football or a controversial line-call in tennis, from a multiplicity of angles to show what 'really' happened. Of course, the idea of an electronic media revolution is now rather hackneyed, and has been widely criticised. For example, Winston maintains that the new electronic media have been fully assimilated into the cultural conservatism which dominates capitalist society.[31] In his view, television drama and investigative items conform to the dominant 'naturalistic' view of reality. They have a beginning, a middle and an end, even if the sequence does not always occur in this order.

Moreover, although television can play up the ambiguity and uncertainty of situations there is always the underlying presumption of authorial direction. That is to say, the conventions of broadcasting require the viewer to assume that the ambiguity and uncertainty of a particular film sequence is staged to convey some kind of message – even if that message is simply the banal observation that the world is an ambiguous and uncertain place. Winston also uses close historical readings of the management of innovation in telecommunications to slay the popular image of a communications 'revolution'. He shows that the research, development and marketing of new communications technology with a revolutionary potential is regularly suppressed and delayed by vested business interests who move to protect their existing market position. Winston concludes that a model of gradual, continuous innovation rather than sudden revolution best fits the facts. This is a powerful critique. However, it concentrates almost exclusively on relations of production in telecommunications. The question of consumption, and more specifically the topic of the uses made of telecommunications as a domestic leisure resource, hardly figure in the account. This is a pity. For, from the standpoint of the consumer, there is a strong sense in which the consumption and application of the new media has had a revolutionary impact.

In the classic bourgeois world there were three main categories of gaining knowledge of the world: personal experience, word of mouth and the graphic image. These categories remain, but they have been extended by audio and televisual communications e.g. television, radio, hi-fi, audio/visual tapes and discs. The electronic media, especially TV and video, are now the most powerful 'machinery of representation' in society.[32] Our exposure to them is concentrated in our leisure time since it is when we are not engaged in paid employment that we have greatest access to them. However, their influence ricochets into all areas of our consciousness. For example, television informs us about the world, but it is also made up of selected information which produces a specific construction of the world. It entertains us, but it does so by making the quotidian into spectacle, the mundane into melodrama, real life into *Dallas* or *The Price is Right*.[33] 'Live' moving and talking pictures, beamed into the living room offer greater opportunities for vicarious involvement and pleasure than older forms of communication. Perception of the world has changed in the process.

Logically, perception cannot be divorced from experience. For how we see things influences how we interpret and act in the world. Modernism unpeeled the classic bourgeois view of social reality. Established attitudes to organisation and representation were violated in the process. With regard to leisure, the alteration is evident in many aspects of practice. However, in order to clarify the point it is worth giving three fairly detailed examples.

Consider first the classic bourgeois view of adult sexuality. It was an extremely narrow view. Males and females were required to join in exclusive, lifelong, heterosexual, procreative union. The husband was defined as the breadwinner of 'his' family. The wife was expected to be the homemaker, the provider of a secure, warm and loving environment for her spouse and 'his' children. Bourgeois domesticity was, in fact, founded upon the economic and erotic dependence of the wife upon her husband. Women were discouraged from taking a fully active part in economic and political life. Professional work for women was non-existent until the closing decades of the century. Even then, it was confined to the traditional household service role, as in nursing, caring for infants and social work. Similarly, women's leisure was severely restricted. The physical movement of women in public places was limited. Manuals of etiquette debarred urban streets, taverns, marketplaces, fairs, and the like, as places of menace and seduction.[34] A woman from a 'good family' who visited such places unchaperoned was said to put her life and reputation at risk.

Bourgeois society did not expect its women to remain idle in their leisure time. The emphasis in 'suitable' leisure pursuits for women was placed on home-based industriousness and sexual humility. Bourgeois women were expected to devote themselves to needlework, dressmaking, cookery, flower-arranging, and so on. Research into nineteenth-century medicine and its approach to 'women's complaints' is revealing in demystifying the classic bourgeois view of 'healthy' adult leisure for females. In particular, it has been argued that depressive conditions were diagnosed as the result of an overabundance of free time and the abnegation of the sufferer from her 'normal' adult role. In the words of Turner:

> Historically, hysteria and melancholy were not simply conditions of women, but specifically of middle-class women. They occurred, according to medical opinion, because the unmarried woman was unoccupied and hence prone to nervous disorders which had their physiological origin within the unoccupied womb. The virgin middle-class woman was thus both socially and physiologically 'lazy'. The remedy was marriage and prayer.[35]

The women's movement, together with the movement for gay rights, has had a profound effect on leisure relations and adult sexuality. It has challenged old, encrusted distinctions between work and leisure, normal and abnormal sexuality, public and private life. It has proclaimed the positive side of diversity, contrariness and dynamism in people's desire. It has refuted the idea of monolithic models of respectable leisure practice. Although there are many counter-arguments, for example, the reactions against promiscuity and homosexuality engendered by the AIDs panic, the bourgeois 'norm' of exclusive, lifelong, heterosexual relationships has withered on the vine. Cohabitation between heterosexual as well as homosexual couples, extramarital sexual relationships, the decision to remain childless or to delay starting a family until much later in life, have all become part and parcel of modern adult sexual relationships. The women's movement and the movement for gay rights, have emphasised that leisure is part of the perpetual remaking of the world. Moreover, it has fixed this in the mind indelibly as a process involving the critical reconstruction of established conventions, habits and routines. In a few words, it has been, and continues to be, a thoroughly modernist phenomenon: endlessly mutating, abounding in contradictions and felling every preconception of fixity and permanence.

The second point refers to the organisation of modern work and leisure relations. In classic bourgeois thought, work and leisure were said to be separated by hard and fast divisions. The workplace was physically removed from the home and the organisation of work relations approximated to what Gouldner has called a 'punishment centred' model[36] – so that, for example workers were expected to clock-in and clock-out at appointed times, fines were laid down for lateness, work tasks were prescribed in detail and closely supervised. I am fully aware that a strong case can be made that all of these features are perpetuated in present-day work relations. However, to make that case without reference to the changes in work organisation which have made the workplace more 'worker-friendly' is to give a one-sided and misleading picture. The introduction of flexi-time and the development of human relations techniques in management have made the workplace less oppressive and monotonous for many workers in the secondary and tertiary sectors. Moreover, technical progress in communications enables paid employment to be conducted from the home. The telephone was initially instrumental in this development. More recently, the growth of home-based computer terminals which can be connected to company headquarters by a simple, standardised, electronic link has greatly enhanced the versatility of the home as a place of paid employment. It would be controversial, contentious and plain wrong to attest that work and leisure have totally converged. This is not my argument. My submission is that the distinctions between work and leisure, public and private life, duty and excitement, have blurred.

Paid employment remains associated with the realm of necessity yet it also, quite overtly, presents opportunities for what are traditionally seen as 'leisurely' activities, like larking around, gambling, playing cards or simply passing the time of day. Similarly leisure remains associated with the realm of freedom. However, in some respects it has taken on some of the characteristics of paid employment.

Thus, society emphasises the virtues of discipline over relaxation, industry over idleness, planning over non-planning in leisure practice. In some areas of leisure (for example, sport, music, photography), there is a strong pressure on participants to 'reach professional standards'. 'Whether you're shooting in the Himalayas or nearer to home, Tudorcolour film will give you professional results,' declared the Tudorcolour Photographic Group Campaign in the summer of 1985. This blurring of the edges between work and leisure is precisely what one would expect under conditions of modernism, i.e. where the meaning of action is said to be ambiguous, dynamic and uncertain. Moreover, it is evident not only in what people actually experience in their work and leisure, but also in the physical design of work and leisure space. This brings me to my third point.

The representation of leisure space in classic bourgeois society mirrored the conceptual distinctions regarding the organisation of leisure practice in classic bourgeois thought. Leisure space was divided from work space. For example, the bourgeois home was presented as an escape from work, the parks and memorial gardens of bourgeois society were paraded as reserves of calm in the bustle of the city. Nowhere was this tendency clearer than in the design of suburban houses for the propertied class. These began to spread out from the overcrowded city centres from the mid-nineteenth century onwards. The spatial layout sought to create boundaries, privacy and a sense of enclosed serenity and to combine with it the advantages of urban industrial life. Mumford comments:

> Following romantic principles, the suburban house and plot and garden were deliberately de-formalized. The street avoided straight lines, even when no curves were given by nature: it might swerve to save a tree, or even to preserve the robust contours of a hill-side.[37]

Such flexibility was impossible in the city, where the whole terrain was subjected to the requirements of manufacturing and commerce. The spatial distribution of work and leisure areas at this time was fairly clear. However, by the end of the century, and even more as the next century unfolded, this clarity grew muddied. The designs of modern architects such as Le Corbusier, Loos, Perret, Mies van der Rohe and Gropius set out to abolish the old and established divisions between work and leisure. Workers' houses, the home environment, luxury apartments for the rich and civic buildings were endowed with the clear analytic lines of the machine. From the desk lamp to the kitchen kettle, household objects began to be designed with adherence to simple geometric form. New techniques of mass production supported this trend towards functionalism and simplicity. Their effects were further visible in the streamlined look of refrigerators, prams, tables, chairs, cutlery and many other industrially-produced objects. Meanwhile, the design of work space explored the potentialities of violating the physical barriers between work and leisure space which classic bourgeois design had striven to erect. Factory walls and factory gates were replaced with wide driveways and verges enabling open access. Factories and offices were set off from public street space by ornamental piazzas or landscaped gardens. Transparency and light became standard design features. Gropius was the first to incorporate large expanses of clear glass in his trend-setting design of the Fagus factory built at Alfeld-on-the-Leine in 1911. The effect, which has been copied on countless occasions since, was to dissolve the traditional distinctions between interior work space and the vast exterior of nature and society. I have said that modernism is a multi-faceted phenomenon. It follows that it would be quite wrong to suppose that modern design acted unilaterally to transform social perception and consciousness. However, modern design certainly contributed to a confusion of aesthetics which, in some cases, has made work space indistinguishable from leisure space and *vice versa*.

In this chapter I have maintained that modernism is the essential context to examine leisure practice. No doubt I shall be accused of 'nihilism'. For this is the charge regularly brought against anyone proposing 'process' and 'movement' as more accurate and useful concepts to explore social relations, including leisure relations, than 'stability' and 'order'. In response to this I can only refer the reader to the pivotal arguments set out in this chapter. I have argued that meaning and perception are central to matters of leisure. Leisure relations are pluralistic relations of power. Questions of 'normality' and 'abnormality', 'health' and 'malaise' in leisure are contested questions. The orderly world of classic bourgeois thought which fetishised the idea of a natural, harmonious balance or exchange between work and leisure, lies in ruins. Campaigns to curb what is labelled as 'obscene' or 'grossly offensive' behaviour are made and will continue to be made. Because the bourgeoisie still enjoys greater access to the apparatus of the state they will have the lion's share in waging these crusades of moral regulation. However, all attempts to 'clean up' society by laying down fixed, immutable and universally binding systems of moral conduct will miscarry. Modernism has blurred the traditional bourgeois distinctions in the organisation of sexuality and work and leisure experience. It has also blurred the divisions between work and leisure space. Under modernism, people look to leisure for experience of creativity, learning and growth. Work becomes a means to finance these ends. The rider to this is that leisure is bound to assume more political significance in social life. Consider, for example, the women's movement, the movement for Gay Rights, the Campaign for Nuclear Disarmament, the Green movement – all sprang from people's 'free' time rather than their work time. Just as leisure replaces work as the experience of greater personal significance, leisure rivals work as the setting for meaningful collective organisation and action.

Notes

1. K. Marx and F. Engels (1968) 'The Communist Manifesto', in *Selected Works in One Volume*, London, Lawrence & Wishart, p. 46.
2. M. Berman (1982) *All That Is Solid Melts into Air*, London, Verso, p. 238.
3. W. Benjamin (1976) *Charles Baudelaire: A Lyric Poet in the Era of High Capitalism*, London, Verso.
4. See F. W. Taylor (1964) *Scientific Management*, New York, Harper & Row.
5. See, for example, H. Braverman (1974) *Labour and Monopoly Capital* New York, Monthly Review Press; A. Gorz (1976) (ed.) *The Division of Labour*, Brighton, Harvester/Humanities Press; G. Salaman (1981) *Class and the Corporation*, Glasgow, Fontana.
6. G. Simmel (1971) 'Eros, Platonic and Modern', in *On Individuality and Social Forms*, University of Chicago Press, p. 238.
7. See, for example, C. Rojek (1985) *Capitalism and Leisure Theory*, London, Tavistock; J. Clarke and C. Critcher (1985) *The Devil Makes Work*, London, Macmillan; J. Kelly (1987) *Freedom To Be*, London, Macmillan.
8. J. M. Brohm (1978) *Sport: A Prison of Measured Time*, London, Interlinks p. 90.

9. Rojek, op. cit.
10. K. Marx (1964) *The Economic and Philosophic Manuscripts of 1844*, New York, International Publishers, p. 157.
11. B. Franklin (1986) *The Autobiography and Other Writings*, Harmondsworth, Penguin.
12. See G. Kolko (1961) 'Max Weber on America: Theory and Evidence', *History and Theory*, Vol. 1, pp. 243–60.
13. For a commentary on Franklin's influence see M. Ossowska, (1986) *Bourgeois Morality*, London, Routledge & Kegan Paul.
14. M. Weber (1984) *The Protestant Ethic and the Spirit of Capitalism*, London, Allen & Unwin.
15. Op. cit. p. 48.
16. S. Smiles (1986) *Self Help*, Harmondsworth, Penguin, p. 174.
17. Op. cit. p. 205.
18. Op. cit. p. 196.
19. F. Gibbon (1934) *William A. Smith of the Boys' Brigade*, Glasgow, Collins, p. 36.
20. See A. Gorz (1980) *Farewell to the Working Class*, London, Pluto; (1983) *Paths to Paradise*, London, Pluto. For a general evaluation of positive discrimination for the 'leisure rich' see A. Veal (1987) *Leisure and the Future*, London, Allen & Unwin.
21. J. Springhall (1977) *Youth, Empire and Society*, London, Croom Helm.
22. Op. cit. pp. 125–6.
23. See, in particular N. Abercrombie, S. Hill and B. S. Turner (1980) *The Dominant Ideology Thesis*, London, Allen and Unwin; (1986) *Sovereign Individuals of Capitalism*, London, Allen and Unwin.
24. See Abercrombie *et al.*, op. cit.
25. P. Bourdieu (1984) *Distinction*, London, Routledge & Kegan Paul.
26. Op. Cit. p. 311.
27. J. Habermas (1974) 'The Public Sphere', *New German Critique* 1:3.
28. Op. cit. p. 176.
29. For a critical assessment of post-structuralism see my (1986) 'Structure Restructured', *Media Education Journal*, 2, 2–6.
30. D. M. Lowe (1982) *History of Bourgeois Perception*, Brighton, Harvester.
31. B. Winston (1986) *Misunderstanding Media*, London, Routledge & Kegan Paul.
32. The phrase is Stuart Hall's. See his 'Media power and class power' (1986) in J. Curran, J. Ecclestone, G. Oakley and A. Richardson (eds) *Bending Reality*, London, Pluto.
33. For a lively study of consumer responses to *Dallas* see I. Ang (1985) *Watching Dallas*, London, Metheun.
34. See A. de Swaan (1981) 'The Politics of Agrophobia' *Theory and Society*, 10, pp. 359–85.
35. B. S. Turner (1984) *The Body and Society*, Oxford, Blackwell, p. 200.
36. A. Gouldner (1954) *Patterns of Industrial Democracy*, Toronto, Collier-Macmillan.
37. L. Mumford (1966) *The City in History*, Harmondsworth, Penguin, p. 557.

Part II
Leisure, Power and Planning

6 Leisure Policy: An Unresolvable Dualism?
Fred Coalter

INTRODUCTION

Although the study of leisure has developed outside the mainstream of social policy analysis, both are united by the duality of their objects of study. This is usually expressed by conceptual couples – social policy and 'liberation and control'; leisure theory and 'freedom and constraint'.

A central concern of sociological theories of leisure has been the question of how individuals and groups are located in the social structure and the degree to which leisure is an area of freedom and constraint, liberation or control. Therefore, such theories are, at root, theories of 'civil society', concerned with the degree to which leisure is a private rather than public sphere, where individuals are free from detailed regulation and constraint to pursue individual needs and desires (Gamble, 1981). It is the nature of this 'civil society' and the 'proper' role of the state which either implicitly or explicitly has been at the centre of theories of leisure and has formed the basis for differing evaluations of post-war developments in leisure policy.

Within the shifting conflicts and paradoxes inherent in the 'freedom and constraint' of leisure and the 'liberation and control' of social policy, I will compare and contrast two differing perspectives. There are other positions, for example Hargreaves, 1984 and 1985; Newman, 1981. However, I have chosen to concentrate on two positions which are competing for the status of 'conventional wisdom'.

1 Social democracy: the 'leisure democracy'

This approach emphasises 'change in continuity'. It is based on a broadly evolutionist perspective in which social change gradually results in lessening social, cultural and economic constraints, giving rise to increased freedoms. Although residual, the role of the state is important in promoting, protecting and providing for new freedoms.

2 Socialism: leisure as cultural conflict
This approach emphasises 'continuity in change'. The tensions and
balance between freedom and constraint vary with the rhythm of
history, indissolubly linked. Leisure is the arena in which ideological
and cultural hegemony is contested, and while the reality of new
freedoms is not denied, the basic exploitative structures of
capitalism remain, sustained by state policy and reproduced in
leisure.
A metaphor might usefully be used to sum up such positions.
Whereas the social democratic position views leisure as having been
deposited by the seas of history on a (usually) sunny beach, the
socialist version views leisure and its eventual destination as undecided
– it is still being tossed on the seas of history.

THE 'LEISURE DEMOCRACY'

Several writers have illustrated that the differences between writers in
the 'conventional wisdom' are as great as the similarities (Rojek, 1985;
Clarke and Critcher, 1985). However, although disagreeing on such
things as the motor of history and the extent and pace of change, they
are united by a tendency to adopt a vague evolutionary perspective on
social change, in which lessening constraints give rise to new freedoms.
The decline of traditional communal and moral constraints and the
emergence of a mass consumer market leads to a decline in localism
and the pluralisation of social life (Coalter and Parry, 1982). In such
circumstances the social system is able increasingly to tolerate more
'play' or 'looseness' and to accommodate cultural diversity (Roberts,
1978). Leisure is gaining an autonomy from other aspects of social and
economic life and tastes; desires and behaviour are increasingly
dissassociated from class and class-based cultures (Smith, Parker and
Smith, 1974; R. and R. N. Rapoport, 1975).
Structural change has been accompanied by ideological change as an
increasing emphasis was placed on the subjectivity of the individual
and freedom of choice (Rapoport, 1975). The sphere of 'leisure',
based on the concepts of sovereignty of the individual and individual
choice, becomes a synonym for civil society. It was in Marx's ironic
phrase the very Eden of the innate rights of man, it is the exclusive
realm of Freedom, Equality, Property and Bentham.
The emergence of the 'leisure democracy' appeared to be the
culmination of historical processes in which already-established civil

and political rights were augmented by social rights of citizenship. Citizenship is achieved through participation and the idea of the ' participative citizen' central to such ideologies of leisure. Participation is both an expression and affirmation of citizenship.

Such a view of the merging citizen is complemented by an evolutionary view of social policy, in which the growth of public provision for leisure is synonomous with the growth and consolidation of rights of citizenship. The development of state policy is viewed as a general movement from 'negative regulation of behaviour to a more positive concept of support for leisure' (Smith, Parker, Smith, 1974).

If citizenship is to be a reality, public provision must provide equal opportunities for all. Within this formulation the strategic commitment of early leisure policy was to increase the supply of facilities in order to provide for existing demand. Bacon (1980) and Pearson (1982) suggest that such policy and provision took place within the context of an implicit, vague ideology of a 'natural', if latent, community – a formulation which denied the salience of class and structured inequalities.

However, the acceptance of recreational provision as 'part of the general fabric of the social services' (DoE, 1975) and continuing inequalities in rates of participation led to the emergence of policies of 'recreational welfare' to cater for 'recreationally disadvantaged' groups. Social policy became concerned not only to cater for existing demand but also to democratise areas of public leisure and actively to encourage participation via promotional policies of 'sport for all' (McIntosh and Charlton, 1984) and the 'democratisation of culture' (Green, 1977). From this perspective, access to recreational opportunities is part of the rights of citizenship – 'the right to share to the full in the social heritage and life of a civilised being according to the standards prevailing in society' (Mishra, 1977).

The 'politics' of such an ideology is social administration. Attempts were made to define the nature of leisure 'need' implied by a social service (R. and R. N. Rapoport, 1975; Mennell, 1979), to improve the administration of leisure services (Travis *et al.* 1978), to improve the fit between provision and need (Dower *et al.*, 1981) and to define recreational disadvantage (DoE, 1977).

Such a fact-based, reforming approach, lacking specific theory or methodology, had obvious appeal to the multi-disciplinary 'leisure studies'. Its concentration on ad hoc, abstracted problems of administration and management, and an implicit belief that rationality was the key to reform, served to depoliticise debate and to accommodate a wide range of 'leisure-committed' opinion (Coalter, Long and Duffield, 1986). Therefore, within the context of a vague notion of 'leisure as citizenship' the task was to improve the coordination, planning and management of public leisure services in order to ensure the extension and consolidation of the new freedoms – leisure policy should seek to liberate, to overcome constraints and to assist in the achievement of the satisfactions sought in leisure (Dower *et al.*, 1981).

However, for some this process had its limits. For example, although Roberts (1978) accepts that one criterion for public leisure provision is 'the pursuit of distributive justice . . . to enhance the standards and quality of life among otherwise disadvantaged citizens', he suggests that the role of the public sector should be an essentially residual one. Such 'reluctant collectivism' (George and Wilding, 1976) derives not so much from a liberal, laissez-faire political philosophy (Bramham and Henry, 1985) but rather from an ideology of leisure. Not only is 'a commitment to service the public's recreational interests too open-ended to be practical' (Roberts, 1978), but a residual social policy is essential to avoid prescription and direction, to preserve the pluralism of the area of a civil society which is 'leisure'. Therefore a pluralist theory of leisure is neatly complemented by a liberal view of the proper role of the state. The state should simultaneously guarantee and respect the private sphere, and the central component of leisure – individual choice – should be exercised through the market, which 'remains one of the most effective participatory mechanisms devised for modern society' (Roberts, 1978).

However, the duality of leisure and social policy is central to certain ambiguities in this position. For example, concern to avoid prescriptive and directive policies is accompanied by an acceptance of the instrumental use of leisure policy to achieve non-leisure objectives – presumably in the context of consensually – agreed goals or in pursuit of the presumed social consensus.

Such ambiguities lay at the heart of public policies for leisure as they developed throughout the 1970's and 1980s. Concerns to extend 'rights' to participaton coexisted with the more prescriptive concerns for social integration and control. The effects of the social changes giving rise to the new 'leisure democracy' were not unambiguous. Although the decline of traditional social and economic constraints served to extend opportunities and create new freedoms, such changes also contained the possibility of diminished social constraints.

Harrison (1973) has remarked that nineteenth-century leisure policies were characterised by a tension between social and moral reform – the former requiring the lessening of constraints on individual liberty, and the latter requiring the building-up of restraints. Such tensions were present in the rhetoric of leisure policy of the 1960s and 1970s – a welcoming of the new 'leisure democracy' was combined with a fear of the deleterious effects of new freedoms (especially on the behaviour of working-class youth). The tensions between freedom and control inherent in much social welfare, were also evident in leisure policy – the non-participating citizen was not only 'recreationally deprived' but also a potential threat – non-participation was not only an issue of individual welfare but also had implications for social stability.

Such tensions are present in the 1975 White Paper, *Sport and Recreation* (DoE, 1975) which points to the dangers to freedom inherent in seeking 'to control or direct the diverse activities of people's leisure'. Nevertheless it also warns of the dangers of social fragmentation and the weakening of institutions of social control in inner urban areas. The line between individual freedom and social constraint is a fine one, and provision for leisure-time activities could contribute not only to individual welfare but also to social stability.

By reducing boredom and urban frustration, participation in active recreation contributes to the reduction of hooliganism and delinquency among young people . . . the social stresses on many young people today are enormous . . . . If we delay too long in tackling the causes [sic] of these stresses constructively, the problems which arise from them will be magnified, and the cost of dealing with their results greatly increased. The need to provide for people to make the best of their leisure must be seen in this context. (DoE, 1975)

Bramham and Henry (1985) argue that the White Paper marked a watershed in leisure policy. It indicated the replacement of social democratic concerns with a 'harder pragmatism', in which the vocabulary of motives became dominated by the 'externalities' associated with leisure provision. the 'recreational welfare' policies of the 1960s (which were not without their ambiguities) became more clearly policies of 'recreation as welfare' – the instrumental use of leisure provision to ameliorate the effects of wider deprivations and to integrate and control groups seen as a threat to social order (Coalter, Long and Duffield, 1986). In 1973 the Quality of Life Experiments were established. These drew on educational models of positive discrimination proposed by Plowden (1967) and they sought, through action-research, to explore ways of improving the quality of urban life through recreational provision. In 1976 the Urban Programme was extended to include recreation provision (DoE, 1976) and the DoE published *Recreation and Deprivation in Inner Urban Areas* (DoE, 1977), which explored types of activity and policies which could increase recreational opportunities for those living in socially and environmentally deprived areas.

Traditional facility-based, demand-led responses were to be augmented by models adopted from social work and youth work practice. The Sports Council outlined the emerging philosophy by suggesting that what was required were: 'leaders . . . capable of making sympathetic approach, assessing needs and wrestling with the problems of integration and segregation' (Sports Council, 1979). And we will continue to work on the social front in relation not only to the unemployed but also in areas of urban and rural deprivation and with schemes for the ethnic minorities and the retired. We have a new social scene emerging' (Sports Council, 1981).

Legitimate attempts to provide increased opportunities and improved social and physical environments could combine with (and conceal) other, more instrumental, purposes. Sport and recreation was a popular, politically neutral and flexible form of social intervention. That it might be being turned into the dustbin of social policy, a cheap, cost-effective and immediate response, was indicated by the nature and immediacy of the response to the 1981 urban riots. The Sports Council allocated £3 million over three years for a demonstration project entitled Action Sport. In line with its developing 'educative' and directive policies, it was aimed to penetrate sections of working-class and ethnic communities which previous initiatives had failed to reach. In line with developing policies this was to be 'people', rather than 'facility'-orientated, aiming to deploy 'street motivators in much larger numbers than anyone had ever tried before in United Kingdom' (Sports Council, 1982). However, in a further move to break down barriers and to assist in the achievement of the policies of social integration and control, these motivators were to be recruited from within the problem communities themselves. Thus 'in the main it is hoped to select ready-made leaders from among the unemployed' (Sports Council, 1982). That the concern was as much with 'recreation as welfare' as with recreational welfare, was indicated by the comment that the campaign was mounted quickly because of the urgency of putting leaders on the street as a result of the deteriorating situation, in terms of unemployment and the problems caused by social unrest in the inner cities (Sports Council, 1982).

The Quality of Life programmes have been referred to as being 'conceived in affluence, born in uncertainty and ended in austerity' (Scottish Arts Council, 1978) and such a description seems more generally applicable to the fate of public leisure policy since the early 1960s. Although shortlived, economic expansion had established the rhetoric of citizenship rights; social change and economic decline served to re-emphasise the more instrumental and utilitarian aspects of public leisure provision – once again issues of integration and control were on the political agenda (Carrington and Leaman, 1982).

It is these aspects of public policy, which seek to displace and defuse social problems by redefining them as 'problems of leisure' which form a major part of the critique of the cultural theories.

LEISURE AS CULTURAL CONFLICT

In the critique, as in pluralism, there is a commitment to an idea of leisure as a realm of autonomy, freedom and self-determination. However, some writers, drawing on Gramsci and aspects of the Frankfurt School, argue that the pluralist position misrecognises the nature of 'leisure' and 'civil society'. For example, while admitting that 'leisure can genuinely be seen as an area of some freedom, where positively evaluated experiences are most keenly felt', Clarke and Critcher (1985) suggest that this sense of choice and self-determination (central to the pluralist case) is largely illusory. This is because they wish to extend the definitional components of leisure beyond subjective feelings of 'freedom' or 'choice' to include, indeed be underpinned by, the more objective concept of 'control'. Here the view of 'participation' extends beyond consumption to include the ability to determine what is produced. Monopolistic capitalist markets, bureaucratic state structures and managerialist practices within public provision serve to substitute the illusion of choice for control and debase the role of active citizen into one of passive consumer.

From this socialist/culturalist perspective the pluralism of civil society is not based on any simple concept of choice, delayed stratified diffusion or contingency (to be ameliorated by policies of positive discrimination). Rather, it is a plurality of structured inequalities which reflect deeper, structural and cultural factors. We do not have change in continuity but rather deep structural continuities masked by change.

The pluralists' concentration on consumption and exchange relationships tends to abstract leisure from more fundamental (capitalist) social relations. As Clarke and Critcher (1985) remark, 'leisure is a social category which is the product of forces which are not leisure'. Leisure ideologies and practices serve to disguise and reproduce basic structural inequalities based on class, gender, age and ethnicity. Although conceding that leisure is an area of relative autonomy and subjectively experienced as 'free', Clarke and Critcher (1985) are nevertheless committed to some form of 'class-domination' theory – for them, the invisible hand of the market is ultimately the iron fist of capitalist social relations. They are therefore committed to the analytical utility of class or, perhaps more accurately, class structure. For them the utility of class and class culture has been wrongly rejected as a result of a process of 'reductionism upwards' (Johnson, 1979) in which the lack of an observable one-to-one correspondence between class and specific modes of behaviour is taken to indicate the lack of utility of class-based analyses. People's relationships to leisure are to be understood as being constructed and mediated by the continuing influences of class-based value systems.

In a sense Clarke and Critcher (1985) recognise the importance of Touraine's (1974) contention that 'leisure' is replacing 'culture' in that they suggest that there is a constant struggle in which leisure ideologies and practices (classless, consumerist) seek either to submerge or marginalise certain cultures. For them leisure is not just in danger of replacing class culture but, more importantly, is an ideological obstacle to the achievement of socialism – class-based cultures do not just have inherent worth, they are also the potential basis for political action. In other words leisure/civil society is the sphere in which the struggle for hegemony occurs (Hall and Jefferson, 1976). As hegemony refers to the power to frame alternatives and certain opportunities, to win and shape 'spontaneous' consent, the processes and ideologies of leisure – the appearance of choice, the experience of freedom and the ideologies of consumerism – are central to the process. Leisure is neither wholly free nor totally determined but is an arena of conflict over cultural meaning. As such it is characterised by a constant struggle to constrain and control, to 'hegemonise', bases of potential opposition. To paraphrase Bailey (1978), the contest for the hearts, minds and pockets of the working class is ongoing.

Like the social democratic theorists, Clarke and Critcher (1985) regard the market as central to the production and reproduction of leisure. The work of hegemony – a dual process of denial and reinforcement of difference, the substitution of an illusion of choice for the concession of control – is achieved through an increasingly monopolistic and restrictive market. Despite its imperfections the market remains one of the most effective mechanisms of control devised by modern society.

The ideology of the market is all-pervasive, and ideologies of the individual 'consumer' underpin public provision and management practices, serving to undermine the market's collective purposes and reduce its ability to provide for need. Also, because of the predominance of the market and commodity forms, the role of the state in leisure policy is residual, 'providing for the deficiencies of market forces' (Clarke and Critcher, 1985). However, the low salience of the state as leisure-provider does not imply that its functions as a regulator and controller are unimportant.

Because leisure is the product of forces which are 'not leisure', the state's presence is ubiquitous – constructing, controlling, regulating and maintaining the institutions of civil society. For example, legislation and policies relating to the family, education and public space serve to regulate and control institutions central to an understanding of the social construction of leisure opportunities and constraints.

Many social policies seek to extend opportunities and to improve the quality of life, often in response to popular demand. However, from this perspective the dual elements of social policy are not equal. Despite the social democratic elements the essential nature of social policy, within an unequal and exploitative system, is explained by the need to regulate and control. In the last instance the progressive intent of social policy is either subordinate to, or undermined by, the primary need to integrate and control – all concessions and compromises take place within the 'taken-for-granted structures of capitalist society (Clarke and Critcher, 1985). For example, consumer-protection legislation merely preserves consumers from the unacceptable forms of capitalism in order that they will be available (and accept) the 'real' thing. In leisure policy, more narrowly defined, the same issues of control and regulation predominate. Arts policies based on the notion of 'democratisation of culture' (Green, 1977) which seek to provide greater access to traditional art forms do so, not (solely) because of a belief in its interest value, but in order to inculcate a broader audience with ruling-class values and to civilise the working class. Although Clarke and Critcher (1985) suggest that such a strategy 'failed', largely because of the inherent class nature of what was defined as 'culture', others question whether such policies went beyond mere rhetoric (Hutchinson, 1982; Green, 1977).

Sport, with its less obvious class nature, has proved to be a more important and successful instrument for social integration and control. Here again the central theme was to 'civilise' certain sections of the working class by 'substituting' rational and improving recreation for more hedonistic and socially disruptive activities. The themes of moral welfare, social integration and control have been consistent elements of the rhetoric of leisure policy (Coalter, Long and Duffield, 1986) – reaching strident proportions as the problems of economic decline, social dislocation and social unrest increased. From the Albermarle Report's (1960) concern with 'a new climate of crime and delinquency' via the 1975 White Paper's reference to 'social stresses on young people' to the Sports Council's (1981) references to 'the deteriorating situation . . . and problems of social unrest in the inner cities', the rhetoric of policies for sport and recreation have contained an uneasy tension between recreational welfare and recreation as welfare.

However, such policies have real cultural limits, as they are based on a failure to recognise that both particular sports and sport in general embody distinctive class, gender and ethnic values and as such are not proper vehicles for strategies of integration. As is the case with the market for leisure, state policies serve simultaneously to deny and reinforce difference, to both include and exclude. Therefore social democratic attempts to reform leisure policy – the acceptance of multi-culturalism, cultural democracy, decentralisation, 'relevant' provision – are doomed to failure because they fail to recognise that 'pluralism' is related not to a diversity of 'needs' but to structured patterns involving relationships of cultural power (see also Green, 1977).

Clarke and Critcher (1985) point to a double failure of social policies for leisure. Firstly, and for them positively, policies of 'recreation as welfare' (Coalter, Long and Duffield, 1986) have failed to achieve the desired levels of integration and control. A mixture of misrecognitions of the structural basis of cultural differences, unintended consequences of management practices and refusals and resistances by sections of the working class, have served to limit policies of integration. This failure is, paradoxically perhaps, related to the second failure – the failure of policies of 'recreational welfare', to extend freedoms and opportunities to all sections of the community.

By retaining a notion of agency ('resistance'; 'contestation'; 'conflict') this position avoids the more deterministic conclusions often associated with Marxist theories of welfare and the structural 'needs' of capitalism. For example Hargreaves (1984; 1985) offers an altogether more deterministic view, in which large sections of civil society are 'hegemonised'. From this perspective the reproduction of class, ethnic and gender differences is neither the result of failures of policies of positive discrimination nor misrecognitions of cultural differences. Rather it results from material obstacles and functional necessity. Financial and resource constraints undermine the ability to provide sufficient facilities and opportunities for all (Hargreaves, 1984).

However, the social limits to participation are not merely cultural but are set by the need to exclude more extreme disruptive and oppositional elements from public provision. Such exclusions are politically functional, serving to reinforce divisions between the lower and upper strata of the working class, thereby contributing to the disunity of this class as a social whole, presumably serving to block the development of socialist politics. Such divisions and exclusions also serve to undermine social integration and identification of subordinate and excluded groups with the nation and the national interest. This is secured at the ideological level through populist ideologies of nationalism promoted by state-sponsored international sporting success – here, hegemony is not a dynamic process of contestation but a 'continuing achievement' (Hargreaves, 1985).

COMMON GROUND?

Clarke and Critcher (1985) do not subscribe to such a deterministic position and at the level of the psychology of leisure they are largely in agreement with the pluralists. They acknowledge the reality of the 'positive evaluation of such freedoms and controls as do exist' in the market, and reject simplistic notions that this is mere 'intellectual stupification induced by the propaganda of monopoly capitalism'. In fact, although the individualising ideology of consumerism is a constraint on the development of the collectivist ideologies of socialism, socialists' failure to acknowledge the material reality on which this psychology of freedom and choice is based is also a barrier. Therefore, although pluralists come under criticism for their failure to recognise the structured nature of inequalities, and the role of the leisure market in reproducing and reinforcing them, there appears to be agreement on the reality of the psychology of leisure.

However, by placing a socialist version of 'control' over the production of leisure opportunities and choices at the centre of their definition of leisure, Clarke and Critcher (1985) place real structural limits on the attainment of freedom and choice within the capitalist market. Here the pluralists' psychology of leisure becomes the culturalists' ideology of leisure – the myth of consumer sovereignty disguises the extent of capital's power to define and constrain choice and opportunity. It is here that the most fundamental differences occur in the evaluations of the central leisure institution. Although the pluralists are not uncritical of the market, its imperfections are acknowledged by the 'safety-net' role allocated to the state. A public leisure policy for commercial provision is based largely on liberal, laissez-faire principles. However, from the socialist perspective, rather than being the realisation of freedom, 'consumer choice' is its antithesis – a contradiction which can only be resolved by superceding capitalist market relations, or at least in the short term using a more distributive form of taxing and licensing to increase real choice and opportunity.

Here there is a belief that the logic of public intervention 'in pursuit of distributive justice' (Roberts, 1978) may be more dynamic, and may entail a greater degree of intervention and direction, than is acknowledged in the pluralists' support of a minimalist leisure policy. Clarke and Critcher (1985) acknowledge that the fear that prescription and 'totalitarianism' might be inherent in policies for leisure is not confined to the pluralists. However, in the context of an increasingly monopolistic market, producing for profit rather than meeting need, such reservations may be in danger of confusing the design of a process with a finished product – of confusing freely-chosen leisure activity with the institutional conditions which facilitate it.

However, although there are deep divisions concerning the nature of market-based freedoms, attitudes towards the non-market leisure sector – public leisure services – seem less polarised. Here the issues to be resolved appear to be conflicts rather than contradictions. By retaining the idea of human agency and rejecting the view that leisure services can be explained simply by the structural 'needs' of capitalism, the cultural perspective acknowledges the possibility of reform 'within the state'. The continuing belief in the liberative potential of public leisure services provides the basis for an analysis of their deficiencies which is similar to that of the pluralists.

Like Dower *et al.* (1981), Clarke and Critcher (1985) suggest that the liberative potential of leisure services is undermined by bureaucratic structures, managerialist ideologies, the growing dominance of professional paternalism in the definition of need and consumerist ideologies. These all serve to produce restrictive definitions of 'appropriate' forms of behaviour and thereby exclude groups whose culture emphasises informality and spontaneity. However, again like Dower et al. (1981) they concede the possibility of progress 'within the state'. Although policies of positive discrimination and community involvement are no more 'than small and difficult steps in new political directions' they nevertheless represent the reduction of paternalism and the extension of control central to leisure and the meeting of need.

Therefore both the pluralists and the cultural theorists point to unresolved dilemmas and conflicts in public leisure services between ideologies of the market and ideologies of welfare. They point to a failure to move beyond rhetoric, to establish the political legitimacy of the welfare status of public leisure services. In all areas of social policy welfare practice is modified by more fundamental political and economic priorities. However, such problems are exacerbated in leisure because of the lack of a coherent philosophy or politics of 'recreational welfare' with which to resist consumerist definitions and managerialist practices (Harrison, 1986; Coalter, 1986). Whether concerned to produce a 'new culture of leisure provision' (Dower et al., 1981), or to increase democratic control and accountability (Clarke and Critcher, 1985), both seem to be agreed on the failings of public leisure services to achieve their liberative potential and to underwrite the freedom and choice inherent in the notion of leisure.

References

Albermarle Report (1960) *The Youth Services in England and Wales*, London, HMSO
Bacon, W. (1980) *Social Planning, Research and the Provision of Leisure Services*, Centre for Leisure Studies, University of Salford.
Bailey, P. (1978) *Leisure and Class in Victorian England*, London, Routledge & Kegan Paul.
Berger, P. *et al.* (1974) *The Homeless Mind*, Harmondsworth, Penguin (Pelican)
Bramham, P. and Henry I. (1985) 'Political Ideology and Leisure Policy in the United Kingdom' *Leisure Studies*, Vol. 4, No. 1.

Burns, T. (1973) 'Leisure in Industrial Society' in M. Smith *et al.* (eds), *Leisure and Society in Britain*, London, Allen Lane, The Penguin Press.

Carrington, B. and Leaman, D. (1982) 'Work for Some and Sport for All' *Youth and Policy* Vol. 1, No. 3.

Clarke, J. and Critcher C. (1985) *The Devil Makes Work: Leisure in Capitalist Britain*, London, Macmillan.

Coalter, F. (1986) 'A Leisure Profession? Definitions and Dilemmas *Local Government Policy Making* (December).

Coalter, F., Long, J. and Duffield, B. (1986) *The Rationale for Public Sector Investment in Leisure*, London, Sports Council/ESRC.

Coalter F. and Parry N. (1982) 'Leisure Sociology or the Sociology of Leisure?' *Papers in Leisure Studies No. 4*, Polytechnic of North London.

Department of the Environment (1976) *Policy for the Innter Cities*, London, HMSO.

Department of the Environment (1977) *Recreation and Deprivation in Inner Urban Areas*, London, HMSO.

Dower, M. *et al.* (1981) *Leisure Provision and People's Needs*, London, HMSO.

Gamble, A. (1981) *An Introduction to Modern Social and Political Thought* London, Macmillan.

George, V. and Wilding, P. (1976) *The Ideology of Welfare*, London, Routledge & Kegan Paul.

Green, M. (1977) *Issues and Problems in the Decentralisation of Cultural Planning*, Centre for Contemporary Cultural Studies, University of Birmingham.

Hall, S. and Jefferson, T. (1976) *Resistance Through Rituals*, London, Hutchinson.

Harrison, B. (1973) 'State Intervention and Moral Reform in Nineteenth Century England' in P. Hollis (ed.) *Pressure from Without in Early Victorian England* London, Edward Arnold.

Harrison, F. (1986) 'The Economic and Political Dimensions of Leisure Services' in Fred Coalter (ed.), *The Politics of Leisure*, London, Leisure Studies Association.

Hargreaves, D. (1984) 'State Intervention in Sport and Hegemony Britain', Paper presented at the Leisure Studies Association International Conference, 'Leisure: People, Planning and Politics'.

Hargreaves, D. (1985) 'From Social Democracy to Authoritarian Populism: State Intervention in Sport and Physical Recreation in Contemporary Britain', *Leisure Studies*, Vo. 4, No. 2, May.

Hutchinson, R. (1982) *The Politics of the Arts Council*, London, Sinclair Brown.

Johnson, R. (1979) 'Three Problematics: Elements of a Theory of Working Class Culture', in J. Clarke, C. Critcher and R. Johnson (eds) *Working Class Culture*, London, Hutchinson.

McIntosh, P. and Charlton, V. (1984) *The Impact of Sport for All Policy, 1966–84 and a Way Forward*, London, Sports Council.

Mennel, S. (1979) 'Theoretical Considerations on Cultural Needs', *Sociology*, Vol. 13, No. 2.

Mishra, R. (1977) *Society and Social Policy*, London, Macmillan.

Fred Coalter 129

Mishra, R. (1986) *The Welfare State in Crisis*, London, Wheatsheaf.
Newman, O. (1981) *Corporatism, Leisure and Collective Consumption*, Centre for Leisure Studies, University of Salford.
Pearson, N. (1982) *The State and the Visual Arts*, Milton Keynes, Open University Press.
Rapaport, R. and Rapaport, R. N. (1975) *Leisure and the Family Life Cycle*, London, Routledge & Kegan Paul.
Roberts, K. (1978) *Contemporary Society and the Growth of Leisure*, London, Longman.
Rojek, C. (1985) *Capitalism and Leisure Theory*, London, Tavistock.
Scottish Arts Council (1978) *Annual Report*, Edinburgh, Scottish Arts Council.
Smith, M., Parker, S. and Smith, C. (1974) *Leisure and Society in Britain*, London, Allen Lane, The Penguin Press.
Sports Council (1975) *Sport and Recreation*, London, HMSO.
Sports Council (1978) *Annual Report 1978–79*, London, Sports Council.
Sports Council (1981) *Annual Report*, London, Sports Council.
Sports Council (1982) *Annual Report*, London, HMSO.
Touraine, A. (1974) *The Post-Industrial Society* London, Wildwood.
Travis, A. S. *et al.* (1978) *The Role of Central Government in Relation to Local Authority Leisure Services in England and Wales*, Centre for Urban and Regional Studies, Birmingham University.

7 The Promise and Problems of Women's Leisure and Sport

Jennifer Hargreaves

WOMEN, LEISURE AND SPORT

Without doubt, men possess greater cultural power than women. In leisure activities in general, and in sport in particular, men spend more time and have access to a wider range of opportunities than women, and sport is a unique feature of cultural life in which women are seriously disadvantaged and where sexism is fostered. But, although the social construction of most sports is based on a long and relentless history of male domination and female subordination, nevertheless, male power in sport has never been absolute. During the late nineteenth and early twentieth centuries, there was a gradual development of female sport, which continued through the interwar and post-war periods and has accelerated in recent years. The situation now is that more women choose to participate in sport in their leisure hours than previously and more women are involved in a greater number of sports than ever before. This change in the sporting profiles of women is shifting traditional male structures of leisure and sport.

The most common interpretation of the increase in leisure opportunities for women, such as sport, is that it is an evolutionary and progressive movement in the history of industrial society.[1] But the vision presented to us is an idealised one which recognises the historic subordination of women in sport, the exaggerates the trend towards equality of opportunity for women and minimises the wielding of, and struggle for, power, which has been an intrinsic aspect of this process. This is a 'liberal' attitude which assumes that any increase in sporting opportunities for women, or redistribution of sports resources in their favour will occur within the existing structures of sport, and this implicitly assumes the 'essential' nature of capitalist society to be a given factor. In contrast, there are a number of radical alternative interpretations which are critical of the role of leisure and sport in capitalist societies and which share an essentially determinist conception of the relationship between the capitalist mode of production and culture. For example, it is argued that sport is exploitative because it props up inherent class and property inequalities and incorporates conflict endemic to capitalism, including antagonistic gender relations and examples of sexism.[2] In this view, it is argued that there has been a failure to shift deep-rooted causes of inequality and that increased female participation is a form of incorporation into a structure of sport that remains, in fundamental ways, a bastion of male power.

Here we are faced by two contrasting attitudes about the position of women in leisure and sport, towards the essential nature of sport itself and towards the nature of society. Each of these approaches tends to exaggerate – on the one hand, the extent of individual freedom and the benefits of sport and, on the other, the restraining and harmful effects of sport. Each of these approaches focuses on male sport – in the first case, as a model to copy and, in the second case, as one to resist. However, neither of them deals adequately with the complexities and contradictions of gender relations in sport: for example, with the idea that most modern sports still subordinate women but at the same time can be a liberating and creative experience for them, or with the observation that women are systematically prevented from participating in sports that also provide a potential space for female liberation. The problem raised here is whether we can explain theoretically the relationship between the possibilities and limitations facing women in the spheres of leisure and sport.

The failure to deal adequately with this problem is, in part, the result of the ways in which theories of leisure and sport have been produced. Most analyses have been written by men and are predominantly about *male* leisure and *male* sport, and, with few exceptions, women in them have been marginalised or even rendered invisible. Throughout the literature, there is a tendency to 'insert' women in previously constructed pictures of male leisure and sport and there is a general failure to examine gender issues. Ironically, women themselves have compounded this problem of neglect and distortion. Women's studies have tended to focus on questions of legal, political, economic, educational and ideological significance. The fields of female leisure and sport are new and relatively undeveloped, and there is little research material about them. As a result, accounts tend to be descriptive and only tentatively theorised. In the 1980's for the first time, there has developed a concern to explore more systematically the relationships between leisure, sport and gender relations which is part of a wider theoretical movement focusing on the cultural level of life and on the significance of ideology and consciousness. It is also an effect of feminist intervention and the developing awareness of the inadequacies of theories that fail to consider the construction of gender divisions as an intrinsic component of the analysis of culture.

A possible way forward is to explore more fully the relationship between women's sport and the theoretical problem of human freedom and constraint. This is an issue that is topical in neo-Marxist approaches in the sociologies of culture, leisure and sport. Debate centres on whether individuals are manipulated in leisure and sport or whether they can be truly free to pursue activities that will be creative and liberating, unhindered by the social and ideological forces of capitalist society. The concern with this problem has developed as a response to the tendencies towards economic and cultural reductionism in orthodox and structural Marxist analyses, and in particular to the way in which the concept of *ideology* has been employed, as if it is 'total' in its effects on a passive population. An alternative is to resist these tendencies by keeping intact what is arguably the inherent *humanism* of Marxism and the sense of culture as a way of life imbued with systems of meanings and values that are actively created by individuals and groups. In this approach, leisure and sport are treated as cultural formations which provide the contexts for the production and reproduction of identities or 'ways of seeing' that amount to a group consciousness, resulting from shared experiences and involvement associated with commonly understood customs, interests, desires, rituals, styles and symbolic representations. At any time, it is possible to discern cultural continuities and discontinuities, because dominant meanings and traditional interests engender opposition and have to be defended, while new meanings and new interests are constantly being worked out and struggled for. Configurations of power are never static, but part of a continual process of change that incorporates negotiation and accommodation.

HEGEMONY, LEISURE AND SPORT

In recent years, Gramsci's work, specifically the concept of *hegemony*, has been used to analyse the complexities of the relationship between freedom and constraint in leisure and sport.[3] Hegemony describes a form of control that is persuasive, rather than coercive, and which depends upon the production and maintenance of values and beliefs that support established social relations and structures of power. Hegemony can be reinforced by coercive means of control, but essentially it operates through more subtle means as a form of ideological persuasion. But it is not an all-or-nothing phenomenon. Dominant and subordinate groups are not necessarily, unambiguously winners or losers. Dominant groups often allow concessions in the face of opposition, in order to retain credibility and overall control. In this way, power relations function to a large extent by the winning of consent and support from subordinate groups for those in positions of power. People comply with, and believe in the reasons for existing power relations that are not always in their best interests. Gramsci uses the concept of hegemony to examine how, in specific historical and social situations, 'a fundamental class is able to establish its *leadership* as distinct from the more coercive forms of domination'.[4] The concept of hegemony recognises instabilities in social relations and the complex ways in which particular forms of domination are produced in different social contexts and institutions, such as families, schools, the media, leisure, and sport. It opposes analyses that assume individuals to be manipulated and passive recipients of culture. In Raymond Williams' words:

A lived hegemony is always a process . . . it does not just passively exist as a form of dominance. It has continually to be renewed, recreated, defended and modified. It is also continually resisted, limited, altered, challenged by pressures not at all its own.[5]

But at the same time the concept of hegemony does not ignore the structural constraints faced by individuals in their everyday lives and the ways in which sport and leisure, for example, are inextricably linked to other aspects of culture and to significant economic, political and social arrangements. It should not be assumed that culture is the 'whole of society', but, rather, that it is analytically distinct from political and economic processes and that, together with them, it makes up the totality of social relations. In other words, hegemony is a structure of power that is represented in varied social processes and consolidated for individuals in different social sites. It proposes a dialectical relationship between individuals and society, a relationship that is both determined and determining, and it allows for cultural experiences such as leisure and sport to be *both* exploitative *and* creative.

Although recent developments in the sociologies of leisure and sport have used the concept of hegemony to explore the contradictory nature of culture, in these accounts, antagonistic class relations have provided the focus, rather than a rigorous exploration of the way class and gender divisions are constructed *together*, or the specific complexities of male hegemony in sport.[6] Because of the relative silence about women's sport and gender divisions, there is generally an implication that class is the root cause of women's as well as men's oppression in sport, and that problems of gender are secondary. These accounts of sport have serious theoretical limitations because they fail to deal with the complexities of the relationship between capitalist relations and patriarchal relations.

It is possible to apply the concept of hegemony specifically to male leadership and domination in leisure and sport in order to show ways in which gender relations intersect with specific features of capitalist social formations. Male interests predominate in most areas of leisure and sport where male hegemony has probably been more complete and resistant to change than in other areas of culture. Nonetheless, I argue here that male hegemony in sport is not total: rather, it is a constantly shifting process that incorporates both reactionary and liberating features. It is clear that women actively accommodate to and collude in existing patterns of discrimination in sport that are specific to capitalism and to male domination, *as well as* opposing them and struggling to alter them. The legitimate use of the female body in sport is constantly being redefined and this process embodies *struggles* over *meanings*. The concept of hegemony invites us to consider how meanings that legitimate male domination in sport are produced, reproduced, struggled over, and changed.

WORK AND LEISURE FOR MEN AND WOMEN

The extent of both women's subordination and women's freedom in leisure and sport is mediated by social and economic criteria which intersect, in fundamental ways, with *symbolic* means of control. Conventional ideas about the nature of work and leisure and the relationship between the two provide a starting point for considering the inequalities between men and women in sport. There is an undeniable link between income, cultural power and gender relations: women have been economically subordinated to men[8], and this state directly affects attitudes, and access to leisure. The nuclear family is effectively an economic unit within which the husband/father is defined as the major wage-earner, whose labour is necessary to satisfy the needs of the home and the family, and who has earned the right to leisure. In contrast, the wife/mother is defined in terms of her dependent role as housewife, for whom money and time for leisure are like 'bonuses'. In its present form, industrial capitalism requires the unpaid domestic labour of women to service the waged labour force and the next generation of workers:

> It is not simply that women's work at home is *different* from that of men – *it is constructed by it* and *subordinate to it*. Women's work reproduces men at work; women's work allows for men's 'existence time' or reproduction, and women's work produces leisure for men.[9]

But many women, as well as men, are in paid work and since the Second World War, the largest increase in employment outside the home has been among married women.[10] Women who are employed are in a contradictory position in terms of their leisure. On the one hand, the public world of work can provide greater financial independence and can broaden social horizons which, in turn, make comparisons with men more significant and raise expectations about leisure, but, on the other hand, women's position in the labour market is marginal to the position of men. Women generally have less well-paid and less secure jobs and they constitute a massive 'reserve army of labour'; they are in demand when labour is scarce, but are readily expendable when jobs are scarce. Moreover, the freedom for leisure activities of most women who work outside the home is curtailed because they have the additional and major, if not exclusive, responsibilities for domestic work and childcare and single parents, particularly, are subject to further constraints.[11]

But whether or not women work outside the home is less important than the *idea* that women's proper place is in the home, because it encompasses the implicaton that the 'real' work is done elsewhere by men. Because money determines value in capitalist societies, labour done at home, including childcare, which is physically demanding, time-consuming and socially essential, is often valued less highly than paid employment. The belief that there is a rigid distinction between the nature of paid work and the nature of domestic work is a way of thinking to which most women demonstrate acceptance through the way they conduct their lives, and is an unequivocally male definition of work, linked to the idea that men should be free to engage in recuperative leisure pursuits so that they can return refreshed to their jobs. Leisure is conceived in such a context as the polar opposite of work because of its therapeutic potential, compensating for the strains and constraints of unrewarding labour. There is a tendency to treat the prevailing sexual domestic division of labour uncritically and to idealise the home, the nuclear family and the woman's role within it, and to ignore the oppressive characteristics of the private sphere of the home, especially for women. In general, men have more disposable time for leisure and sport than women, and they find it easier to indulge *of their own free will* in leisure activities. Ironically, for vast numbers of women, it is likely that 'leisure' is a highly regulated area of life and has little connection with freedom. Although there are differences in the extent and forms of the limitations on leisure between, for example, women from different class and ethnic backgrounds, there are certain features that one can apply to women in general.[12]

CONSTRAINTS ON WOMEN'S LEISURE AND SPORT

Lack of time is an obvious limitation on women's leisure and, after marriage, any discrepancy that already exists between men's and women's leisure opportunities tends to increase. Women with young children who also go out to work are in the worst position. Because married women do most of the housework themselves, any leisure is fitted in between essential childcare, cooking, washing, shopping, and cleaning, etc. Women in the home have no real notion of 'time off' and hence the distinction between work and leisure becomes blurred. Domiciled and family-based leisure becomes the norm for married women, especially those with young children. Watching television, for example, which is the most popular leisure activity for married women with children, can be done at the same time as keeping an eye on the children, or doing the ironing or mendings.[13] Women's responsibilities in the home and for children restrict leisure activities outside the home and so, not suprisingly, sport is a minority activity.[14] When women marry, they usually stop participating in sport, even if they previously had an interest in it. However, even given sufficient free time, the energy required for vigorous forms of physical activity is itself a disincentive for women to participate in sport. Because domestic labour is physically tiring, sport may well be the worst sort of leisure activity for women with a young family: it is in no way invigorating and recuperative for them but, instead, can cause exhaustion and poor health.[15] Furthermore, leisure outside the home, and sport in particular, can be a costly affair. Getting transport, paying a childminder and finding entry fees, for example, are particularly difficult for the low-paid, for single parents and for women who are unemployed or whose husbands or partners are unemployed. In many families, money for leisure is almost exclusively in the control of the male, since earnings tend to be seen as belonging to the person who earned them, and housekeeping money or welfare payments are not seen as available for personal use.

Male control of female leisure occurs also in ways that are connected with the wielding of power in a more personal sense. There is evidence that men control the amount of time their wives or girlfriends or daughters may spend on any type of social activity, and there is evidence, too, of violence being used by husbands against their wives for questioning their authority. In addition, women feel frightened or nervous about going out alone, or even in twos or threes, which is not the case for men, especially when going to traditional male venues, such as pubs, working men's clubs, some sports clubs, leisure centres and health clubs. This is a limitation that is imposed on women and mediated by male and female attitudes towards sexuality. Unless women are accompanied by a man, they tend to be defined as 'loose' or, less pejoratively, 'looking for a man', and women feel threatened by the sexual harassment of men in these contexts. The pattern that women tend to follow, after they get into a permanent relationship with a man, is to adjust to new forms of leisure structured by their positions as girlfriends, wives, or mothers, whereas men more often continue the leisure interests that they had before they were married. Women will, for example, accompany their men to the pub or act as their sporting 'accoutrements', in the roles of tea-ladies, laundresses and ticket-collectors.

The evidence available about women's leisure is based upon empirical material, including women's own accounts of how they perceive their lives, and it suggests that it is possible to generalise about women as a group who experience their leisure in ways that are different from, and subordinate to, men. It can be very misleading, however, to treat women as a homogeneous group. For example, class inequalities accentuate gender inequalities in leisure and sport. Most of the examples of constraints on women's leisure are greater for working-class women than for middle-class women, who are more likely to have some sort of help in the home and with childcare, and who, more typically, have more money for leisure and access to private transport. There are, not surprisingly, many more middle-class than working-class women involved in sport. However, although there has been a marked increase recently in the provision for women of health clubs, keep-fit groups, aerobics classes, body-building gymnasia and saunas, the fitness boom for women has hardly affected the lives of working-class women at all.

There has been a long tradition of symbolic violence against women associated with middle-class male sport – the vilification of women in the rituals of rugby songs provide a graphic example.[16] But some of the most blatant sexist attacks against women in sport have been in pubs and in working-men's clubs, which are traditional centres of working-class male culture and male bonding. In these places, women have supported men's sporting roles (for example in playing darts or snooker or soccer), but they have been denied equal rights with men to vote, hold office or to play. The convention of separate leisure for men and women is not so discrete for middle-class families, however, so that mixed sport and family sport are predominantly middle-class phenomena.

There is a serious lack of information about women's leisure and sport, but as new evidence becomes available, it shows that there is a consistent gap between middle-class and working-class participation, that there is a big dropout during adolescence, and that very few older women participate in sport at all. But other factors, such as regional variations, different ethnic patterns of participation, and the effects of religious imperatives and cultural affinities, make the account of women's sport more complex.

GENDER IMAGES, LEISURE AND SPORT

It may be a mistake to attempt to construct a unitary discourse about women's subordinate position in leisure and sport in relation to men, but the paradoxes of women's position are precisely the features of it that highlight the nature of male hegemony. Although there are differences among women in their relations with men, there are also similarities. A unifying feature of the subordination of women is the implicit belief that differences between men and women are biologically determined and hence immutable. The natural capacity of women to bear children has psychological and social repercussions, allocating women to primarily reproductive, mothering and childcare roles. The ideology of domesticity, that keeps women out of the labour market and in a state of dependence on men, is the result of the production of stereotypes about 'natural' or 'appropriate' male and female behaviour. It is not argued here that staying at home and being responsible for the welfare of the children is, necessarily, a more onerous and alienating way of life than selling one's labour power in a repetitive, inflexible and uncreative job. Looking after children can be a uniquely rewarding experience. The point is that the sexual division of labour is considered to be 'in the natural order of things' and supports popular ideas about male superiority.

Any account of human behaviour that is rooted in the body is most difficult to disclaim, because the attempt to do so threatens a person's identity or very 'sense of being'. In this way, ideology is a powerful, material force. Many women themselves believe that they are inherently endowed with characteristics that make them different from men, and better suited than men, in particular, to care for children. Hence they place marriage and family above satisfaction in other spheres, such as at work or in leisure and sport, and thus they reinforce their own subordination. This is an example of *control by consent* and illustrates the way in which male hegemony is confirmed for men and women by the reality of their lives. It constitutes the essence of the problem of change for women, though it is, of course, a problem for men as well. The ways in which differences, rather than similarities, between the sexes are presented as important, is a product of culture that underpins the 'different ways of life' experienced by men and women. The *fact* that only women can have babies gives rise to the *idea* that they are the only ones who can care for them adequately, and thus men's abilities to nurture and to experience conditions and emotions conventionally assigned to women, are repressed. It has been argued that, if men in general were to learn to nurture children,

> this would reduce men's needs to guard their masculinity and their control of social and cultural spheres which treat and define women as secondary and powerless, and would help women to develop the autonomy which too much embeddedness in relationship has often taken from them.[17]

The essence of male hegemony is embodied in this quotation. It is not a static condition, but a *process of legitimation*. Changes in relationships between men and women can be explained if human beings are seen as active rather than passive agents, and if the link between leisure, sport and ideological influences is seen as dialectical and not mechanical. Increasing numbers of women challenge conventional female roles in the home, and this reduces the effectiveness of the domination of men, so that a more equal division of domestic labour and shared parenting become aspects of non-exploitative relationships in the home, enabling women as well as men to enjoy leisure outside the home.

Dominant images of masculinity and femininity have a double effect upon women's attitudes to sport. The popular, chauvinist model of British sport embodies an entrenched belief that men and women have fixed biological and psychological natures that are essentially different and that sport is the 'natural' domain of men. Sporting masculinity tends to be equated with a 'commonsense' model of masculine biology – that is, to be good at sport is to be active, skilful, powerful and muscular and to exhibit such traits as competitiveness, aggression, assertiveness and courage, as well as a positive orientation to work. In contrast, athletic prowess does not accord with popular definitions of femininity, which are associated with relative weakness, gentleness, cooperation, submissiveness, grace and agility. Some men still celebrate, and defend vehemently, extreme and reactionary ideas about the 'values of manliness', as if there were transhistorical and transcultural masculine and feminine identities:

> Women should once again be prohibited from sport: they are the true defenders of the humanist values that emanate from the household, the values of tenderness, nurture, and compassion, and this most important role must not be confused by the military and political values inherent in sport. Likewise sport should not be muzzled by humanist values: it is the living arena for the great virtue of manliness.[18]

Sport is thus a major source of gender divisions and the sportsman is the symbolic focus of male power. The strength and aggression required in sports such as boxing, rugby, American football and ice-hockey render men, by implication, fit also for work and battle. The appropriate discourse for the practice of power invested in the male sporting body is a military discourse of war and combat, of struggles, confrontations, strategies and tactics. By contrast, 'feminine-appropriate' sports such as gymnastics, synchronised swimming and ice-skating, which emphasise balance, coordination, flexibility and grace, idealise popular images of femininity. In addition, women are involved in non-performance, subordinate roles, as fans, members of supporters' clubs, cheerleaders, tea-ladies and ticket-collectors. There has been a long history of excluding women from sports which require a lot of power, aggression and body contact, but women have been excluded also from such sports as golf, angling, snooker, and darts, that require very little muscular energy, but have traditionally been male leisure preserves and important sites for collective male behaviour. Sport thus reinforces traditional male and female gender identities by supporting the idea that the existing sexual division of labour – at work and at home – is the 'natural' state of affairs.

Constructions of masculine and feminine subjectivities in sport and leisure do not exist in isolation. They are reinforced by similar ideological formations in other spheres, such as the family, the school, places of work and the media. Take the example of Richard Dyer's discussion of the male pin-up. He points out that 'sport is the most common contemporary source of male imagery – not only of pin-ups of sportsmen, but in the sports activities of film stars, popstars and so on'.[19] The popular, dominant image of masculine identity is presented for us to look at and to think about as if it were the norm. Male subjects are 'active' subjects, usually doing something like carrying a huge boulder or vigorously playing a sport, and 'even when not actually caught in the act, the male image still promises activity in the way it is posed'.[20] Well-defined, hard, and taut muscles imply physical strength and aggression that, it is assumed, women do not possess. As John Berger points out, 'men act and women appear'.[21] Muscularity is thus a 'sign' of male power which implies sexuality. Women, in contrast are presented predominantly in their roles as mothers and housewives, frequently in the context of the home, or as 'essentially feminine' as the partner of a man, and as sexually attractive to men, but rarely participating in a vigorous physical activity.[22]

Dominant gender images are constructed for us in the home and reinforced through the years of schooling and adolescence.[23] The relation between young women, leisure and romanticism illustrates the connection between gender images and sports participation. For female school-leavers, the construction of femininity in terms of heterosexual attractiveness is a major aspect of leisure and it is seen as relevant to their social and economic positions. 'Working, to find a man takes a lot of time and effort for university graduates as well as young working girls. Female networks put pressure on young women to conform, and the cult of romanticism, bedroom- and fashion-culture, and talking on the telephone provide the contexts for female-bonding that is probably the nearest equivalent to male-bonding in sports. The idea that 'getting or keeping a man' is the most important ambition for a young woman is confirmed for us in magazines such as *Jackie, Just Seventeen, 19* and *Photolove*, produced for teenage consumption, and in popular journalism for older women, which reminds them that they should assume the major responsibility for the house and the children and that they have an obligation to foster an image of themselves as sexual objects.[24] There is an obvious conflict between involvement in vigorous sport and these images of femininity. Not surprisingly, it is usually 'feminine-appropriate' sports, such as tennis, gymnastics, figure-skating, or swimming that are depicted in women's popular magazines, and often with females in attractive and sometimes sexually provocative poses, presented as commodities for male pleasure. Most commonly featured are work-outs, dance, keep-fit, and aerobics, which are not in opposition to 'essential femininity'. They are presented as activities that will improve the figure and, together with a good diet and appropriate skin, hair, and nail care, will enhance a woman's appeal to a man. The new, fit and beautiful 'superwoman' fits the romance blueprint. The assumption that women should exercise in order to prepare themselves for male 'consumption' is illustrated by a book on female body-building, written by a man: 'My ideal modern woman is perfectly fit, with a well-balanced figure, and entirely feminine.'[25] Such images are reinforced by media coverage.

Generally speaking, the media cover male sport, presented as a 'natural' activity associated with male identity and chauvinism. The coverage of female sport is minimal by comparison, and conventonal sporting ideologies about women cohere around images of femininity and motherhood. In the popular press, sportswomen are almost always portrayed first as females and then as athletes. They tend to be described essentially through their sexuality – how leggy and pretty they are – rather than on their sports skills and techniques. Female athletes who exemplify the stereotype of 'femininity' are treated explicitly as sporting sex-symbols, in celebration of the male/female distinction, like 'pretty Miss Mary Decker who, in this Amazonian world, wears make-up on the track and shaves her legs'.[25] Alternatively, we read that female athletes are, by implication, unfeminine, gay or 'butch', like Jarmilla Kratochvilova, 'the girl with the body of a man'.[27] In such ways, personal sporting identities are shaped by social structures and media sport reinforces conventional patriarchal values.

ALTERNATIVE IMAGES OF FEMALE SPORT

The symbolic articulation of differences between men and women in sporting images have an important controlling effect upon people's participation in sport. However, the dominant images are not the only ones. Sport, like other cultural instances, embodies conflict, and alternative and varied images of femininity in sport are emerging. This throws further light upon the nature of male hegemony in sport. The somewhat bleak picture that has emerged of the social, economic, and symbolic controls upon women's participation in leisure and sport may tend to mask ideas and practices that are marginal, or even oppositional, to the dominant ones. Male hegemony in sport has always embodied struggles and contradictions, and has not remained static and inviolable. For example, in 1896, during the first Olympics in Greece, which was unequivocally a bastion of bourgeois male privilege, a single, unofficial female competitor who 'crashed' the marathon – a Greek woman call Melpomene – symbolised the efforts of women to overcome male dominance. Since that time, gradually more women have struggled against fierce opposition to be allowed to participate in different sports and different events. It is no longer exceptional for a woman to run a marathon, and yet it was not untl 1984, after a long and bitter battle against mythical accounts of female inferiority, that the marathon became an official Olympic event for women.[28] Successes of female athletes, and the production of sporting heroines, for example, co-exist with, and in contradiction to, reactionary attitudes about female participation, and there is no inevitability about the outcome of such differences and conflict.

For example, there is general ignorance, but growing knowledge, about evidence which can dispel myths about the relation between women's biology and sporting potential.[29] It is true that men are, on average, taller, stronger and heavier than women, with broader shoulders, narrower hips and a higher centre of gravity. They have more muscle mass, a greater lung capacity, larger hearts and therefore a more efficient delivery of oxygen to the working muscles. Sportsmen are, therefore, generally stronger, speedier and more powerful than sportswomen: they can run faster, jump higher and throw further. However, although most females have a lesser muscle mass, more body fat and are more fragile and flexible, though they are slower, weaker and less powerful than men, it does not follow that events demanding speed and power are only suited to men. There are far greater physical differences *within* a sex than *between* sexes, and fitness, skill, agility and coordination can be more important considerations. Women do also have to accommodate to the physiological changes which occur during menstruation, pregnancy, childbirth and the menopause, but problems associated with these processes are less common among women who take regular exercise. It is not common knowledge that Olympic medals, world records, and personal best performances have been won and produced by female athletes at all phases of the menstrual cycle. Furthermore, during early pregnancy, and shortly after childbirth, women have competed successfully at all levels of competitive sport. Fanny Blankers-Koehn, nicknamed 'the flying Dutch Housewife', provides one of the best-known examples that supreme athletic ability is not incompatible with normal procreative functioning. In 1948, she won four Olympic atheltics medals when she was pregnant, and then, as a mother, she went on to set four world records. It is also a popular misconception that women's reproductive systems are more susceptible to injury than men's: in fact the female reproductive organs are securely held and protected inside the body and cannot be dislodged or injured by vigorous exercise. Furthermore, protective apparatus can be worn by women and by men, and ethical reasons for condemning dangerous sports are as applicable to men as they are to women. Although female biology is different from male biology, an increasing minority of people recognise that there is no medical or physiological reason to prevent healthy women participating in any sport whatsoever.

It may be too early to say that male hegemony in sport is fragile, but it contains oppositional elements and is a contested zone, as women challenge traditional sporting identities. 'Femininity' in sport is not a static phenomenon, but a concept encompassing varied images of women which can be understood as manifestations of *struggles over meanings* which are in a constant state of flux and negotiation. By their entry into more sports, and through the successes of competitive athletes, women are themselves changing 'commonsense' thinking about their biology and potential in sport. In some events the best women are beating men's past records, and women are out-performing men in some direct sporting competitions which have become open to both sexes. The trend towards equivalence with, and superiority over men, is most dramatic in long-distance events in swimming, walking, cycling, ice-skating, roller-skating, and the marathon. There is some evidence that women may be physiologically better-suited than men in endurance events, although, ironically, women have only a brief history of participation in these events because they have encountered fierce and sustained opposition.

The conflict between conventional notions of femininity and sporting prowess is greatest in traditionally masculine sports – in particular those which involve body-contact, or demand individual displays of strength, speed and skill, such as team games, combative sports, power events and speed events. However, in spite of opposition and prejudice, these have all become sports in which increasing numbers of women are participating. In these contexts, the subordination of women is constantly being reproduced *and* subverted, as men struggle to retain control and women make more demands and tangible gains for themselves.

The politics of women's sport is concerned in part with struggles over resources, and the result has been a gradual shift towards equality with men. More women are participating in more sports than in previous years, and in a greater variety of roles: there are increasing numbers of female sports reporters, commentators, administrators, referees, and coaches. Much of this development is the result of women taking action for themselves, which, to some extent, is one of the effects of the women's movement. The inauguration of the Women's Sports Foundation has provided coordination for the development of women's sport in Britain. It provides an information service for women interested in sport, organises working parties to examine particular areas of discrimination, and acts as a pressure group on the sports establishment. Until recent years, most of the expansion of women's sport had occurred within the established structures of sport, which had been to a large extent in competitive models of sport in the club network. More recently, there has been a development of non-competitive sport at local level, often as an independent, voluntary venture, but with links with, or funding from, local authorities, official bodies of sport, or charitable or commercial sponsors. Such schemes for women's sport are intended to be inexpensive, enjoyable, non-élitist and beneficial to health. In some situations, strategies of positive discrimination have been adopted, and special days and weekends of sport for women and regular classes in convenient venues and with crèche facilities are becoming more common. Some local authorities have employed women's sports development officers; women's committees have a stronger influence in local politics and it is likely that authorities that continue to marginalise women's sport will come under a lot of pressure.

Most of the impetus has come from white, middle-class women, but there is a growing concern to make sport accessible to working-class women and to those from ethnic minorities. Although the concept of the 'whole community' is incorporated in the rhetoric of public provision of sport, the largest group of users is middle-class white males.[30] The 'community network approach' has been inaugurated specifically to attract people from other social backgrounds and sporting dispositions, especially women. In Merseyside, for example, a number of sports projects make links with other services, such as the city health centre, with the aim of offering facilities for varied types of exercise and sports, presented in a way that will make women 'feel at home' and have fun, in contrast to the 'male, aggressive, competitive model of sport that puts women off.'[31] For example, there are keep-fit, aerobic, and badminton classes in inner-city schools, rambling and dancing for the over-sixties, and the 'Sisters' Network' for those women who want to run. Snooker, rock-climbing, swimming, a variety of watersports, and other minority sports are introduced to beginners. There is a general consensus among people working in these schemes, that

> the health approach has been effective because it has attracted such women as those 'classic' ones who have done nothing since leaving school, those who would never have dreamed of taking exercise. For example, overweight women, those who have young children, and the elderly.[32]

If sport becomes part of a 'way of life' for increasing numbers of women, such a trend can begin to change the perception of other poeple about what is appropriate behaviour for women. Such a movement does not immediately eliminate male hegemony, but it shifts its construction and the extent of its effectiveness. In fact, opposition to traditional male models of sport and the desire for alternative ones has come not only from women, but from men as well. There is, in fact, no fixed model of male oppression in sport: some men and some women are supportive of traditional models and some men and some women oppose them. Male hegemony is not a simple male *vs* female opposition, and to be opposed to male domination in sport is not the same as being opposed to men. There are examples of mixed sports which stress health, enjoyment and cooperation and de-emphasise competition, in which the experiences of men and women coincide and where men and women work reciprocally. The specific ways in which sexism is experienced by women in relation to sport need to be explored, as do the effects of sexism on men.

This chapter attempts to suggest how we might understand women's sport. For a fuller analysis, many other factors need to be considered, such as the effect of women's sport on the 'quality of life'. It has only been possible here to look at some examples of the possibilities for, and constraints on, women in sport. The struggle to remove discrimination is a struggle to remove the practical and symbolic means of perpetuating discrimination. It concerns the social and economic constraints on women's sport (what is *possible*), the connection with ideology and symbolic forms of control (what is *permissible*), and self-determination and the articulation and fulfilment of desire (what is *pleasurable*).

Notes

1. Some examples of texts that represent this view are: J. Dumazedier, (1974) *The Sociology of Leisure*, Amsterdam, Elsevier; M. A. Smith, S. Parker and C. Smith (eds.) (1973) *Leisure and Society in Britain*, London, Allen Lane, The Penguin Press; S. Parker (1979) *The Sociology of Leisure*, 3rd ed., London, Allen & Unwin; K. Roberts (1981) *Leisure*, London, Longman.

2. See for example J.-M. Brohm (1978) *Sport: A Prison of Measured Time*, London, Ink Links; P. Hoch (1972) *Rip Off the Big Game*, New York, Doubleday; G. Vinnai (1973) *Football Mania*, London, Ocean Books.

3. The concept of hegemony is central in the work of J. Clarke and C. Critcher (1985) *The Devil Makes Work: Leisure in Capitalist Britain*, London, Macmillan; R. Gruneau (1983) *Class, Sports and Social Development*, Amhurst, University of Massachusetts Press; Jennifer Hargreaves (ed.) 1982) *Sport, Culture and Ideology*, London, Routledge & Kegan Paul; John Hargreaves (1986) *Sport, Power and Culture*, Cambridge, Polity Press.

4. Quoted in T. Bennett, G. Martin, G. Mercer and J. Woollacott (eds.) (1983) *Culture, Ideology and Social Process* (Milton Keynes, Open University Press, p. 187.

5. R. Williams (1973) 'Base and Superstructure', *New Left Review*, No. 82, (Nov./Dec.) p. 9.

6. See for example Clarke and Critcher, op.cit., Gruneau, op. cit. and Hargreaves op. cit.

7. A debate about the relationship between patriarchal relations and capitalist relations is found in the following publications on women's sport: *Arena Review* (July 1984); Jennifer Hargreaves (1986) 'Where's the Virtue? Where's the Grace? A Discussion of the Social production of Gender Through Sport', *Theory, Culture and Society*, Vol. 3, No. 1; M. Boutilier and L. San Giovanni (1983) *The Sporting Woman*, Champaign, Illinois, Human Kinetics.

8. V. Beechey, 'Some Notes on Female Wage Labour in Capitalist

Production' and M. Benston, 'The Political Economy of Women's Liberation', both in M. Evans (ed.) (1982) *The Woman Question*, Oxford, Fontana; S. McIntosh, 'Leisure Studies and Women', in A. Tomlinson (ed.) (1981) *Leisure and Social Control*, Brighton Polytechnic.

9. C. Griffin, D. Hobson, S. MacIntosh and T. McCabe (1982), 'Women and Leisure' in Jennifer Hargreaves, op. cit. p. 94.
10. A. Giddens (1982) *Sociology: A Brief but Critical Introduction*, London, Macmillan, p. 131.
11. E. Green, S. Hebron and D. Woodward, 'A Woman's Work' (1985) *Sport and Leisure*, London, Sports Council (July-August), and 'Everyday Life and Women's Leisure: Ideologies of Domesticity and Processes of Social Control' (Paper presented at Centre for Leisure Studies, University of Tilburg, The Netherlands: 1985) and *Women, Leisure and Social Control* (unpublished: 1986); C. Griffin, D. Hobson, S. MacIntosh and T. McCabe, 'Women and Leisure', in Jennifer Hargreaves (1982), op. cit.; E. Wimbush (1986) *Women, Leisure and Well-Being*, Edinburgh, Centre for Leisure Research.
12. The next section on 'Constraints on Women's Leisure and Sport', is based on research in the following studies: R. Deem (1986) *All Work and No Play? The Sociology of Women and Leisure*, Milton Keynes, Open University Press; Green *et al.* ibid; Griffin *et al.*, ibid.; Wimbush, ibid.
13. For example, the publications by Green et al, ibid., are based on a research project, jointly funded by the Sports Council and the ESRC. 97% of the married women in their survey (altogether 707 women between the ages of 18 and 59), do the major part of the housework themselves. The major leisure activity for 66% of the married women was watching television.
14. Ibid. 21% played some form of sport, but participation was much lower among the older women. Official Sports Council reports *General Household Survey* London, (HMSO, 1983), and *Social Trends* London, HMSO 1985, show no more than 17% of women in the population who participate in sport.
15. Wimbush, op. cit.
16. E. Dunning (1986) 'Sport as a Male Preserve: Notes on the Social Sources of Masculine Identity and its Transformations', *Theory, Culture and Society*, Vol. 3, No. 1, pp. 79–90.
17. N. Chodorow (1978) *The Reproduction of Mothering*, Berkeley, University of California Press, p. 218.
18. J. Carroll (1986), 'Sport: Virtue and Grace', *Theory, Culture and Society*, Vol. 3, No. 1, p. 98.
19. R. Dyer (1982) 'Don't Look Now', *Screen*, Vol. 23, No. 3 – 4, p. 68.
20. Ibid. p. 67.
21. J. Berger (1972), *Ways of Seeing*, Harmondsworth, Penguin, p. 47.
22. See, for example, F. Borzello, A. Kuhn, J. Pack and C. Wedd (1985), 'Living Dolls and "real women"', In A. Kuhn, *The Power of the Image: Essays on Representation and Sexuality*, London, Routledge & Kegan Paul; N. Henley (1977), *Body Politics: Power, Sex and Nonverbal Communication*, Englewood Cliffs, NJ, Prentice-Hall.

23. See, for example, G. Belotti (1975) *Little Girls*, London, Writers' and Readers' Publishing Cooperative; P. Browne, L. Matzen and J. Whyld, 'Physical Education', in J. Whyld (ed.) (1983) *Sexism in the Secondary School*, London, Harper & Row; S. Delamont (1980) *The Sociology of Women*, London, Allen & Unwin; S. Delamont (1980) *Sex Roles and the School*, London, Methuen; ILEA, *Providing Equal Opportunities for Girls and Boys in Physical Education (1984)* Swindon, GLC Supplies Dept; O. Leamon, *Sit on the Sidelines and Watch the Boys Play* (1984) London, Longman; S. Scraton, 'Images of Femininity and the Teaching of Girls' Physical Education', in J. Evans (ed.) (1986) *Physical Education, Sport and Schooling*, Lewes, Falmer Press; S. Sharpe, *Just Like a Girl: How Girls Learn to be Women* (1976) Harmondsworth, Penguin.

24. See, for example, Henley, op. cit.; A. McRobbie (1978) 'Jackie: An ideology of adolescent femininity', *Women take Issue*, Birmingham, CCCS; A. McRobbie, 'Just Like a Jackie Story', in A. McRobbie and T. McCabe (eds.) (1981) *Feminism for Girls*, London, Routledge & Kegan Paul.

25. O. Heidenstam (1984) *Body Beautiful*, London, William Foulsham, p. 65.

26. P. Freedman, 'The Fastest Painted Lady in the World', *The Sunday Times*, 27 May 1984.

27. Ibid.

28. For an account of the history of women in the Olympics, see my 'Women and the Olympic Phenomenon', in A. Tomlinson and G. Whannel (eds.) (1984) *The Five Ring Circus*, London, Pluto Press and my article (1984) 'Taking Men On At Their Games', *Marxism Today*, Vol. 28, No. 8.

29. The information here and further details about the relation between women's biology and sports participation can be found in K. Dyer (1982) *Catching Up The Men*, London, Junction Books, and E. Ferris (1981) 'Attitudes to Women in Sport: A Prolegomena towards a sociological theory', in *Equal Opportunities International*, Vol. 1, No. 2, p. 32–39.

30. See for example the Sports Council Report, *Sport in the Community*, 1983; and *General Household Survey*, London, HMSO, 1983.

31. Interview with Robin Ireland, memeber of the Merseyside Health and Recreation Team, 18 August 1986.

32. Ibid.

8 Leisure and the Informal Economy

Jeff Bishop and Paul Hoggett

INTRODUCTION

In a territory as yet so little explored as 'leisure' there can hardly be said to be 'traditions' of analysis and debate, terms and definitions. At the same time, any cursory glance at the burgeoning literature would show quite clearly some emerging points of consensus as well as some more questionable assumptions. One particularly healthy aspect of recent debate has been the attempts to root leisure theory in the context of wider social theory; to see leisure in relation to employment, commercialisation, privatisation, the family, developing social relations and so forth; (see for example Parker, 1976; Roberts, 1978; Dumazedier, 1978; Rojek, 1985). The less healthy side of this has been the concentration on seeking areas of leisure which reinforce already-held theoretical positions, for example on autonomy, professionalism or the dominance of consumption over production.

To the uninitiated reader the impression to be gleaned from recent literature would be that leisure is almost entirely an individualised activity, often determined into a model of passive consumption, increasingly focused on a socially isolated and home-centred 'family' unit; an area in which social relations are mere replications of those laid down by capitalist systems of production, consumption and exchange values rather than use values. Thus the authors of a recent book are able to assert that 'there is no social agency within leisure' (Critcher and Clarke, 1985) (and presumably individual agency is also unlikely).

If this were a *complete* description there would be little point in attempting to deal with parallels or links between leisure and the informal economy. The worlds would not be separable in the first place and the nature of leisure discourse would be determined solely as a subset of broader socio-economic discourse. In terms of many aspects of leisure – professionalised sport, for example – we would not question the need to place leisure debate in such a context. We do,

150

however, question the completeness of the basic description of the world of leisure, and would suggest that it misses out what is arguably the 'largest' (a sloppy word we will illustrate more fully later) area of current leisure activity. For want of a better phrse we will call this area 'communal leisure' but it is more commonly thought of as the 'voluntary sector'. Perhaps it is no coincidence that this area is left out of much leisure debate because examination of the world of netball clubs, lapidary societies, drama groups and so forth makes it far less easy to assert the dominance of established capitalist modes of production, consumption, exchange, use of 'labour' and so forth.

By focusing on this gigantic area of mostly unrecorded and unvalued activity, we will in particular be arguing that one can gain important insights into the developing area of the 'informal economy' and even begin to see some ways forward for new forms of emancipatory work. We will be arguing that the leisure world is not at the moment totally dominated by passive consumerism; that there are – even in economic terms – more notions of 'value' than is often argued, that there is a major and unrecognised social dimension to much leisure activity, which demands new modes of 'economic' thinking and that we can see in small-scale communal leisure organisation a reassertion of crucial aspects of 'first nature'.

The chapter will begin by describing those areas of leisure activity which offer insights into new (or are they old?) forms of social organisation for the production of goods and services. Its prime emphasis will be on small 'voluntary' groups but we should make it very clear that these are not the exclusive venue for such forms of exchange. The core of this description and analysis will be taken from a large research project on 'The Operation of the Voluntary Sector in Leisure' for the Joint Committee of the Sports Council and Economic and Social Research Council (Hoggett and Bishop, 1985); one of a series of innovatory social science projects in the leisure area. Despite the project being 'large' it was perhaps the first to look at and even expose what we have already described as a gigantic area of activity and is therefore still relatively small and partial. The second part of the chapter will consider various definitions and dimensions of the 'informal economy', seeking to relate these to the world of communal leisure. The chapter then ends with some possible implications of pulling together themes from our two worlds, hinting particularly at the delicate balance between emancipation and entrapment, inevitable if one is to attempt to build from those beginnings we will have described.

COMMUNAL LEISURE (AND THE INFORMAL ECONOMY)

Ask a local authority leisure worker to suggest what is meant by the 'voluntary sector in leisure' and one is likely to receive an answer which covers some mixture of the following:

Scouts, football clubs, drama groups, mums and toddlers groups, pensioners circles, art societies, youth clubs, photographic societies, swimming clubs (and so on).

Clearly, some of these activities can only be undertaken communally (say, drama or a netball match), while others (for example, painting or photography) can equally well be undertaken by individuals at home, and others by small casual groups (such as two friends playing squash). In our work we were astonished at the number of essentially individual activities around which groups and clubs formed and soon realised that the reason for such collectivisation is not simply necessity (for the activity itself). In trying to make sense of this diversity we first suggested some divisions by activity. Thus there are *single activity groups* (badminton, clocks, gardening) and *multi-activity groups* (in which the group undertakes perhaps a walk one week, bingo the next, and listens to a talk the week after). Within the single activities we then suggested four categories of *sports, arts, crafts and hobbies* although boundaries (for example, those of ice-dancing or photography) are often unclear. Within multi-activity groups there are some dealing with a specific *client group* (women, young people, the elderly) and others based around a particular *geographical* community (community associations, for example). Such surface classifications will, however, become rather peripheral as we begin to penetrate deeper into purpose and structures. Before doing so, let us consider the scale and extent of communal leisure.

Our study focused on two geographical areas – one a suburban swathe of East Bristol and the other a centre-to-periphery segment of Leicester (mainly including more deprived neighbourhoods). When we had to curtail our detective work in East Bristol we had a list of over 300 groups and yet were aware of many others (such as pub skittles leagues) not contacted. Establishing average memberships is extremely difficult, but we could suggest that there are perhaps 25 000 to 28 000 people in Kingswood (the East Bristol district) who are members of at least one leisure group. That is from a total population of 88 000. We suspect that such figures represent one end of a spectrum of which Leicester is perhaps more typical. Here we found far fewer groups, and many of those were extremely new, formed during (and as a result of) the Urban Programme interventions. Nevertheless we estimated, to take just one example, that many more people are playing football in Leicestershire on a winter Saturday than would ever go to see the professional Leicester City club play. The scale is immense and traditionally uncounted. At the simplest possible level, if one were to put some form of economic value (as per the paid housework example) on all such leisure activity, the sums involved would dwarf all other direct, formal economy contributions.

In our attempts to come to terms with such a huge and diverse area of communal activity, we found ourselves forced – if somewhat reluctantly – to consider what features the myriad groups have in common and which might distinguish them from (a) other areas of leisure activity and (b) other parts of voluntary action. Despite that reluctance (shaped by a concern about cataloguing together many groups which consider themselves to be virtually on different planets to others), we consider that there are several key common features. We would argue that these groups are 'Collectivities which are self-organised, productive and, by and large, consume their own products' (Bishop and Hoggett, 1986).

Notice first that this definition excludes any mention of leisure. We are assuming that 'leisure' says something about the meaning and quality of people's experience of some activity (although even that word 'activity' has connotations of a rather functional concept of activism). Thus a canal restoration society, for whom the activity is sheer hard work (to most people) is in their own terms a leisure group and somebody spending twenty hours a week administering a swimming club – but never smimming – can also be indulging in leisure.

Here then is our first potential insight into the informal economy because we are suggesting that there are no easy boundaries between work and leisure defined by the nature of the activity itself. The canal example and the light engineering 'work' of a railway preservation society, or even the gardening society accounts done as leisure by someone who works professionally as an accountant, all show that we cannot construe a top-down economic model to which leisure activities are mere anecdotal additions at the very bottom of the scale. We could also point to recent examples of people for whom (for example) silk-screen printing started as a hobby but who now (perhaps since redundancy but just as often out of choice) run a small shop, printing T-shirts.

Returning to the core of our definition, we will avoid elaboration of terms such as 'collectivity' and 'self-organised' and move to the more important and superficially more surprising use of the terms 'production', 'consumption' and 'product'. At the more obvious end a play is often termed a production, beekeepers produce pots of honey, gardeners produce plants and vegetables and dressmakers produce clothes. While such direct physical products are easy to conceive, we would also argue that an orchestra recital, some folk dances, a brass band concert, a photographic exhibition or collections of stamps are distinctive products. Surely it is not then fanciful to consider a hockey match, an aerobics display, a chess tournament, a caving convention and so forth as a form of 'product' for their groups?

With many of the latter activities (especially sports) it is only in their professionalised or semi-professionalised stream that clear and marketable products are available as outputs; a small cricket club would not dream of charging its few supporters to watch the match. To relate this again to the informal economy, there are a number of 'products' of strictly amateur groups for which money changes hands. Products or produce may be sold by fishermen, beekeepers, lapidarists, gardeners, wine-makers, philatelists, photographers, metal-detector users, numismatists, clock collectors (and many other collectors), artists (pictures, sculpture, etc.), lacemakers, upholsterers, and so on. And this exchange is not the preserve of collectivised activity – it may happen just as much as a result of individual endeavour. Group membership does, however, allow the exchange of expertise (say, on growing leeks), wider opportunities to market products (such as the annual show) as well as enabling expensive equipment (perhaps a gem tumbler) to be made available, or ordinary materials (like jars and labels for honey) to be acquired at bulk discount prices.

Many groups also provide opportunities for people to see – and pay for – their products through a variety of types of performance or display. Tickets will be sold for a play, a marching band may charge a fee, a railway preservation society charges admission to its stations or for rides and the Morris dancers pass around the hat.

It is important to notice that we have now blurred part of our own definition by describing a range of circumstances in which groups would appear to be producing for consumption by others. This was done to explore the boundary with the informal economy but we would now reassert two key points. Firstly that such monetary exchange is the exception rather than the rule for leisure groups, and secondly that the status and meaning even of such blatantly economic activity makes it of secondary or minor significance in comparison to other dimensions of a group's life.

Drama offers a good example because it is intrinsically about performance and cannot therefore be about self-consumption; or can it? In our contacts with drama groups we noticed that all the preparation tasks – rehearsals, costumes, lighting, sets, and so on – were clearly immensely valuable activities for those groups in their own right, rather than just as means to the end production. We also noticed that most amateur drama groups do, in a manner of speaking, perform to themselves because the majority of any audience is invariably made up of friends, relatives and neighbours – 'people like us' rather than outsiders. The charges made for performance can therefore be seen to be no more than a way of making the important activities happen rather than a transfer of a product – mediated through money – from the group to others.

The same appeared to be true for photographic societies or gardening clubs in that any sales of products/produce was a fortuitous by-product of an exhibition or show rather than being in any way its *raison d'être*. Clearly, however, there are again some delicate boundaries. A photographic society in which its members suddenly found themselves unemployed might be tempted to sustain its existence by deliberately exhibiting to sell, or a beekeepers' group might be tempted by public admiration for their honey to start packaging and promoting it 'properly'. More commonly such shifts are unconsciously resisted and the monetary element remains no more than a group of equivalent of 'pocket money work' (Handy, 1984).

What we are arguing is that, despite the occasional exchange of goods and services for cash, the main purpose of any group is to produce something for its own members. We can take this further – and again with relevance to the informal economy – by suggesting that it is essential to take a far broader concept of the notion of product than is often the case in economically determined discourse. In the drama example we would argue not only that the final peformance is a product but also that the many social occasions during which it was assembled can also be considered as a type of 'product'. To complete this argument we consider that a group itself – its character, identity, shape, tensions and dynamic – is at least as important a 'product' to the members as any external output of its prime activity (Kropotkin, 1976).

While it may be an exaggeration to suggest that a Naturalists Society is really no more than an exuse for a group of people to come together socially, we would assert that the balance between internal and external justifications is very different to that of most units of capitalist production. In most industry the pressure to create the product has effectively destroyed the potential for social exchange and solidarisation at and through the workplace. Membership of a leisure group is both an end in itself (the social dimension) as well as a means to an end (playing lacrosse, etc.), yet the domination of discourse by economic patterns and language is so strong that people do indeed almost have to invent functional, activity-based 'excuses' simply to come together.

Groups such as those we have described offer a unique opportunity in our society. They offer a mutual-aid model of production for self-consumption, and do so in a way which celebrates and values the organisation and existence of the group itself as an independent object. They offer people a place to 'be someone' rather than just a place to 'do something'; an attribute often ignored but essential to any development of debate about the informal economy (Robertson, 1986).

THE INFORMAL ECONOMY (AND LEISURE)

During the last few years the informal economy seems to have been going through something of a rediscovery. Academics and politicians, conservatives and socialists are talking about it, and a number of wild and extravagant claims are being made on its behalf. For some, the existence of a large, organised informal economy is proof that the impact of unemployment and recession has not been as devastating as has been thought – people have used their natural entrepreneurial instincts to find ways of 'making out', even if these ways have been slightly illicit. For others the boom within the informal economy is an indication of the further degradation of work – the marginalisation of a sector of the workforce, particularly women, youth and ethnic minorities, into insecure, unregulated 'sweated' jobs. Yet others interpret this development in a quite different way, as heralding the inauguration of a post-industrial leisured society where people work less and play more.

What then do we mean by the informal economy and how does it relate to leisure? Are there grounds for believing that this sphere of human activity is becoming increasingly important as the formal world of work goes through some kind of crisis? As a starting point we try to encapsulate some of the main components of the informal economy within Table 8.1.

Table 8.1. The unrecognised economy

	Circulation of goods and services within the formal economy	Circulation of goods and services within the community	Circulation of goods and services within the household
	The Unregulated Economy		
Relationships mediated by exchange-values	1. Home/outworking 2. Sub-contracting 3. Cottage industry 4. The black economy		
		The Communal Economy	The Household Economy
Relationships mediated by use values		1. Pocket-money work 2. Mutual aid (including communal leisure) 3. Informal care, volunteering 4. Barter, particularly of skills	1. Housework 2. Self-servicing 3. Home-based enthusiasms

In Table 8.1 a number of distinctions are made which require some explanation. Firstly it is possible to think in terms of three sites in which goods and services are informally produced, exchanged and consumed – entirely within the household, outside of households but within the community and outside of household and community. Secondly, we can distinguish between two forms of exchange relationship, and hence between two different forms of production and consumption. Where production is primarily a means to an end, the end being money or profit, we can talk of the production of exchange values (the value of the product lies only in what can be got for it). Where production occurs primarily because it is intrinsically valuable or useful to the producer herself or assumes the form of a gift for others to enjoy and benefit from, then we can talk of the production of use values. A woman who knits mohair jumpers for herself or for friends and relatives is engaged in use-value production, a woman who does this in order to sell to the anonymous 'other' of the market is engaged in the production of exchange values. The distinction between the two forms of exchange relationship is not hard and fast. Use-value production can lead to monetary gain – a friend may pay the woman for the jumper produced – but the monetary transaction is subordinate to and contained within the existing social relationship and not the other way around.

We can elaborate the three main headings of the diagram as follows: *The unregulated economy* Activity within this sector is very akin to the formal economy, the main difference being that it is unregulated. The use of lump labour by large building firms is a classic example of the sub-contractual form. Another important and, as we shall see, perhaps rapidly growing area is 'out-working' (Hakim, 1984; Huws, 1984). Here large companies totally decentralise elements of subcomponent production into small sweat shops or into workers' homes. Within such companies the production process therefore straddles informal and formal sectors, the latter now involved only in the assembly of sub-components produced 'informally' outside the company. Such forms of decentralised production are rapidly becoming the norm in Italy and Japan (F. Murray, 1983; R. Murray, 1985).

In all of the examples above the division of labour is highly extended. This is not the case for 'cottage industry'. Here the worker is much more in control of what he or she produces by virtue of his/her domestic capital or skills – market gardening, catering services (particularly for business), craft production and various forms of personal services related to tourism (from the charter of fishing craft to bed and breakfast) are among the many examples. However, the similarity of this work with out-work lies in the fact that the goods and services produced do not circulate within the local economy of home and community: rather they are produced for consumption by an 'outside other'.

What we call the 'black economy' differs from out-working in that the work involved is typically less fragmented and one is more likely to be working for oneself or a small local firm. The work itself requires less domestic capital and skill than many forms of cottage industry. One of the distinctive features of the black economy, however, is the way in which much of the production and consumption of 'black' goods and services is contained within a locality. The consumers often 'know' the producers, who may be 'friends of friends'. This is quite unlike most forms of out-working and cottage industry. It is the only major form of exchange-value production within the local economy.

The communal economy This refers to the circulation of goods and services within the community and informal local networks largely through direct exchange unmediated by money. The one excepton here is 'pocket-money work' (Handy, 1982) emerging from the pursuit of particular enthusiasms. The gardener who sells surplus produce, the amateur artist or lapidarist who manages to sell a few pieces of work, judges at horticultural shows or fancying shows (caged birds, 'show mice', 'fancy rats', etc.), 'callers' at square-dancing evenings, and so on. Here the individual enthusiasts, through the skills that they have acquired, sell their products or skills to friends, relatives and workmates, typically ploughing the money gained, back into their enthusiasm. Such activity is often a stepping-stone into cottage industry, and hence from leisure into self-employment.

Forms of mutual aid are an important element of the informal communal economy. Here people consume the goods and services that they have collectively produced. With one exception, forms of mutual aid are now comparatively scarce in Britain though elsewhere, particularly in under- or partially-developed societies, these traditions are still strong. One interesting example is the phenomenon of self-build housing in southern Italy. In some of the most advanced industrial countries, particularly Germany and Sweden, patterns of mutual aid have undergone something of a revival with the development of housing, retail and distribution co-ops.

There is, however, one form of mutual aid which is very widespread in Britain and, with the possible exception of Holland, has no real parallel in the rest of Europe. This is the realm of self-organised leisure, of clubs and societies devoted to sport, the arts, crafts and hobbies that we described in detail at the beginning of this chapter.
The household economy Many goods and services are produced and consumed within the home itself. The boundary between necessary and chosen activity here is very tenuous. Many recent commentators (Gershuny and Miles, 1983) have pointed to the impact of domestic capital goods upon the household economy. According to these writers, a new generation of goods are becoming available which provide households with their own means of production, releasing them from dependence upon the tertiary sector of the economy for the provision of services – washing machines, electric drills and saws, hydraulic jacks, etc. enable families to become more self-servicing. It is useful to distinguish between domestic capital goods which are essentially means of production and others, such as videos or hi-fi, which are essentially means of consumption. Illich's (1973) distinction between 'programmed' and 'convivial' tools is also useful here. A programmed tool essentially places its user in the position of dependence and passivity – in a sense one is oneself consumed by the machine just as the worker is consumed by the means of production

within the factory. The programmed tool itself provides, at the most, very limited possibilities for the realisation of the user's skill and imagination. The convivial possibilities inherent in many household machines can often only be realised when the user has acquired appropriate skill – for many families home computers are just another programmed tool, a self-service space-invader arcade; for others, however, they can become means of self-development.

Whilst some domestic capital goods are used primarily as a means of performing necessary household tasks, others are also means of leisure production. The sphere of family leisure is a very 'grey' area, incorporating both necessary and discretionary labour. Thus domestic capital goods like food processors are used both for necessary chores and creative cookery whereas washing machines (to our knowledge) have no leisure uses.

There may be grounds for extending Gershuny and Miles' (1983) concept of domestic capital goods so that it includes items which are clearly leisure goods. The impact of technological innovation and diffusion upon leisure activity has gone largely unresearched. This is a great pity, as a cursory glance at the area indicates the mushrooming of completely new enthusiasms based upon technologically advanced goods (hang-gliding, video, home computing, electronics . . .) or the development of élite pursuits into mass pursuits as technological advances cheapen the cost of leisure activities (the Mirror class of sailing dinghy is a classic example). To some extent we feel a parallel development is occurring in the sphere of leisure to self-servicing within the home. The huge expansion in the production of leisure equipment has meant that more and more people have the means to 'do' leisure rather than consume leisure services provided by others. More and more people are doing painting, silk screen printing, photographic development, picture framing, sound-mixing (the list is endless) because the means of doing these things now appear to be within the reach of the average family.

THE INFORMAL AS AN UNRECOGNISED ECONOMY

Having described some of the main elements of the informal economy and illustrated the manner in which it assumes three quite distinct forms, is it possible to give a sharper definition to the informal economy than one which simply sees it as the underbelly of the formal one? The very possibility of conceptualising an economy differentiated into formal and informal sectors is relatively recent (Lozano, 1983). Nineteenth-century capitalism, for instance, did not permit such a distinction. It contained a much greater degree of direct subsistence production, exchange of goods for money as immediate equivalent of value (that is, no surplus value), informal exchange of useful services, barter, non-contractual wage employment and cottage industry. One of the distinctive features of industrial capitalism is therefore the way in which it gathered up production and tore it out of the texture of home and community. It is probably also true to say that the emergence of a formal 'world of work' provided the counterpoint to the development of a formal 'world of leisure'; before this point recreative activity was much more an integral part of informal everyday life than a separate and discrete sphere to which one could ascribe the term 'leisure'.

The simplest definition of the informal economy is probably one that centres upon whether an economic activity is regulated by the state or not. For example, enterprises where wage levels are unrelated to the official minimum, where there is no social or health and safety protection could be defined as unregulated and hence informal. A further defining element is the enumeration of economic activity, and its appearance in national accounts. Work that should be, but is not, declared or is only partially declared, would therefore be defined as an informal sector activity.

The problem with such definitions is that they exclude work that is unpaid but which is nevertheless work, that is, performed out of necessity. In other words, housework is excluded by such definitions, not just the work of cooking, cleaning and child care, but also of home maintenance, the production of items of food and clothing, etc. All of this work could be performed by paid workers from the formal economy; indeed some privileged households do employ maids, nannies, gardeners, handymen, and so on to perform it.

This sector of economic activity, often referred to as the domestic or household economy, is clearly vast and, although it refers primarily to work undertaken by women it also includes traditional forms of male activity (such as DIY). Because our society only tends to value activities which are paid or create capital, housework has been traditionally undervalued. This has led some feminists to argue for 'wages for housework' as a way of giving status back to women's work. But the problem surely is to create a society where 'value' has become liberated from monetary equivalence (exchange value) and not to try and give all human activity commodity value.

An examination of housework is therefore useful as it enables us to see how many activities within the informal economy have been given only limited and marginal value. As Handy notes:

> the home, it is estimated, uses, in aggregate, half as much labour as the whole of the formal economy, not just in cooking and cleaning, but principally in the care of the young, the old and the infirm. Transferred to the state, or to private concerns, these services would cost billions and would, incidentally, magnificently boost the official wealth of the nation. (Handy, 1984)

The idea that 'the only valid measure of wealth is the exchange-value of goods and services produced for exchange' (Boddington, George, Michaelson, 1979) has become quite shrilly proclaimed by monetarism throughout the world. In Britain this attitude has obtained quite sacred connotations. But if the 'wealth creators' have become blessed we are also left in no doubt that these good souls are the entrepreneurs and businessmen who 'put money to work' rather than the women who look after their dependent relatives, the organisers of local horticultural societies, the 'good neighbours' or amateur aquarists who may have acquired a national reputation for breeding discus fish or large guppies. All of these latter activities do not really count in the estimation of a nation's wealth. We might feel justified then in suggesting that a stronger definition of 'informal' than the terms 'unregulated' or 'unpaid' would be to use the term 'unrecognised'. This is particularly useful given the double meaning of 'unrecognised' – it includes activities which are unseen (for instance, the unregulated black economy) and undervalued (such as housework, volunteering and so on).

As we have just hinted, there is indeed a huge realm of activity which is valuable, that is, which creates value, but which under capitalism goes unrecognised. Indeed classical Marxism has always accepted the existence of a source of value in human activity above and beyond the exchange value of the product of the activity itself. This alternative source of value lies not in terms of how much money can be made from the activity but rather in terms of how useful that activity is in meeting one's own or others' needs. From this perspective a missile which can be sold for millions of pounds is less valuable than the hours a neighbour might spend with a bereaved pensioner – the missile *creates* no use-value whatsover.

From this angle, then, the rediscovery of the informal economy is

equivalent to the rediscovery of a different and unrecognised world of
value from that of the commodity market place. As such it becomes
part of a critique of contemporary capitalism and its particularistic
allocation of value to human behaviour. To cite Gorz, one of the
leading exponents of this anti-capitalist critique:

> Only with capitalism does work, or the heteronomous production of
> exchange values, become a full time activity, and the self-supply of
> goods and services (by the family or community) become a marginal
> and subordinate activity. (Gorz, 1982)

THE INFORMAL ECONOMY: PATHWAY TO IMMISERA-
TION OR EMANCIPATION?

All of this brings us into an important contemporary debate. Whilst
most contemporary research suggests that the informal economy is
growing, two quite contradictory accounts have developed of the
social and political implications of this growth. One analysis sees the
expansion of the informal economy as taking us towards some kind of
dystopia. This 'dual society' thesis (Gordon, Edwards and Reich,
1982) perceives the growth of the informal economy ('informalisation'
as some writers have termed it (Miles, 1985)), as an expression of a
fundamental fissure emerging within the labour market of advanced
capitalism between 'core' and 'peripheral' jobs. This tendency has
been exacerbated by developments in new technology which have
accentuated the deskilling process. As a consequence a shrinking
number of core jobs are established concerned with design,
operational research, marketing, production control and sub-
component assembly, requiring relatively high skill-requirements and
providing reasonable job security, wages and conditions. At the same
time much of the labour process becomes decentralised outside the
parent company altogether and is conducted by separate small firms
engaged in cut-throat competition for the sub-component crumbs
which fall from the parent company's table. Many of those small firms
are themselves no more than boss-agents for networks of home
workers. Such peripheral jobs demand low skill-levels and unsurpri-
singly job security, wages, conditions and unionisation are all poor.
As Mattera comments,

This decentralisation of production occurred most dramatically in Italy, but the same process gradually appeared in the US, Britain and other advanced countries as well . . . As many as a third of the vehicles sold with Toyota and Nissan labels have at times been manufactured in large part by employees of other, smaller firms. (Mattera, 1985, p. 32)

From this perspective the growth of the informal economy is equivalent to the growth of immiseration, not to the emergence of a 'leisure society'. This argument is reinforced by recent research on household time and expenditure budgets in the UK, which suggests that ownership of domestic capital goods is very much dependent upon one's position within the labour market – those who are unemployed are least likely to possess tools and equipment which could enable them to enter informal work or leisure (Miles, 1983; Glyptis and MacInness, 1987). The prospect emerges then of a new basis of inequality 'between information-rich and information-poor people' (Miles, 1985).

We should, however, be wary of overgeneralisation, because research also points to considerable national and regional variations. Pahl's (1984) study of the Isle of Sheppey suggests that individuals with most access to the informal economy are those with most access to the formal economy – the latter provides the cash, the skills, the materials and the contacts for workers to involve themselves in the former. At the same time, some evidence from Italy appears to point to quite different conclusions. If we take Mingione's (1977) research on the petrochemical industry in Syracuse, his more recent research in Messina and Reggio Calabria (1985), or the research of Cetro on the automobile industry in Pomigliano D'Arco (1977), all of this appears to suggest that those Italian households with jobs within the formal economy have virtually no involvement in the informal economy.

Yet there is also considerable evidence to suggest that the informal economy within Italy is not an homogeneous phenomenon. Vinay's (1985) research on the informal economy in central Italy was based on a sample of households which had one key attribute in common – the households nearly all had some access to land, a smallholding or a large garden or something of that proportion. In other words her research was based upon the informal economy in predominantly agricultural areas. Her sample was based on 'non-agricultural families', 40 per cent of which nevertheless had a large kitchen garden, and over 20 per cent of which were involved in poultry-breeding and other forms of husbandry. Not only was access to land important but the presence of an extended family and kinship network was also paramount in the ability of these families to extend and enlarge the pool of labour available for informal work. As Vinay noted,

The families we have studied appear to be highly adequate to face economic crises and unemployment in the formal economy because of the persistence in the area studied, of extended families and of wide kinship ties, the wide range of skills required by their members – through the traditional socialisation of the family labour force to a wide variety of work tasks. The strong ties with the land which constitute both the component of the family budget and a refuge in times of crisis, the diffusion of home ownership commonly, and finally, the deep roots these families have in the local community and in the local culture, these communities being often relatively small, with little immigration or emigration, and with strong social networks.

However, whilst Vinay remarks that the families in her sample were undoubtedly more able to cope with unemployment than other families which perhaps lacked such skills and resources, the very success of such household survival strategies perhaps contributed conservatively to issues of social change in southern Italy. Thus there is a strong feeling that the informal sector is both a survival strategy and a potential trap to households in Italy.

Such national and regional variations should make us cautious of any analysis which appears sweepingly deterministic. We should be wary of those who write as if they were bearing witness to the emergence of some new and inexorable trend. Not only do such forms of argument ignore particular conditions; more importantly they fail to consider the role of human choice or political struggle in determining the outcome of such mutations.

In this context the writings of Andre Gorz provide a welcome antidote to some of the more structuralist theories. Gorz (1982, 1985) is probably the most noted advocate of the 'informal economy as emancipation' thesis. For Gorz the key impact of the current technological revolution is not so much the decentralisation of production and the creation of a dual economy but the displacement of labour by automated machinery and the diffusion of domestic capital goods enabling the self-supply of goods and services (1982, p. 84). As far as Gorz is concerned automation forces us (and particularly the

Labour movement) to choose between an equitable distribution of the labour time which is available (through reducing overtime, struggling for a shorter working week, promoting job sharing, etc.) and collusion with the dual labour market strategy in which a privileged, unionised labour aristocracy continues to work more than 45 hours a week while the rest of us (the 'neo-proletariat') are unemployed or scratch about in the informal economy. For Gorz the choice is clear: only by fighting for the former can we avoid the aggravation of social inequalities and divisions within the working class. Moreover, whereas unemployment yields 'empty time' – time without end, time without rhythm or punctuation, time without the material means (skills, tools, etc.) to put it to use – the redistribution of work could provide us all with more 'free time', that is, time which could free us for productive leisure without incapacitating us. Gorz therefore envisages an expanding realm of human autonomy alongside a shrinking sphere of increasingly automated heteronomous production (necessary mass production of those goods and services necessary for a 'viable society' and the creation of convivial tools). He sketches a future in which the informal economy is massively expanded as people make use of free time and accessible convivial tools. As he notes,

> the priority task of a post industrial left must therefore be to extend self motivated, self rewarding activity within, and above all, outside the family . . . (1985, 87).

One of the problems for Gorz is his penchant for florid language and the provocative turn of phrase. Does he really mean that the period of industrialisation is over? And when he says 'automation, therefore, takes us beyond capitalism and socialism' (1985, p. 32) does he mean us to take him seriously? The problem is that whereas some of the proponents of the 'dual economy' theory write as if such changes have gradually caught up on us, Gorz often writes in the quasi-apocalyptic style of the sudden, unprecedented rupture. What we require is a way of conceptualising the development of industrial capitalism which stresses the discontinuities of non-incrementalism of its trajectory whilst also acknowledging its propensity for equilibrium.

The search for such a model could lead to a series of developing ideas framed around the concept of long wave theory in which it is argued that economic restructuring, far from being unprecedented, has in fact several precedents. From amongst the many variants of this theory, (such as Mandel 1980, Freeman, Clark and Soete 1982,

Mensch 1979), one can elicit ways of interpreting the interplay of technology, economy and culture which enable us to place current upheavals and crises in a proper historical setting.

A general consensus seems to be emerging (e.g. Aglietta, 1979) that we are currently at the crisis-ridden end of a long wave of economic development in which mass consumption and production were regulated strongly by the state. It is also argued that further economic and technological development requires changes within the socio-institutional framework, but that this is not always a matter of the cultural and social being dragged into line behind the economic. As Miles notes,

> Ways of life are themselves dynamic elements in the process of socio-economic change . . . it is not so much a question of cultural lag, with social changes following on the needs of production, but one of a web of interdependant changes in formal and informal production; changes which effect and interact with each other so as to shape the development of the whole system. (1985)

Long wave theory would lead us to suggest a number of alternative scenarios for that wave which follows the end of the current state-regulated period. The full automation scenario points towards a permanently enlarged reservoir of technological unemployment while another points to a massive movement of labour into the 'low-tech' areas of the service sector. Gorz's scenario of a hugely reduced working week would fit here, countered with another possibility of dramatic decentralisation of productive processes, as computers enable processes to be moved away geographically whilst still retaining a crucial degree of central control. The related aspects of worker exploitation or worker control, social and cultural change, remain impossible to predict, being a matter for political choice and struggle rather than sociological stargazing.

IMPLICATIONS

We have argued that the benefit of the concept of the 'unrecognised economy' is that it challenges prevailing notions of value and usefulness. Individual, family and communal leisure, in its productive rather than consumerist form, along with housework, informal care and neighbourliness, volunteering, mutual aid and community action are all aspects of this unrecognised economy. It is vast in its proportions and, excluding a few alienated souls, remains the chief source of value for all of us throughout our lives. Yet the wealth of nations is never measured against the richness of its everyday life.

We have also tried to demonstrate that the creation of the formal world of work and the commodification of value is only a quite recent phenomenon. As such it is the equivalent to a 'second nature' that we have acquired and which stands in opposition to, yet feeds upon, the tensions and weaknesses within a perhaps more significant, and certainly lost, 'first nature'. It is in part lost because we have no language for it and, because our only available language is economically determined, it is that much more difficult to reassert. We ourselves have been forced to use words such as 'product' when describing the identity and sense, value and meaning of a leisure group and have fallen into the trap of defining groups in terms of their activities rather than forms of relationship.

In searching for the roots of any change to such dramatic imbalance, we have argued caution about any theorisation which suggests that civil society and culture are some kind of secondary superstructure having no power over the economic and technological spheres. While technological change plays a major role, to see everyday life as 'first nature' enables us to move decisively from deterministic theories of social change in which the sphere of civil society is, at best, noted through presence of 'cultural lag'. Social relations are not infinitely malleable and wherever one looks for the unrecognised economy, including the communal black economy, it is thriving – even in Russia (Mattera, 1985), where the utmost effort has been taken to regulate and formalise all aspects of life.

Gorz understands this realm of life as first nature when he says:

> The sphere of individual sovereignty is not based on a mere desire to consume . . . it is based more profoundly on activities . . . which are in themselves communication, giving, creating and aesthetic enjoyment, the production and reproduction of life, tenderness, the realisation of physical, sensuous and intellectual capacities, the creation of non-commodity use values (shared goods and services). (1983)

It may be that our arguments are already too late; that the world of 'leisure' has been colonialised so fully that the very term is now almost synonymous with a productivist and economically determined form of consumerism. What then of the numerous groups and individuals to whom we spoke during our research and that we now know to be creating in the manner Gorz describes? If the term has already been colonialised, how long before the activities, groups and individuals give up the uneven fight to retain a precious autonomy?

Within all the clubs and societies we have studied, even the most 'professional' and competitive, an equilibrium between doing and being, between activity and sociability and between individual and group aspirations, was vital for their continued existence. This merely reflects the basic fact that, as human beings, we are social and that it is through socialisation that our creative and productive capacities are most fully developed (Winnicott 1985). By arguing that such areas of creative and productive social exchange have much to tell us about the informal economy now, and in suggesting that they may offer us clues towards a reformulation of broader economic and cultural structures in the future, are we in danger of damaging that precious though limited area of autonomy?

References

Articles
Cetro, R. (1977) 'Lavoro A Domicilio A Pomigliano d'Arco', *Inchiesta*, 33.
Hakim, C. (1984) 'Homework and Outwork', *Employment Gazette*, (January).
Huws, U. (1984) 'New Technology Homeworkers', *Employment Gazette* (Janaury).
Lozano, B. (1983) 'Informal Sector Workers: Walking Out The System's Front Door', *International Journal of Urban and Regional Research*, 7, 3.
Miles, I. (1985) 'The New Post-Industrial State', *Futures*, 17, 6.
Murray, F. (1983) 'The Decentralisation of Production: The Decline of the Mass Collective Worker', *Capital and Class*, 19.
Murray, R. (1985) 'Benett on Britain: The New Economic Order', *Marxism Today*, (November).
Vinay, P. (1985) 'Family Life Cycle and the Informal Economy in Central Italy', *International Journal of Urban and Regional Research*, 9, 1.

Books
Aglietta, M. (1979) *A Theory of Capitalist Regulation: The US Experience*, London, New Left Books.
Bishop, J. and Hoggett, P. (1987) *Organising Around Enthusiasms: Mutual Aid in Leisure*, London, Comedia.

Boddington, S., George, M. and Michaelson, J. (1979) *Developing the Socially Useful Economy*, London, Macmillan.
Critcher, C. and Clarke, J. (1985) *The Devil Makes Work: Leisure in Capitalist Britain*, London, Macmillan.
Dumazadier, J. (1978) *The Sociology of Leisure*, Amsterdam, Elsevier.
Freeman, C., Clark, J. and Soete, L. (1982) *Unemployment and Technical Innovations: A Study of Long Waves and Economic Development*, London, Pinter.
Gershuny, J. and Miles, I. (1983) *The New Service Economy*, London, Pinter.
Gordon, D., Edwards, R. and Reich, M. (1982) *Segmented Work, Divided Workers*, Cambridge, Cambridge University Press.
Gorz, A. (1982) *Farewell to the Working Class*, London, Pluto.
Gorz, A. *Paths to Paradise*, London, Pluto.
Glyptis, S. and MacInnes, H. (1987) *Leisure and the Home*, London, ESRC/Sports Council.
Handy, C. (1982) *The Informal Economy*, ARVAC Pamphlet No. 3.
Handy, C. (1984) *The Future of Work*, Oxford, Blackwell.
Hoggett, P. and Bishop, J. (1985) *The Social Organisation of Leisure: A Study of Groups in their Voluntary Sector Context*, London, Sports Council/ESRC.
Illich, I. *Tools for Conviviality*, London, Calder & Boyars.
Kropotkin, P. (repr. 1976) *Mutual Aid*, New York, Porter Sargent.
Mandel, E. (1980) *Long Waves of Capitalist Development*, Cambridge Cambridge University Press.
Mattera, P. (1985) *Off the Books: The Rise of the Undergound Economy*, London, Pluto.
Mensch, G. (1979) *Stalemate in Technology*, Cambridge, Mass., Ballinger.
Miles, I. (1983) *Adaptation to Unemployment*, SPRU Occasional Paper No. 20, Brighton, Falmer.
Mingione, E. (ed.) (1977) *Ricerca Sociologica sui Polidi Suiluppo Industriale nel mendione*, Rome, mimeo.
Pahl, R. *Divisions of Labour*, Oxford, Blackwell.
Parker, S. (1976) *The Sociology of Leisure*, London, Allen & Unwin.
Roberts, K. (1978) *Contemporary Society and the Growth of Leisure*, London, Longman.
Rojek, C. (1985) *Capitalism and Leisure Theory*, London, Tavistock.
Winnicott, D. (1985) *Playing and Reality*, Harmondsworth, Penguin.

Chapters
Mingione, E. (1985) 'Social Reproduction of the Surplus Labour Force: The Case of Southern Italy', in N. Redclift and E. Mingione (eds) *Beyond Employment*, Oxford, Blackwell.
Robertson, J. (1986) 'What Comes After Full Employment', in P. Ekins (ed.) *The Living Economy*, London, Routledge & Kegan Paul.

9　Drugs and Leisure, Prohibition and Pleasure: From Subculture to the Drugalogue[1]

Nicholas Dorn and Nigel South

This is not an essay about *all* drugs, legal and illegal, nor about whether the use of drugs is an activity best characterised as a leisure activity, or about whether drug-use gives rise to pleasure or problems. Instead we offer a brief review of some of the existing sociological literature (almost entirely from outside the 'leisure studies' field) which touches upon the use of illegal drugs in relation to leisure or wider lifestyles. We then move on to a broadening of our subject matter which introduces additional perspectives and issues in a way which we hope will challenge prevalent narrow thinking about drug-use and recreational practices. Thus while drug-use is a common and regular activity for many people today[2] this is significant, not only for the users, but also for their families and friends (and many others who may be involved in responding to any resulting problems).[3]

The paper focuses then on illegal drugs and, in its main sections, on the central life preoccupations that can arise for people following the heavy involvement of a family member in the use of heroin. In examining the broader impact of heroin (and other drug) use we seek to raise issues about family life, the public and private spheres of our everyday worlds, and about gender, power and other social relations. Drawing out such issues brings into question conventional analytical as well as commonsense categories of, for example, leisure and labour. The theoretically discrete nature of such categories makes little sense in practice when applied to the ways in which discourses about drug-use and drug-related problems can become a form of recreation and self-development for people engaged in what is termed here, the drugalogue.

DRUGS, LEISURE AND LABOUR IN THE LITERATURE ON THE SOCIOLOGY OF DEVIANCE AND YOUTH CULTURES

Today's concern and debate about drugs principally revolves around heroin; through the 1960s and 1970s liberal and conservative positions were generally drawn up over the use of so called 'soft' drugs. For some people, the use of marijuana was liberation beyond leisure, subverting the very notion of any need for time to be divided out in such a way. Yet the audience that received Richard Neville's *Playpower* (1970), with such chapter titles as 'Johnny Pot wears gold sandals and a black derby hat' and who saw an alternative culture of freedom and pleasure unfolding must by now be sadly disappointed.

In general, like Neville's and other manifestos of the time, the sociological accounts of drug-use and, importantly, what it represented for participants, focused on it as a deviant activity but one which fulfilled certain ends. In a shift from positivistic and functionalist accounts of drug-use which explained behaviour in terms of 'normlessness', 'mindless implulsive behaviour' or psychopathy (cf. Young, 1973a, 17) a new sociology of deviance developed which placed drug-use within a framework which tried to understand the meanings and values of drug-users, interpreting them as a challenge to conventional values about the work ethic and 'straight' expectations of the responsible, proper, healthy and constructive use of *earned* leisure time.

Where previously drug-users were viewed as retreating or withdrawing into their own privatised space and experience (cf. Cloward and Ohlin, 1960, following Merton, 1957), the new perspectives such as labelling theory began to actually locate drug-users either in the cultures and social contexts that they moved in (Becker, 1963; Finestone, 1964) or else within conceptualisations of the alternative or subterranean value systems (Matza and Sykes, 1961) that they were developing or to which they adhered. Becker's important contributions in *Outsiders* were based on observation and interviews with jazz musicians and others who smoked marijuana. The experience analysed here was emphatically a social one, involving a process of being initiated into use of the drug by others, of learning to enjoy the effects, and of being in a social network that must value secrecy in order to ensure supply of the drugs in the face of social control. Finestone (1964) offered an account of an *alternative* value and status system among lower-class (male) blacks in Chicago, identifying these as an inversion of traditional middle-class American values. The work ethic was spurned and the image of the cool hustler operating in an expressive and hedonistic culture was emphasised. Freedom, voluntarism and 'play' were keynotes.

In the work of Matza (1961) and Matza and Sykes (1961) a scheme of formal and subterranean values was elaborated in which the latter lays stress on what are normally conceived of as leisure activities that should more properly fit into the institutionalised routines of the workaday world. This approach is developed in Young's (1973a) early analysis of middle-class British 'bohemian' youth in which 'use of drugs, sexual excess, lack of planning or deferment of impulse' is related to a 'general subterranean value' of short-term hedonism. According to Young (1973a; 1971) *legal* drugs are 'an adjunct to the conventional balance between formal and subterranean values' and are therefore rejected by the bohemian as under the 'hegemony of the wider culture', whereas marijuana is used, at least in part, because it 'enhances' the subterranean view of society while providing the means of exploration of the psychic self. It is pharmacologically suited to this goal and hence 'fits' the culture (Young, 1971); it is important in terms of accessibility (of what is after all illegal); and it is available 'in the type of area where individuals are likely to reside' (1973a: 27). Interestingly, whereas some of this early work by Young carries an optimistic and almost celebratory tone about aspects of the values and artefacts of the bohemian culture, his analysis of 'The Hippie Solution: an essay in the politics of leisure' (1973b), developed in the same period, has a much more pessimistic flavour in discussing the limitations of the hippy/bohemian alternative subcultures and the contribution to change and personal enhancement of self that drugs could offer. In this vision the hegemony of the dominant culture would inevitably win unless *social structure* as well as individual conscious-ness and interpersonal social relationships could be changed.

Both sociological and various subcultures' own home-grown theories and philosophies had posited the imminent radical transcend-ence of conventional social values following from the widespread recreational use of hallucinogenic drugs. Perhaps it was unsurprising then, that some subsequent commentators came to adopt an almost atheoretical and pluralist perspective on drug-taking – albeit not without some corrective value. Thus Plant in discussing his sample of *Drugtakers in an English Town*, observed that:

The study group was so varied that no single theory adequately explains their behaviour. Most did not seem problematic in terms of the factors examined. *Often, drug taking was simply a leisure activity or a token of idealism.* (1975: 258; emphasis added).

On occasion some of the literature on 'youth cultures' has made reference to drug-use and 'leisure' – although surprisingly rarely. Willis (1978) describes two groups, the motorbike boys and the hippies in his ethnographic study *Profane Culture*. Although other biker groups are reported as having made significant use of drugs (especially in North America) (Thompson, 1970) the motorbike boys in Willis's study 'hated' rather than 'revered' drugs, relying 'directly on the strength and control of their own agency' (p.13). Drugs were seen as 'a threat to the ability to act and make decisions autonomously' (p. 14). Reflecting a theme central to the discussion that we develop later in this paper, the use of drugs was seen as a serious undermining of masculinity:

Tim: They can't be men if they take drugs . . . there must be something wrong with them . . .
Mick: It's the same as beer isn't it. I mean you get a lot of people, they've got to have a drink before they'll bleeding hit anybody. If I couldn't hit anybody without beer or drugs . . . I wouldn't be much. (p. 14)

Among the hippies, however:

there was avid discussion about the effects of various drugs, and great interest taken in their supposed different properties. It was common for drug experiences to be recounted, marked over and analysed at great length. (p. 135)

Again anticipating a central element of the analysis that we shall offer later, Willis draws out how it is more than the use of drugs *per se* which is important to the hippie culture – it is the whole set of practices and discourses around the subject that preoccupies. For the hippies, appreciation of Eastern mysticism and of Western rock music, was facilitated by hallucinogenic drug-use (pp. 143–8). The hippies attitude to heroin was, however, rather more ambivalent – it was not perceived in the same way as a drug that provided an experience that could be 'influenced and moulded'.

Its force demanded respect. Its secret meanings could be the last ones you would know . . . In this sense we see a very clear limitation of cultural meaning set by the pharmacological base of a drug. (151)

Elsewhere in the literature on youth cultures there are scattered references to drug-use – Pearson and Twohig (1976), for example, raise a pharmacological-effects challenge to the 'learning the effects of marijuana' model proposed by Becker (op. cit.) and developed by Auld (1981), and suggest that such commentators 'change their dealers' – but overall, detailed work that might usefully be discussed in relation to 'leisure' is scarce. it should be emphasised that the literature on leisure studies is even less illuminating. To take just one example, a major survey of studies and findings on *Youth and Leisure* by Roberts (1983) mentions drugs on just four pages out of 192, despite acknowledging that:

> pills and joints have . . . become parts of the teenage scene in virtually all corners of the country (Plant, 1975). Glue sniffing is cheaper . . . [and] the majority of young people know about and, if they wish, can purchase illegal drugs. (p. 30)

More recent work, broadly influenced by cultural studies and criminological perspectives, has been stimulated by the emergence of a serious and widespread heroin problem. This has begun to raise a wider range of questions in order to investigate previously neglected social relations that the use of drugs throws into sharp relief. This development has followed not simply from the fact of a rise in heroin-use, but also from the impact of critiques within sociological theory (for example, with regard to the neglect of gender in youth culture studies, McRobbie, 1980; Dorn and South, 1983), and from fundamental changes in social structure with the rise of economic depression and high unemployment in many areas of the country (e.g. Pearson, 1987) (in marked contrast to the 'affluent society' of the 1960s which influenced styles of drug-use then and sociological accounts of it).

Auld *et al.* (1986) refer to the little that is known about young women heroin-users in Britain, and point to the existence of 'specific cultural impediments to use of "heavy" drugs by young women' which 'may both restrict women's drug use and shape it in particular ways' (p. 176).[4] As McRobbie suggests,

> for a complex of reasons, the imaginary solutions which drugs may

offer boys do not have the same attraction for girls. One reason is probably the commonsense wisdom inscribed in most women's consciousness – that boys don't like girls who drink, take speed and so on; that losing control spells danger; and that drinking and taking drugs harms physical appearances' (McRobbie, 1980, p. 46).

Such 'commonsense wisdom' is rooted deep and we highlight it further in a subsequent section of this chapter which draws upon an interview with a group of mothers talking about their perceptions of drug-use and gender-divisions. Auld *et al.* develop some discussion of differentiated gender roles as they are articulated around drug-use in taking up a further suggestion that McRobbie makes, that 'the wasted male junkie can in popular mythology, in novels and films, retain a helpless sexual attraction which places women in the role of potential nurse or social worker' (ibid). As in myth so in life, and Auld *et al.* point to how the occasion of having to 'come off' heroin gives male users an 'emotional lever' to use in their relationships with women (girlfriends, wives, mothers). Familiar role-expectations of women to provide care and emotional (and to some extent financial) support are magnified (Auld *et al.*, op. cit., pp. 176–80). These are themes which are returned to in this chapter.

The recent work of Pearson (1987) makes a contribution to the debate about the difficulty of conceptualising 'leisure' for the unemployed, drawing on fieldwork among young heroin-users in the North of England (Pearson *et al.*, 1986). In an article on 'Social deprivation, unemployment and patterns of heroin use', he points to the necessary commitment to activity, networking and sheer hard work that is required to maintain a lifestyle as a heroin-user (cf. also Auld *et al.*, 1986; Preble and Casey, 1969). Thus whilst heroin-use and the enjoyment of or need for its effects may be construed as a gratification analogous to earned recreation after labour, the practice is in reality so heavily bound up with and framed by other facets of the lifestyle as to make the application of 'leisure' as an analytical category extremely misleading. Understanding of the time-structuring of a heroin-using and *obtaining* lifestyle is obscured by trying to differentiate between leisure and other activities within the context of unemployment and economic depression.

As we have seen, sociological treatments of drug-use and, importantly, of the contexts in which drugs are used, and the experiences interpreted and given meaning, have progressively broadened their focus from a narrow concentration on the pathological or privatised, retreatist individual to more fully place the user within social networks or movements, elaborated alternative value systems and material social circumstances. Themes of challenge to consensus, conformity and prohibition; of drug-use as part of a lifestyle, with consequences for other social relations, and of the centrality of *talk*, the exploration and articulation of meanings, values, and experiences, associated with drug-use – all are consistent features of the research and accounts referred to above. In the main sections of this paper these themes recur in our analysis of interviews with those (usually family members) who have had to cope with and respond to problems arising from serious drug-use. For those responding, as well as for users, conventional notions of leisure and pleasure are fractured. Yet it seems that engagement in the hard work of dealing with such a problem can merge labour and leisure in a discourse (the drugalogue) which can offer, albeit in a refracted fashion, familiar aspects of challenge, self-discovery, social engagement and satisfaction as might be conventionally sought in something called 'leisure'.

PARENTS, PROHIBITIONS AND PLEASURE

In his *History of Sexuality*, Michel Foucault drew attention to the manner in which a field of pleasure, sexuality, was constituted in the nineteenth-century through discourses of surveillance, constraint and control. His point was that the very possibility of talking about pleasure in sex is generated through and by an emphasis upon fear of discovery, guilt and demands for 'reform'. Intrinsic in the possibility of speaking and thinking about pleasure was the giving of covert recognition of that pleasure whilst allowing this to co-exist with, rather than undermine the necessity for constraint. Pleasure – above all, pleasure that is given through the attention that one may give to one's own body, was made speakable and comprehensible in the public realm, by its articulation as an object of surveillance and control.

This account raises an acute question. Is forbidden, secret or guilty pleasure comprehensible within existing theories of leisure? What then are the implications of Rojek's contention that 'leisure relations should not be studied as relations of self-determination and freedom. Leisure relations are relations of permissible behaviour' (Rojek, 1985, p. 177)? Was there no experience of pleasure before control announced it? No sexual pleasure before Victorian constraint? And, by analogy, no pleasure in intoxicaton before (a) temperance movements and their anti-opiate sequelae, (b) the Defence of the Realm Act or (c) the anti-drug concerns of the post-war period? What were the drinkers of previous centuries, the opium-users of the nineteenth century industrial period (Berridge and Edwards, 1981), the amphetamine-using mods and cannabis-using hippies of the 1960s, the multi-drug users of the 1970s and beyond, and the heroin-users of recent decades doing? Were they totally reliant for articulation of their pleasure upon an internalisation of a sense of prohibition? There is a definitional problem here. Unless pleasure is defined in a particular, nineteenth-century way, (*pace* Foucault), then one would have to rule out of court any possibility that intoxication *per se* held any attraction. One would have to discount the importance of that very object which in discourse analysis is held up as the centre of things; one would have to deny the materiality of the body. One does, after all is said and done, have some difficulty with the idea that 'it's all in the mind', whether it be sexual practices or the use of intoxicants that concerns one.[5]

The 'social problem' of drug-misuse provides an illustration of the articulation of pleasures through a discursive grid of constraint. When drug-use becomes an issue within families, the recognition of individual (particularly, adolescent) pleasure is closely tied up with social (paticularly, parental) pain.

It is striking that parents and other family-members – struggling as individuals, couples, neighbours and sometimes organised self-help groups or community activists – very clearly construe the issue of drug-use as one of power. The constant internal rumination and the pleasure and relief felt in talking with others – the pleasures of the *drugalogue*, as one parent described it to us – are concerned with the issue of power in two ways. In the first instance, there is a taking-up of an empirical notion of power *over* what is seen as an intruder, into normal family relationships of home and leisure, work and external responsibilities; the issue is how to overcome that malign power with the resources of the parents themselves, of doctors, police and so on.

Secondly, there dawns a realisation that this attempt to locate and defeat an enemy does not work (at least, not in the short term, not in most cases), and so family-members increasingly adopt a more complex series of interlinked discourses on the nature of the problem. Two which we shall illustrate here are concerned with a splitting-off and rejection of the offending family-member and of other drug-users, and with a contrary attempt to hold them close and infuse them with so much goodness that the crisis passes. Such discourses may alternate, or a stable adherence to one may obtain.

Finally, arising out of 'the drugalogue' and transcending it to some extent, there is a fourth discourse within which surveillance switches from the drug-users, back to those who previously tried to constrain and then to 'understand' them. The speaker begins to apply the knowledge of the human sciences to him or herself, reconstituting him or herself in the process. This shift, epitomised most clearly in the work of Families Anonymous (but by no means restricted to this group) is of considerable interest for two reasons. It is an example of a truly *popular* cultural form, a discourse that is hegemonic in the sense that it has no serious rival in terms of its ability to articulate a set of political concerns – the family; law and order; permissiveness; the discovery of an individualism that transcends obligations to others. Furthermore, this subjectivity involves a substitution of the identity of *gendered subject* (woman who lives for herself; man able to feel and cry) for previous positions of wife (duty to family, primacy of the tasks of motherhood) and of husband (heads of family).

In this way the drug problem, as apprehended by the pro-family movement, becomes, for some of those involved, a new arena for the discovery of self and the subsequent abandonment of the original notion of family responsibility. Drug-use is hardly a site of leisure for those drug-users who get heavily involved – a point elaborated in several research projects in the United States and in Britain, and epitomised by the title, 'Taking care of business' (Preble and Casey, 1969; Johnson *et al.*, 1985; Auld *et al.*, 1986; Pearson, 1987) – but *responding* to drug-users can for many parents and other family members herald an opportunity for that most well-developed leisure activity, the discovery of self, in new engendered forms.

In the following sections of this paper, we draw upon a series of taped interviews, group discussions and less structured interactions with parents and other family-members in most regions of England. The work was conducted during late 1985 and the first half of 1986, and has given rise to a short book for families as well as to other work (Dorn *et al.*, 1987). The account given here presents a revised perspective on our set of qualitative data, arranging it more tightly as four discourses on the family which cut across categorisations of social activity such as labour or leisure: (1) the attempt to reimpose a form of parental authority that is sensed to have been threatened or lost; (2) the splitting-off from the family of that which threatens parental authority; (3) the attempt to compensate for failure of control by emphasising the caring element of family life, treating the drug-user as a sick person to be succoured; and (4) the shift away from preoccupation with the care and control of the user, turning instead to the cultivation of self.

RE-IMPOSITION OF RULE

The degree of shock experienced in the discovery that one's son or daughter is involved in forms of drug-use unfamiliar to parents should not be underestimated. Although involvement with drugs may be preceded by other behaviour that disturbs the mother and/or father (and/or other family-members) the discovery that drugs are involved can be dramatic and can precipitate both psychological and physical conflict.

The subsequent struggle to reimpose previous familial relations can involve a continual clash of wills, often on a daily basis over several years.

> It has been swings and roundabouts, he's been up and down, there's been constant rows, all the emotions, I've had him cowering in the corner . . . he's locked himself in his bedroom – you're not allowed in there – it's a clash of wills, him and I, I'm strong and he's been fighting – I'm not strong really. I'll tell you now, like this morning, Ian's on the dole and I give him his money – I don't want to keep control, to help him I'm doing it, he has his dole daily and that's his beer money every day and he's on what the doctor prescribes him, and today he wanted an extra pound. Now it's easy to give him the extra pound and to let him handle his tablets, but he abuses it, you know, I say to him you can do what you like with your dole money, Ian, but you're not drinking my money, so there was a row there this morning over that. So we've got that conflict still all the time.
>
> (Annie)

Two external agencies that parents typically turn to in the attempt to overcome the problem are the police and the medical profession – although satisfaction is not always forthcoming. One complaint commonly levelled against the police is that they simply do not take action when they might be expected to support the parents in their attempt to reimpose discipline.

> the [parents] say things like, 'We've rung the police and told them but they say they can't do anything, I see drug dealing in pubs but the police don't do anything about it', you know, those are the sort of comments. . . . They tend to be very pro-police in anything else, but in this they're – anti is the wrong word – critical, because they can't see much being done about it.

And on the medical profession:

> They're quite anti-clinics because they think it's not confidential, I'm not quite sure what they think of the local GPs, there's a little bit of mixed opinion, but I don't think they have a lot of faith in them. I believe also that they – I heard a story, I don't know if it's true, that one GP provided one week's supply three times a week to one of these lads – so they haven't a high opinion of them from that point of view.
>
> (Probation Officer leading local parents' group)

Such a view of medical services is, naturally, not universal. Although we found a number of cases in which psychiatrists had been found unhelpful and ordinary GPs reportedly naive, there is extensive evidence that GPs are increasingly being approached by drug-users and their families (Glanz and Taylor, 1986) and in many cases being found helpful.

Nonetheless, amongst many parent-groups attempting to reimpose previously dominant familial relations, there is a persistent feeling of having been let down by the state. Either police, social workers, doctors and other professionals are criticised for not taking firm and decisive action in support of parents or, in a more radical critique of the 'nanny state', the latter is blamed for actually undermining parental authority. One mother and father who had feared that their daughter might be using drugs when she moved to a different town had initially felt confident that at least if she lost her job then she would have to return home.

> She didn't, and social security paid her rent and no questions asked, and yet they say 'Oh, it's the parents' fault', the state takes the child over at sixteen, or can do, and you have no rights anymore.
>
> (Group based in a south coast town)

Here is a fuller articulation of similar concerns:

It's the political side that's caused half of it.

They don't force you to try in schools anymore, they say it's up to you if you want to do what you want . . .

. . . there's no caring anymore, the same with the police . . . Now there's all young policemen, there's gang warfare and all the fighting, there's a young fella same age as all these out of work pushing his weight around, it used to be a fella you could look up to, and there's too many laws . . .

Or if they're caught singing on a Friday night, it's breach of the peace.

They're getting their backs up, they can't do anything.

They've only got to be in a crowd and the police will walk up to them and start aggravation, they're forgetting the serious things, letting them slide. I think so anyway. All these comprehensive schools and there again you can't tell the government, all these laws about legal rights, that's a load of rubbish: equal rights where work's concerned yes, but the man is stronger than the woman.

These women libbers get on my nerves.

The lads around here have got no confidence have they?

Interviewer: Is it, where you mention political things – is it unemployment?

I think that's the root of it.

A lot of them have had good jobs.

I wouldn't say that, most of them have never had a job.

You come out of school and you know you're going to end up on the dole or on a 12-month scheme, and that's it.

I find now with all these laws about women, girls are brought up in the same way as lads, taught the same as lads, the girls aren't treated like girls, they're one of the chaps. I mean I don't like being treated as one of the chaps. And they're all f-ing and blinding together, they're all doing the same thing. Females aren't the same as males, it's as simple as that. I think all these things together, that's what it's created, it's a lot of things together.

(Group in South Merseyside)

The strength of McRobbie's (1980) 'commonsense wisdom' about sexual divisions and appropriate behaviour is clear enough here. Mapped on to such a personal politics, the issue of drug-use within the family evokes a sharp reaction by parents and often the failure of straightforward attempts to reimpose their authority leaves a bitter (yet familiar) taste in their mouths. One possible response to this failure is to reduce one's frustration by giving up the attempt to control and instead to reject the embodiment of the problem – the user.

SPLITTING OFF THE PROBLEM: REJECTION OF THE USER

Most of the attempts to reimpose parental rule over drug-using offspring fail. Although some drug-users respond to parental or spousely distress by promising to desist, this promise – exacted in the context of often quite heavy pressure – is rarely honoured. What sense can be made of this? One response is to exonerate the user by placing the blame *outside*. Three main opportunities for externalisation of the blame for continued drug-use exist. They are: possession of the user by outside forces (which may be construed as the drug itself, and/or those who bind the user to the drug); or some fault in the user; or some attribution of the fault to social and political conditions, such as a vaguely-defined but deeply-felt resentment at the state of the world. As an example of the first discourse – the projection of blame on to the demonic qualities of drugs, consider the following extract from an interview with members of a group choosing the name, Parents in Pain.

> *Mother*: If you can sort of . . . imagine them as they were before they used, and look at the person that you know, and when that person has stopped using they're back to that person again. It is the drug itself that is making them do all the things that they're doing. If you look at it like that it doesn't hurt as much.
> *Father*: It is in fact a possession . . .
>
> (Parents in Pain)

The feeling that the drug is to blame is mediated by *gender*. As we shall describe in the next section of this chapter, the gender of s/he who responds/defines the problem is one side of this, mothers and wives being more 'tolerant', less likely to split off the user as evil than are husbands and fathers. But the gender of the user is also relevant – for both males and females responding. The following extract from a group discussion illustrates this.

> *Alice*: Somehow they get more degraded the girls you know.
> *Barbara*: . . . I think any girl who is on it, to be honest with you is a bit simple, each one I've met . . .

Marcia: Mostly though it's the lads, their boyfriends who influence them . . .

Tony: But the lads say . . . I'm a lad right, and if I saw a girl on it, it would disgust me, even the lads who are on it themselves, it disgusts them to see girls on it. They just look like prostitutes.

Alice: With a female there's got to be that caution there, hasn't there?

Interviewer: Like with heavy drinking?

Alice: Yes, well, all lads do things they're not supposed to do, it's in them, isn't it, they're male. But it's not in a woman and I think any woman who does that is not right up there and you can see it by looking at them.

Tony: But I know loads of girls that've had it.

Alice: Well each one I've seen – they're not right.

Barbara: They'll have a go, they'll take a chance, yes. I know all about that because all youngsters will have a go, but those that persist in staying on it, they don't look right in the head. They definitely don't look right, there's something missing. They belong in the lunatic asylum to me, you know, I can only say the ones I've seen, I haven't met that many, but the lads seem quite normal, but they've just done it, but the girls don't to me, they're much worse somehow, they're more evil . . . I think they're all evil – addicts – to me they are, but the girls always seem worse, hardest to handle altogether . . .

(Group in South Merseyside)

Here, drug-use can be seen as relatively easy to understand in the context of patterns of *male* recreational use of intoxicants, while expectations based on sexual divisions are writ large, and girls losing control through involvement in drug-use are viewed as incomprehensible and carrying the stigma of the 'fallen women'.

MAKING THINGS OK AGAIN: CARE AND GENDER

The accounts of mothers, corroborated in some of our interviews with fathers, point to the hypothesis that much of the task of reimposing parental role, childhood innocence and 'normal' expectations of work and play, is quite beyond the capabilities or motivation of many fathers. It is the mothers who usually take on this task, as reported by this volunteer counsellor who has herself experienced the situation.

Four out of five of the problems have been this: the fathers were more concerned not about the health of the addict but that there would be trouble, that they would be picked up by the police, their address would be in the paper, people at work would know. It is embarrassing and you know you can understand those feelings – they are quite natural, but the mother also goes out to work and she has got the same worries but she still has to cope with the problems of addiction and try and get help for them.

(Angela, Derby)

The differential reactions of mothers and fathers need not necessarily be ascribed to a greater 'psychological' or other maternal need on the part of mothers to care for the child. Certainly there is some anecdotal evidence that drug-using young men, in particular, 'work on' mothers and other female friends and relatives to extract extraordinary levels of care and attention, making claims about the allegedly unusually high needs of drug-users, coercing the woman into giving what is demanded (cf. our earlier discussion; Auld *et al.*, op. cit.). At the same time, it is equally the case that the location of power and strength of emotional leverage in such relationships can shift in other directions, as we describe in the next section.

ENDING THE DRUGALOGUE: DISENGAGING FROM THE USER AND LOOKING TO ONE'S OWN NEEDS

There is a social movement – epitomised in the self-help organisation Families Anonymous but broader than it alone – which questions the value of close surveillance and other forms of social engagement with drug-users. As one member of FA puts it, there are limitations to any strategy of close care and supervision:

I devoted an enormous amount of time to trying to trap her, to trying to find out what she was actually doing. . . . It didn't make any difference. . . . All those sort of strategies, searching, questioning, it's no point in asking a question unless you are going to believe the answer.

(Margaret, London)

On joining a group in which the prescribed norm is to talk about oneself, rather than about the user whom one has tried to care for and control, parents and other family-members are at first taken aback. Those who stay, adopt a new style of talk and with this begin to talk – and talk, and talk!

> They learn it. People who can't say boo to a goose for the first month and so on, suddenly start talking – you know the number of newcomers who've said I just can't believe the way you all talk, you're all so fluent and so articulate. Nothing is rehearsed. It's all just straight off the cuff – it makes for a deep feeling and the freedom to talk exactly as you want to talk . . .
>
> (Margaret, London)

However, the opportunity for parents – primarily mothers – to talk together can result in a shift in the topic of conversation.

> What generally happens first is that with a new person (attending a group) you get a long recital of the awful things that have happened and what he or she (the drug-user) is doing and so on. And then the emphasis will be to try and turn that round on to what the parent or person is actually feeling and how they are reacting. We try to keep it off the . . . what we call the drugalogue. You know, a long sort of cycle of what they (the user) did and what they look like and so on, because that actually doesn't lead anywhere. One of our principles is start with yourself, turn the focus of attention away from the addicted person on to yourself, on to the way that you are reacting to it rather than the situation itself.
>
> (Margaret, London)

The shift in surveillance from the user to oneself heralds a relinquishment of the sense of identity that is posited in the role of parenthood and entry or to a terrain which is, for many, quite new. This is the terrain of 'taking our own needs seriously for a change' – a psychology of self-valuation that is broadly Rogerian in its inclination, if not explicitly so. On this ground, notions of leisure, self-awareness, creative experience, self-gratification and labouring at the hard work involved, all coalesce and blur artificial distinctions which typologise individual and social experience.

The quest for the 'discovery of self' involves a questioning of those aspects of gender identity that previously underpinned the hegemony of 'parenthood'. For mothers, this means the giving-up of those aspects of 'femininity' that previously underpinned modes of motherly care, nurturance and support that have come to be seen as counter-productive. For fathers, it means (for the relative minority who stay the course) a degree of conscious 'feminisation' as they struggle with themselves to find ways of relating in other than authoritarian ways. Women, it is claimed, learn to care and to take power for themselves for the first time; men learn to care for the first time.

Turn the focus of attention away from the addicted person onto yourself . . . I remember (my daughter) saying to me, after about six weeks that I'd been going to meetings of the parent group – 'How long are you going to keep this up? . . . 'I don't think it's doing you any good'. When of course what she meant was, 'It's not doing ME any good'.

(Frances, London)

Perhaps – you've got a sort of reflection of masculine values on one side with the young man trying to prove himself, and the father perhaps responding in a way that is not understanding because it is not how the father would see masculine behaviour.

(Fred, Essex group)

A lot of men think, it's just for women these groups, well if someone like Graham will turn round and say, 'I cried', well it makes them feel better if they've already cried . . .

(Veronica, Lancashire)

It is perhaps unexpected that it is in the relatively 'conservative' and 'pro-family' arena of the parents' anti-drug movement that we find concerns also associated with feminism, personal politics and the so-called anti-sexist men's movement. However, the shift in voice from 'parenthood' to 'personhood' (valuation of self, the masculine in the feminine and *vice versa*) can be detected in a wide variety of settings in contemporary society. Cathy Urwin, for example, has observed that mothers of young babies who get to know each other on the basis of this shared position and identity may subsequently come to question the 'naturalness' of motherhood.

[T]alk with other mothers enabled some mothers to discover their own feelings of ambivalence about their situations, and towards their babies, were not so peculiar or abnormal as they feared. For instance, it was through talking to other mothers that Mrs Taplow came to the conclusion that 'maternal instinct was a myth'.

(Urwin, 1985, p. 199)

Hence parenthood (and particularly motherhood) can generate conditions in which the 'naturalness' of the role and identity becomes questioned. This is so for mothers of the newly-born and for parents (particulary mothers) of adolescents who have 'gone wrong' (for example by using heroin). The shift from private problem to public speech, the incitement to discourse – first resulting in a 'drugalogue' but developing into a conversation about oneself – may perhaps be especially refreshing to those mothers who did not find much opportunity to distance themselves from the mothering role when their child was younger. In any event, a shifting of surveillance away from the user brings a new experience of power to the parent.

CONCLUSION

It may be fruitful to try to make further links between the growing literature on language, motherhood and pedagogies from the nineteenth-century to the present day; the ways in which re-evaluation of parenthood and cultivation of self can arise in the context of anti-drug self-help groups; and the expansion in the post-war period of a more general interest in therapy, 'personal growth', fitness and associated consumer practices. These arenas, not so far studied in conjunction, are sites of a more general discursive shift from 'social responsibility' to 'personal discovery'.

Within this shift, practices of leisure and recreation for personal growth and development are strongly mediated by other agendas; responding to a 'social problem' like drug-misuse in the family is but one example which in itself calls into question gender, power, age and myriad other relations. No longer (if it ever could) can social theory adequately talk of a sphere of social practice called 'leisure' as if it were something discrete and distanced from the articulation and material consequences of other personal and social practices.

Notes

1. Our grateful thanks to Lorraine Lucas for all her usual help; we look forward to her forthcoming guide '*Word processing Under Pressure*'.

Thanks also to Jane Ribbens who worked with us on the project that this paper draws on, and to our colleague Christine James for her patience whilst our time and attention has been taken from other joint work.

2. As we have observed elsewhere, by weighting the results of local studies, the Government has produced estimates 'suggesting that there were between 25 000 and 40 000 regular users of heroin in the early 1980s (ACMD, 1982, p. 24; Hartnoll *et al.*, 1984, p. 23). Since that time heroin-use – particularly irregular or episodic smoking and snorting – has considerably increased, and it would probably be safe to say that numbers of ever-users of heroin exceeded 100 000 by the mid-1980s' (Auld *et al.*, 1986, p. 171). For more detailed information see ISDD, 1986.

3. Obviously the most commonly-used drugs in western societies are the legal ones such as coffee, tea, alcohol, tobacco, tranquilisers and so forth. Although there is much of interest to explore in the social patterns and styles of using these drugs – as in, for example, the work of Hilary Graham (1976) on smoking in pregnancy – these matters are beyond the scope of our interests in the present paper.

4. Although some limited evidence suggests a closing of the gap between male and female heroin use.

5. cf. Pearson and Twohig's suggestion that Becker should change his dealer on the basis of his argument that initiates to marijuana use must *learn* to appreciate the effects of the drug.

References

Advisory Council on Misuse of Drugs (1982) *Treatment and Rehabilitation*, London, DHSS/HMSO.

Auld, J. (1981) *Marijuana Use and Social Control*. London, Academic Press.

Auld, J., Dorn, N. and South, N. (1986), 'Irregular Work, Irregular Pleasures: Heroin in the 1980s', in Matthews, R. and Young, J. (eds.) *Confronting Crime*, London, Sage.

Becker, H. (1963) *Outsiders*, New York, Free Press.

Berridge, V. and Edwards, G. (1981) *Opium and the People*, London, Allen Lane, The Penguin Press.

Cloward, R. and Ohlin, L. (1960) *Delinquency and Opportunity*, New York, Free Press.

Dorn, N., Ribbens, J. and South, N. (eds) (1987) *Coping with a Nightmare: Family Feelings About Long Term Drug Use*, London, ISDD.

Dorn, N. and South, N. (1983) 'Of Males and Markets: A critical review of youth culture theory', *Research Paper 1*, (Enfield: Centre for Occupational and Community Research, Middlesex Polytechnic.

Dorn, N. and South, N. (eds) (1987) *A Land fit for Heroin?: Drug policies, prevention and practice*, London, Macmillan.

Finestone, H. (1964), 'Cats, Kicks and Colour' in Becker, H. (ed.) *The Other Side*, New York, Free Press.

Glanz, A. and Taylor, C. (1986) 'The role of General Practitioners in the Treatment of Opiate Misuse', *British Medical Journal*, 293, pp. 427–30.

Graham, H. (1976) 'Smoking in Pregnancy: the attitudes of expectant mothers', *Social Science and Medicine*, 10, pp. 399–405.

Hartnoll, R., Lewis, R. and Bryer, S. (1984) 'Recent Trends in Drugs Use in Britain', *Druglink*, 19 (Spring) pp. 22–4.

ISDD Publications Unit (1986) *Surveys and Statistics on Drugtaking in Britain*, London, ISDD.

Johnson, B., Goldstein, P., Preble, E., Schmeidler, J., Lipton, D., Spunt, B. and Miller, T. (1985) *Taking Care of Business: the economics of crime by heroin abusers*, Lexington, D. C. Heath.

Matza, D. (1961) 'Subterranean Traditions of Youth', *Annals of the American Academy*.

Matza, D. and Sykes, G. (1961) 'Juvenile Deliquency and Subterranean Values', *American Sociological Review*, 33, p. 716.

McRobbie, A. (1980) 'Settling Accounts with Subcultures: A feminist critique', *Screen Education*, 34 (Spring).

Merton, R. (1957) *Social Theory and Social Structure*, revised edition, New York, Free Press.

Neville, R. (1970) *Playpower*, London, Johnathan Cape.

Pearson, G. (1987) 'Social Deprivation, Unemployment and Patterns of Heroin Use', in Dorn, N., Ribbens, J. and South, N. (eds) *Coping with a Nightmare: Family Feelings About Long Term Drug-use, London, ISDD*.

Pearson, G., Gilman, M. and McIver, S. (1986) *Heroin in the North of England*, London, Health Education Council.

Pearson, G. and Twohig, J. (1976), 'Ethnography Through the Looking Glass', in Hall, S. and Jefferson, T. (eds) *Resistant Through Rituals*, London, Hutchinson.

Plant, M. (1975) *Drugtakers in an English Town*, London, Tavistock.

Preble, E. and Casey, J. (1969), 'Taking Care of Business: the heroin user's life on the streets', *International Journal of Addictions*, 4, 1, pp. 1–24.

Roberts, K. (1983) *Youth and Leisure* London: Allen and Unwin.

Rojek, C. (1985) *Capitalism and Leisure Theory*, London, Tavistock.

Thompson, H. 'Hell's Angels: Hoodlum Circus and Statutory Rape of Base Lake' (1970) in Douglas J. (ed.) *Observations of Deviance*, New York, Random House.

Urwin, C. (1985) 'Constructing Motherhood: the persuasion of normal development' in Walkerdine, V., Urwin, C. and Steedman, C. (eds) *Language, Gender and Childhood*, London, Routledge & Kegan Paul.

Willis, P. *Profane Culture* (1978) London, Routledge & Kegan Paul

Young, J. *The Drugtakers: the social meaning of drug use*, London, Paladin.

Young, J. (1973a) 'Student Drug Use and Middle Class Delinquency', in Baily, R. and Young, J. (eds) *Contemporary Social Problems in Britain*, Farnborough: Saxon House.

Young, J. (1973b) 'The Hippie Solution: an essay in the politics of leisure', in Taylor, I. and Taylor, L. (eds) *Politics and Deviance*, Harmondsworth: Penguin.

10 Leisure Time and Leisure Space

Chris Rojek

Leisure time and leisure space are not fixed and definite features of society. 'Nineteenth and twentieth century life,' writes Yeo,[1] 'has been full of attempts to divide performing from spectating, street space from play space, education and welfare from recreation, politics from the rest of life, values and choices from production, work from creativity.' Leisure relations, it might be said, involve continuous struggle, negotiation and bargaining.

Evidence of this is all around us. With regard to leisure time it is perhaps most vividly expressed in the collective bargaining process which has a well-established commitment to reduce the working-week and increase paid holiday entitlements. However, it is wrong to confine the matter solely to the struggle between capital and labour. More specific disputes over leisure time in Britain currently include the movement to extend pub-licensing hours in England, Wales and Northern Ireland; the attempts of various voluntary organisations to increase the opening-time of art galleries, museums, libraries and local-authority sports facilities; and the campaign for Sunday racing, which is supported by the Racehorse Association, the Racehorse Owners' Association and the Jockey Club.

Disputes over leisure space are no less various. Open access to public space does not apply as a uniform rule in Britain. Official agencies, notably the police, have wide discretionary powers to judge what constitutes 'lawful assembly' and 'orderly conduct' in public places, e.g. streets, squares, parks, wasteland, and so on. Not surprisingly, conflict over public leisure space occurs regularly. Clarke and Critcher[2] report that confrontation over the use of public street space in inner cities was a major factor in igniting the riots of the 1980s. Public leisure space is also contested formally by a number of private voluntary organisations. These range all the way from the local Neighbourhood Association which battles to keep play-space free for children, to regional and national organisations which seek to protect and conserve 'the national heritage'. Of the latter, by far the most important is the National Trust. In 1985 its membership stood at 1 322 996. It owns and manages huge tracts of land and maintains a large number of historic buildings. Moreover, it acts as a troubleshooter in cases where private land and private buildings which are defined as being of national importance are put at risk.

Struggle, contest and negotiation do not occur in a vacuum. Even the few examples listed here show that our liberty to exploit and develop our faculties and energies in our 'free' time is limited. In capitalist society these limits assume a distinctive form. Thus, there are strong historical pressures which make paying for leisure come to stand for participating in leisure; the policing of collective leisure to stand for orderly collective leisure; and private competition for fun and excitement. Moreover, these distinctions are embodied in the law, mediated through the socialisation process, consecrated in the media and backed up by the full panoply of the forces of law and order. Through these means, historically- and socially-conditioned forms of leisure are turned into 'natural', 'inevitable', 'healthy' forms. History is turned into nature.

I have stated that strong historical pressures operate to shape our leisure relations. And indeed this is the case.[3] However, the consequences of these pressures are very far from being monolithic and perfect. I have already stated that leisure relations involve continuous struggle, negotiation and bargaining. Attempts to regiment leisure promotes reaction; force promotes resistance. If we are to avoid building models which present social actors in leisure as acting mechanically in predetermined ways it is vital to keep these points in mind.

In what follows I shall consider two examples of reaction and resistance to the regimentation of leisure time and leisure space: the opposition to Sunday trading and the Stonehenge hippy convoy. These examples happen to be drawn from the events of 1986 in England, but they are selected for their indicative power rather than their mere topicality. Capitalism, as Marx observed, is a world system of domination. It is certainly the case that resistance to processes of regimentation have occurred throughout history. A number of historical studies now exist which recognise this, and the reader may be referred to them for a perspective which adds depth to my own account.[4]

NEVER ON A SUNDAY

On 15 April the second reading of the Shops Bill to deregulate Sunday trading was defeated in the House of Commons by 296 votes to 282. The result was generally agreed to be remarkable: it involved the defeat of a government with a notional majority of 138; it was built on a revolt by 68 Conservative MPs and the abstention of a further 20; it was the first major defeat suffered by the Thatcher administration in seven years; it was a Bill which had mustered a significant body of support notably from the popular press, the Consumers' Association, the Retailers Consortium and Open Shop (the group of retailers agitating for Sunday shopping); moreover, as proponents of the Bill never wearied of pointing out, Sunday shopping was already an established fact of life in some areas of England because many councils did not enforce the law.

The defeat was brought about by a combination of economic and religious pressure groups. On the economic front, the Union of Shop, Distributive and Allied Workers (USDAW) had lobbied strongly against the Bill. The USDAW General Secretary argued that it would put up to 50 000 jobs at risk in the retail sector and would produce higher prices and lower standards for the consumer. Religious and moral opinion was mobilised by the Keep Sunday Special campaign and the Board for Social Responsibility of the Church of England. Dr Michael Schluter, the founder and director of the Keep Sunday Special campaign, argued that deregulation threatened family life. He was quoted as saying that some 250 000 children would be put at risk by not having a parent home on Sunday if the Bill went through.[5] History does not relate by what occult process Dr Schluter magicked up this exact figure. Yet it cannot be denied that he marshalled a strong emotional argument – who can disagree that a society which abandons its children is anything other than a monstrosity?

However, it does not get to the heart of the deepest moral objection to Sunday trading. What was invoked time and time again by Church leaders, and also by Parliamentarians who spoke against the Bill, was the governments' duty to keep Sunday special, to preserve the traditional British Sunday. Sunday, it was said, is a day of rest. It is a day for 'walking, lunching, sleeping, gardening, visiting the relatives or the launderette, washing the car and reading at leisure newspapers.' Furthermore, 'one does not have to be remotely religious to appreciate a day which is different from the others, to enjoy walking through High streets and suburbs that are, for once, deserted.'[6] This charming defence of the virtues of the traditional Sunday enraged the *petite bourgeoisie*. An editorial in the *Daily Mail* denounced it as 'humbug'.[7] The *Daily Express*,[8] after pointing out that liberalising Sunday trading means extending 'our' freedom of choice, condemned the defeat of the Shops Bill as forcing Britain to remain 'a six-day-a-week nation in a seven-day-a-week world.' Palpably, the British Sunday arouses strong passions. But what is the origin of these passions? And what light do they shed on how leisure time is distributed and regulated in modern British society?

The recognition that Sunday is a special day has its origin in the third Commandment, and Christianity has played the lion's role in promoting Sunday observance. However, it was not until 1234 when Gregory IX issued his papal doctrine, that abstention from servile labour on Sunday was embodied in the general law of the Roman Catholic Church. Nevertheless, much earlier injunctions against abusing the special character of Sunday are on record in English history. In 906 King Edward the Elder forbade executions on Sundays. In 925 King Athelstan forbade Sunday trading. In 1020 King Canute proclaimed that no trading or assembling was permitted on Sunday. As Wigley notes,[9] in a country which lacked a centralised and uniform system of policing, such laws were difficult to enforce. Abstention was common. However, this did not stop the trend of outlawing certain activities on Sunday. For example, in 1388 Richard II forbade labourers to play tennis or football on Sundays. In 1448 an act of King Henry VI prohibited the sale of goods at fairs and markets on the principal feast days, Good Friday and Sundays. Richard's law, like King James's *Book of Sports* which appeared in 1618, illustrated some of the tensions present in official attitudes to Sunday observance. For both encouraged *some* sporting activities on Sunday, notably the practice of archery, leaping and vaulting. Such pastimes,if has often been noted, were easily transferable to the field of war. Both statutes are generally regarded to have as much to do with raising the country's stock of military skills as preserving the character of the Christian Sunday.

Sabbatarianism did exert a genuine and widespread influence over popular consciousness during the Renaissance. At this time the Crown and the clergy combined to try and reform the morals of the people. Folk customs, carnival festivities, dancing, play-acting and ale-drinking were all attacked and many texts lamenting the low state of misrule were published (e.g. Philip Stubbes' *Anatomy of Abuse*: J. Northbrooke's *Distraction of the Sabbath* and C. Featherston's

Dialogue Against Dancing). The zealous temper of mind is well expressed in a passage from the *Westminster Confessions of 1644*:

> The Sabbath is then kept holy unto the Lord, which men, after a due preparing of their hearts and ordering of their common affairs beforehand, do not only observe an holy rest all of the day from their own works, words and thoughts about their worldly employments and recreations; but also are taken up the whole time in the public and private excercise of His worship, and in the duties of necessity and mercy.[10]

Sabbatarianism at this time aimed to militate against all forms of distraction that might divert the individual from contemplating the Lord and His works on His day. It sought to instill standards of decency, self-control, gravity, orderliness, reason and this-worldly asceticism in the people. These were the signs of social 'health', the keystones of 'normality'.

The Restoration reversed this trend, albeit only partially. However, in the late eighteenth and early nineteenth centuries the movement enjoyed a revival. Cunningham[11] writes of groups like the Society for the Suppression of Vice, the Society for the Reformation of Manners and the caucus of Evangelical MPs and their activities to prevent Sabbath-breaking. As the nineteenth-century progressed, and especially after the 1820s, Sabbatarianism grew to exert a major influence on moral and economic life throughout the country. Sabbatarian principles were incarnated in the publications of the Lords Day Observance Society, the Evangelical Alliance and the Religious Tract Society. Wigley writes most perceptively on this phenomenon. He argues that the social origins and economic circumstances of active Sabbatarians in the nineteenth-century were congruent. The material conditions of their lives translated into a common consciousness of their place in the social ladder, the validity of the existing order in society and the threats and opportunities posed to their own place by other social classes. Nineteenth-century Sabbatarianism, Wigley concludes, was an expression of the rising class-consciousness of the bourgeoisie which sought to provide an 'objective' interpretation of their social circumstances and the circumstances of society in general. An important element of the bourgeois attachment to Sabbatarianism then, was class-insecurity. As Wigley puts it:

> Sabbatarians were generally property owners who were literate but read mainly the Bible, possessed political influence but excercised

authority over their inferiors, and often suffered economic hardship but received little protection. Sabbatarianism arose out of their religious preoccupations, but freed them from competition, enabled them a chance to discipline and instruct the lower orders, for whom (like the aristocracy), the doctrine had less appeal and purpose.[12]

The monotonous message of the glut of sermons, pamphlets and other writings which the Sabbatarians produced was that Sunday was a day for beholding the works of God and putting faith in His glory. But if Sunday was 'His' day it was also 'their' day too. For in observing respect for the creator on the Sabbath, 'His' mouthpiece (the Sabbatarians), were also awarded respect. Thus, placing faith in the creator also placed faith in bourgeois values and, by extension, bourgeois law. Again, it is very important to observe that this process was not monolithic. Sunday observance was not a 'total' mechanism of discipline and control. It promoted resistance and reaction among both the working class and the aristocracy. Nonetheless, a mechanism of social control it certainly was. In short, the 'rational' recreation demanded of everyone by the bourgeoisie on Sunday was designed to reinforce the sanctity of the bourgeois way of life. The piety of the Sabbatarians lay in their conviction that Sunday observance was promoted by fear of the Lord. The reality of the Victorian Sunday was that religious observance was used to promote the moral regulation of the self – that is, it was used as a mechanism of shaping social conduct, for bending behaviour, to the values and precepts of one social class.

Sabbatarian fundamentalism has receded as a force in the land. But the bourgeoisie and the Victorian values enshrined in Sunday observance remain. Sunday *is* different. We do not need the defeat of the Shops Bill in the House of Commons to verify this – although it *is* confirmation. It is obvious in the lived experience of Sunday life in Britain. Thus, the public transport systems of most British cities operate a much restricted service. Museums, art galleries, theatres, cinemas and other recreational outlets are either closed or remain open for much shorter hours than on a 'normal' weekday. Opportunities for betting and gambling are severely restricted. Discotheques, night clubs and other places where young people of both sexes can meet are also either closed or open for shorter hours. Television and radio broadcasting stations alter their programme schedules. Religious shows, moral talk programmes, nature and country life shows receive a much higher profile. Sunday is the day when BBC Radio 4 broadcasts *The Week's Good Cause* – a show which invites listeners to make donations to a featured charity. BBC and Independent Television also regularly broadcast charity appeals on Sundays. In sum, the British broadcasting schedules show Sunday to be a day for reflection, for staying at home and for taking stock of the plight of others less fortunate than oneself. And this indeed reflects the restricted opportunities for public interaction that prevail on Sunday.

There is a vigorous paradox here. For Sunday, it can be safely said, is the one day of the week in which most of the working population do not engage in paid employment. It is therefore the day when the capacity of the masses to engage in freely-chosen, spontaneous, self-determined, flexible activity (the *sine qua non* of leisure relations in 'formalist' theory[13]) is most fully extended. Yet, as I have tried to demonstrate in the foregoing discussion, it is the one day in the week in which society drastically curtails access to many basic opportunities for social interaction, e.g. shops, discotheques, night clubs, race courses, galleries, museums, exhibitions, and so on. This is not a matter of happenstance. The official and semi-official regulation of public leisure on Sundays operates to endorse a quite specific view of the 'normal' and 'healthy' use of time. The hale life on the Lord's day is a day of temperance, modesty and quiet. It is a day for the family. 'Typical' Sunday activities include going to church, playing with the children, doing the garden, cleaning the house, and taking a turn in the local park or memorial flower gardens. In brief, it is assumed that the 'normal' Sunday is a day spent in the bosom of the family. Sunday is a day in which husbands and wives are meant to offer special devotion not only to God, but also to the home, their own parents and the children.

Feminist writers have for long argued that the model of home life which is consecrated in welfare state legislation and the teachings of the Church is narrow and misleading.[14] It consists, of course, of the nuclear family which is defined as a married heterosexual' couple living with their children and in which it is assumed that the man of the household is the main breadwinner. This model is said to be endorsed by the media, the schools and the main recreational outlets.

However, the gap between the ideology of the family and how people actually live is very large indeed. Thus, the 1981 state census reported that only 26 per cent of all households consisted of a married heterosexual couple with one or two dependent children. In other words, only something like one in four households conform to the nuclear family 'norm'. Furthermore, the census showed that 22 per cent of all households consisted of only one person and 32 per cent of all households consisted of only two people. In the Shops Bill debate a frontbench spokesman referred to 'taking the family out to lunch or visiting a leisure centre or stately home with ones' wife and children' as standard and healthy forms of Sunday leisure practice.[15] What the census data shows is that this model of Sunday leisure is remote from the experience of most people in Britain. At best it is applicable to only a little more than a quarter of households, so that leisure relations are far more diverse and contrary than the simple nuclear family model of Sunday leisure suggests.

To accept that leisure activity is socially constructed is very different from saying that leisure activity is socially determined. I have argued that leisure relations are enabled and constrained by quite specific social pressures. I do believe that this is the case, and it is just as true of other days of the week besides Sunday. However, I also think that it is quite wrong to deduce from this that the same pressures apply equally to all people in society or that people lack any choice regarding how they spend their leisure time. Structural influences of class, gender, race, degrees of physical wellbeing, age, to name but a few, obviously come into play. I have set out my position here at greater length in Chapter 5 of this book. However, I can further illustrate the effect of structure on leisure practice and, moreover, the contested, negotiated character of modern leisure relations, by moving away from the question of leisure time to the question of leisure space. The next section is devoted to this task.

THE STONEHENGE HIPPY CONVOY

Space needs people to give it meaning. Erving Goffman's fascinating and important work on 'frames of social interaction' and 'strips of activity', shows that the meaning which people attached to space is not fixed, definite or universal.[16] The social scientist and city-planner may routinely divide space into hard-and-fast polarities, such as public space and private space, work areas and recreation areas, urban areas and wasteland. However, people are far more inventive and prolific in giving meanings to space than these simple divisions suggest. Jane Jacobs[17] also recognised this and gave a brilliant example of it in her famous analysis of the cultural meanings and uses made of city sidewalks.

Leisure relations are certainly rich in examples of how the meanings and uses of leisure space are challenged, modified and sometimes radically subverted. In the leisure industry a strong and important movement is presently underway to transform traditional work space into modern leisure space. For example, the old Victorian workcentre of Albert Dock in Liverpool has been transformed into a major city leisure amenity with a built-in complex of shops, office, TV studios and restaurants. Major dockland recreation development schemes are also underway in Glasgow, Cardiff and London. The movement is by no means confined to dockland areas. A large number of Victorian and Edwardian work centres – forges, factories, mines, farms – have been transformed into leisure and recreation centres. For example, the Camden industrial works in Bath is now run as a regional lesiure attraction. The city tourist information leaflet in 1986, a leaflet it should be noted, 'for all the family', describes the works as 'the fascinating world of J. B. Bowler, Victorian engineer, brass founder and mineral water manufacturer . . . discover what it was like to work for a local family firm around the turn of the century.' The key words here, of course, are 'discover what it was like to work'. The leisure industry in Britain, at a time of unprecedented mass unemployment, is skilfully exploiting and developing a nostalgia not for a rural, but for a dead industrial past. It is worth noting in passing that these transformations in the cultural meanings of work space and leisure space appear to be accomplished quite smoothly. The public is apparently ready to accept that old workplaces can be turned into new play and recreational areas. In the context of the general deindustrialisation of the British economy, such acceptance merits careful attention. For it suggests that existing urban and industrial environments may be far more adaptable to a society based on a shorter working week or permanent mass unemployment than many writers on leisure currently suppose.

Still, it must not be thought that the appropriation of space for leisure relates exclusively to history and is basically a matter of taking over old work space. Struggles over leisure space in the United Kingdom occupy a much wider canvas. In 1986 a particularly graphic and well-documented incident occurred. On 29 May *The Times* ran a small news item about a disturbance in the West Country. Les Attwell, a local farmer, was reported to be seeking court action to evict a group of hippies that had trespassed on to his 101-acre farm near Yeovil on 23 May. The hippies had migrated to the West country in preparation for attendance at the regular summer solstice free festival held at Stonehenge. This was the first bulletin that the general British public had received about a dispute which was destined to escalate into one of the most public and acrimonious battles over leisure space that has occurred in recent years. The police enforced the provisions of the Police and Criminal Evidence Act (1984) which gives them the power to enter private land and make arrests and evictions if there is judged to be a breach of the peace. The hippies were forced to decamp. They made their way first to the village of Corfe in Dorset. Here they again met with public protest and police action. After a short interval, the hippies moved on, ending up in early June at Stoney Cross in the New Forest district of Hampshire.

By this stage in the proceedings the hippy camp was the lead feature in the week's news. It was reported that while still in Somerset some 80 hippies had gone to the Department of Health and Social Security and received £3000 in benefits.[18] Radio and TV transmissions had drawn attention to the hippy 'peace camp' where, it was alleged, 'dogs and goats run freely and children beg for money and cigarettes.'[19] The term 'peace camp' was apparently the self-styled label used by the hippy leaders to describe their confederates. It was an inspired piece of public relations. For the term carried strong echoes of the longstanding womens' peace camp which had established itself at the Greenham Common Nuclear base in Berkshire to protest against the existence of nuclear weapons. The womens' camp had incurred the hostile impatience of the government, yet it had also attracted strong support from many liberal and left-wing sections of the public. Later the hippy leaders would introduce the term 'peace convoy', with its powerful overtones of the Falklands episode, to describe their activities.

At Stoney Cross the irritation and discomfort that the hippy convoy had caused in some official quarters escalated into a full-scale moral panic. John Duke, the Chief Constable of Hampshire, commented that 'these anarchists are here spoiling a beauty spot and harassing both residents and holidaymakers.[20] He went on to reassure the public that the police are ready, and the words are his, 'to neutralise this invasion'. The next day Mrs Thatcher was reported to have received a telegram from the Chairman of the New Forest Consultation Panel, who complained that 'the fair face of this unique area is being disfigured and fouled' by the hippy presence.[21] On the same day, in the House of Commons, the Home Secretary branded the convoy as 'a band of medieval brigands'.[22] On 6 June it was reported that the Cabinet had spent 30 minutes discussing the matter. It set up a special committee composed of ministers from the Departments of the Environment, Transport, Health and Social Security and the Ministry of Agriculture to look into the laws against travelling people such as the hippies. On 9 June at 4.40 a.m., in an operation called 'Daybreak', some 400 police officers from the counties of Hampshire, Wiltshire, Somerset, Dorset and Avon converged on the camp. They impounded nearly all of the 150 vehicles belonging to the convoy and dispersed the camp. Some hippies were escorted to a reception centre and given rail warrants to vacate the area. Others left under their own steam. Some 70 decided to walk to Glastonbury to attend a CND festival. Their journey was flanked all the way by several dozen police. Chief Constable Duke, in a press statement, said, 'for over a week there has been a very angry and resentful fear in our community at Stoney Cross which has been threatened by the presence of this invasion. The invaders, as elsewhere, have shown a reckless disregard to peace and how anyone can think of that as a convoy of peace defies my imagination . . . (the convoy was made up of) misguided Huckleberry Finn-type characters and children deprived of normal family environment.'[23]

The routing of the hippy convoy is more than a vivid and interesting backnumber in recent British and cultural history. It shows, more than mere words, that the meaning of leisure space is neither fixed or definite. Leisure space is contested space. In the case of Stonehenge and the hippies it has been contested for some time. The first alternative Stonehenge free festival to celebrate the summer solstice was held in 1973. The site is owned by the Department of the Environment, and the land around it is owned jointly by the Department and the National Trust. The owners have always disputed the right of young people to play live music and camp on their land. Official permission to hold the festival has never been granted. From the earliest days the authorities have resorted to the use of barbed wire and physical force to prevent 'trespass' into the stone circle. Nevertheless, as the seventies progressed the festival established itself as a regular annual feature in the alternative events calendar. Indeed, as Clarke notes,[24] by the late 1970s the festival had received the semi-official tolerance and cooperation of the local authorities and voluntary services. For example, the local authorities provided refuse sacks to clear the site at the end of the event, and Release, together with the Festival Welfare Service Organisation (funded by the Home Office) gave regular welfare support.

As the eighties unfolded things changed. By the middle of the decade, in the midst of a more severe economic and moral climate, the authorities moved to stamp out the festival. In 1985 English Heritage and the National Trust issued an order to prevent the festival. Police roadblocks were used to halt the convoy about 6 miles from the site. Violent confrontation between the police, some dressed in riot gear, and members of the convoy ensued. Some 537 people were arrested. An enquiry into the use of police force published by the Police Complaints Authority admitted that police officers had used excessive force to disperse the convoy. The testimony of members of the public that incidents occurred in which police were observed hitting members of the convoy with truncheons was corroborated. However, since 1363 officers were employed in the operation it was decided that the perpetrators could not be identified, so no disciplinary proceedings could take place. The Chief Constable of Wiltshire, Donald Smith, commented: 'I shall always remain exceptionally proud of the way in which the vast majority of the Wiltshire Constabulary and the officers who assisted them acquitted themselves on that day when confronted by a determined group of people whose use of violence knew no bounds.'[25] In 1986 the hippies made a fresh attempt to reach Stonehenge and the events recounted in this essay unfolded.

The conflict over the festival centres on the disagreement over the cultural meaning and use of the site. The authorities see Stonehenge as a major cultural asset for the nation. This involves policing it to ensure that access to the site is restricted to officially-approved viewing areas. Anything else, argues the Director-General of the National Trust, threatens 'the landscape of this incomparable archaeological area' and the 'monument itself.'[26] The paradox involved here is not lost on the hippies who contend that Stonehenge was not built as a memorial, but as a living spiritual centre. Stonehenge, maintain the hippy leaders, is 'holy land' and access to it cannot be rightly curtailed from any man or woman. 'We come to Stonehenge,' argue the hippies, 'because in an unstable world it is proper that people should look for stability to the past in order to learn for the future.'[27] They repudiate the allegation that the hippy presence constitutes a risk to the site. Indeed the hippies submit that the site is at greater risk from the activities of the authorities. 'Exceedingly large tracts of land,' argue the hippies, 'are covered by military camps and tank ranges. One military exercise does more damage to the landscape than we could possible do in 20 years.'[28] The hippies demand that the authorities grant open access to the site and dismantle the restrictions relating to the playing of live music, dancing, assembly, etc. It is worth noting in passing that there is nothing new in the point about open access. Hardwicke Rawnsely, a founder member of the National Trust, made the case as early as 1900. 'Stonehenge', he asserted, 'is a place where men's feet all up the ages have been as free as air to come and go.'[29] Like the hippies, Rawnsley concludes that to limit access to the site is to interfere with the natural rights of a free-born people.

CONCLUSION

It is not my purpose to comment on the rights and wrongs of the dispute over Sunday trading or the conflict over the use of Stonehenge as a leisure resource. Instead I want to emphasise the important theoretical points that both cases illustrate: leisure time and space do not merely or automatically exist in society. On the contrary, leisure time and leisure space are continuously made and remade by the actions of people. Moreover, these actions often involve basic conflicts over the meanings and uses of leisure time and leisure space. In saying this I am trying to draw attention to the fact that leisure activity is value-laden activity. The conflict and tension entailed in the real leisure relations of people is often lost in the glib slogans of leisure planners and administrators who speak of 'the leisure society' or a policy of 'recreation for all'. Against this I want to stress that the provision of leisure time and leisure space is a political process. It requires social agents to take decisions about the meaning and purpose of time and physical space; and it requires individuals to police space and time from competing interests and demands.

Notes

1. E. Yeo and S. Yeo (1981) 'Ways of Seeing: Control and Leisure versus Class and Struggle,' in Yeo, E. and Yeo S. (eds) *Popular Culture and Class Conflict 1590–1914: Explorations in History of Labour and Leisure*, Brighton, Harvester Press.
2. J. Clarke and C. Critcher (1985) *The Devil Makes Work: Leisure in Capitalist Britain*, London, Macmillan.
3. See my (1985) *Capitalism and Leisure Theory*, London, Tavistock. Here I argue that leisure practice is shaped by processes of commercialisation, individuation, privatisation and pacification.
4. See, for example, E. P. Thompson (1967) 'Time, Work Discipline and Industrial Capitalism,' *Past and Present*, No. 38, pp 56–97; H. Cunningham (1980) *Leisure in the Industrial Revolution*, London, Croom Helm; J. Walton and J. Walvin (eds) (1983) *Leisure in Britain*

1780–1939, Manchester, Manchester University Press; S. G. Jones
(1986) *Workers At Play*, London, Routledge & Kegan Paul.
5.   *The Daily Telegraph* 16 April 1986.
6.   Both quotes from *The Observer* 10 November 1985.
7.   *Daily Mail* 16 April 1986.
8.   *Daily Express* 16 April 1986.
9.   J. Wigley (1980) *The Rise and Fall of the Victorian Sunday*, Manchester,
     Manchester University Press.
10. Quoted in J. K. Carter (1957) 'Sunday Observance in Scotland
     1500–1606,' unpublished PhD thesis, Edinburgh University, p. 41.
11. Op. cit.
12. Op. cit. p. 183.
13. See Rojek, op. cit., pp. 85–105.
14. See, in particular, E. Wilson (1977) *Women and the Welfare State*,
     London, Tavistock; M. Barrett and M. McIntosh (1982)*The Anti-Social
     Family*, London, Verso; C. Ungerson (ed.) (1985) *Women and Social
     Policy*, London, Macmillan.
15. Douglas Hurd, Home Secretary, *The Times* 15 April 1986.
16. See E. Goffman (1959 *The Presentation of Self In Everyday Life*,
     Harmondsworth, Penguin; (1974) *Frame Analysis*, New York, Harper &
     Row.
17. J. Jacobs (1961) *The Death and Life of Great American Cities*,
     Harmondsworth, Penguin.
18. *The Times* 30 May 1986.
19. *Daily Telegraph* 29 May 1986.
20. *The Times* 3 June 1986.
21. *Daily Telegraph* 4 June 1986.
22. *Daily Telegraph* 4 June 1986.
23. *Daily Telegraph* 10 June 1986.
24. M. Clarke (1982) *The Politics of Pop Festivals*, London, Junction Books.
25. *The Times* 25 March 1987.
26. *The Times* 22 June 1978.
27. *The Times* 28 June 1986.
28. *The Times* 28 June 1978.
29. Quoted in P. Wright (1985) *On Living in an Old Country*, London,
     Verso, p. 54.

Author Index

Subject Index